Anonymous

Musings and memories

Being chiefly a collection of anecdotes and reflections of a religious character, on various subjects

Anonymous

Musings and memories
Being chiefly a collection of anecdotes and reflections of a religious character, on various subjects

ISBN/EAN: 9783337728175

Printed in Europe, USA, Canada, Australia, Japan

Cover: Foto ©ninafisch / pixelio.de

More available books at **www.hansebooks.com**

MUSINGS AND MEMORIES.

BEING CHIEFLY A COLLECTION OF

ANECDOTES AND REFLECTIONS

OF A RELIGIOUS CHARACTER,

ON VARIOUS SUBJECTS.

PHILADELPHIA:
PUBLISHED BY
THE TRACT ASSOCIATION OF FRIENDS,
No. 304 ARCH STREET.
1875.

Entered, according to Act of Congress, in the year 1874, by
THE TRACT ASSOCIATION OF FRIENDS,
in the Office of the Librarian of Congress, at Washington.

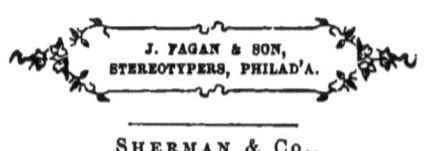

SHERMAN & CO.,
Printers, Phila.

PREFACE.

MORAL and religious truth can frequently be more clearly illustrated in connection with a simple incident, so as to leave a profitable impression on the mind, than by a more elaborate essay.

With this view, the narratives and comments contained in the following pages have been compiled.

PHILADELPHIA, 12th mo., 1874.

CONTENTS

	PAGE
KINDNESS	9
INDIVIDUAL INFLUENCE	28
SHORTNESS AND UNCERTAINTY OF LIFE	44
RICHES	57
WAR	65
RELIGIOUS DUTIES	101
WATCHFULNESS OVER SELF	118
CHILDREN	149
PROVIDENTIAL DELIVERANCES	163
TRIALS	227
FAITH	252
INFIDELITY	269
INTEMPERANCE	283
DEATH	297
INFLUENCE OF THE HOLY SPIRIT	315
MINISTRY	337

MUSINGS AND MEMORIES.

KINDNESS.

GENTLENESS AND GRATITUDE.

GENTLENESS is enumerated, by the apostle, among the fruits of the Spirit, and yet there are some apparently religious men to be met with in whose characters it does not hold a conspicuous place. How it enhances our esteem for the Christian who possesses a large share of it. How it enlarges his sphere of usefulness, and adds a grace to his profession of religion. The rough, honest-hearted man may do good in the world, through the self-denial he manifests, and the true and holy faith which is in him; but of far greater efficacy would his life-labor in the service of his Divine Master be, if in his daily walk he abundantly exemplified the gentleness of Christ, and set forth an example of the true love, heavenly meekness, and courtesy of a saint.

Do good graciously. Let old and young bear in mind that a kind act done in a rough spirit may hurt more than it heals. A rough manner obliterates the obligation conferred, and sometimes leaves unpleasant remembrances concerning those who have labored for our good.

Almost every heart has within it a store of kindly affections, and if there was only a more general effort made to manifest the warmth of our love, and the gentleness of true Christian courtesy, a change for the better would appear in most families, a great and radical improvement in many. A recent writer says, " I am one of those whose lot in life has been to go out into an unfriendly world at an early age; and of nearly twenty families in which I have made my home in the course of about nine years, there were only three or four that could be properly designated as happy families, and the source of trouble was not so much the lack of love, as the lack of care to manifest it." A writer, in commenting on this passage, says, " The closing words of this sentence give us the fruitful source of family alienations, of heartaches innumerable, of sad faces and gloomy home circles. 'Not so much the lack of love, as lack of care to manifest it.' What a world of misery is suggested by this brief remark! Not over three or four happy homes in twenty, and the cause so manifest and so easily remedied! Ah, in the 'small, sweet courtesies of life,' what power resides! In a look, a word, a tone, how much of happiness or disquietude may be communicated. Think of it, reader, and take the lesson home."

Mercies in rich abundance are showered down upon us from the Giver of all good gifts, and if we are grateful, let us manifest it by the kindness and love we exercise towards his children around us. Let us in our own little circle do our duty towards spreading an atmosphere of love and Christian gentleness. Let us not permit kind acts to be done to us, even if they are done roughly, without showing, by our smiles of love and the gentle acknowledgments of affection, that we feel them. Such acknowledgments may have the happy effect of producing similar conduct from others, and tend to spread a bright and holy influence which may reach eventually every member of the home circle. An influence, which it were greatly to be wished, might enter every cot, and spread through every place wherein a group of immortal beings congregate on this earth. Do not receive the kindness of others in silent coldness. The expression of love tends to awaken love.

KINDNESS REWARDED.

Kind acts are often recompensed, even in this life, although the Christian is to do good, hoping for nothing again. Doing his works of charity for the dear Master's sake, and out of Christian love for his fellow-creatures, his reward is in having the Lord's favor, and the feeling that his own heart does not condemn him. He has not turned a deaf ear to the sorrow of those around him, and he knows that the Master, not because he has had compassion on others, but of his own mercy, will show every kindness to him.

An anecdote of the late George Whiting of New York, a worthy, consistent, tender-hearted Christian, illustrates this. Many years since, he was an agent in this country for the Edinburgh Encyclopedia, and had at times large numbers of those costly volumes in an attic over his office. One day a poor man applied to him for work, and looked so distressed, that George was satisfied he was in great destitution. Remembering that he had at that time a large number of the Encyclopedias lying loose, he took the poor man into the attic, and told him if he would pile them up neatly he would pay him for his labor. The man gladly undertook it, and George rejoiced that for the work, which really seemed unnecessary, he could pay him that which would send him home comfortable.

In the course of a few weeks after this, the building was burned, and these volumes were all destroyed. There was an insurance on them, but as George was unable to specify the number of the volumes, and the amount consumed, the company refused to pay, and in the prospect of a loss of the whole insurance, he was dispirited and perplexed.

Still he endeavored to fill up his duty towards others, and whilst engaged in a Christian work of benevolence, he observed a poor man, sick and confined to his bed, gazing on him intently. It was the poor man who had piled up his books. The sick man made himself known; and George then told him of the disastrous fire, and inquired of him if he could remember distinctly the number of books he had handled. As it proved, the man had marked down on a piece of coarse paper the total number, and the number of volumes in each pile, and he still had the paper in his possession. By the aid of the sick man's testimony, and the list he had preserved, George Whiting's evidence of his loss was completed, and his insurance was paid to him.

THE POWER OF KINDNESS.

In the winter of 1855-6, an employee in a family living in Odessa, Delaware, found on a snow-drift near the house what appeared to be the dead body of a sparrow. Picking the bird up tenderly, and gently enclosing it in his warm hands, he soon found, from some motion about the heart, that life was not entirely extinct. He took the bird into the house, where animation was restored, and after some days it was able to fly about the warm conservatory, in which it was left at liberty. With increasing strength its happiness seemed to increase, as was manifest by quick, pleasant motions and cheerful notes. The members of the household called their bird Bessie, and she seemed completely tamed by the kindness manifested to her, and the loving care which ministered to all her wants.

When spring returned, little birds were heard outside of the house piping, trilling, or twittering; but Bessie appeared to pay no heed, until one day a shrill, peculiar note thoroughly aroused her. She immediately began flying around the conservatory, anxiously endeavoring, for the first time, to get out. The sash was opened, and full of love and happiness she joined her mate, whose note she had so quickly recognized.

The happy pair remained in the vicinity of the house all through the summer; and their little ones, when able to fly, were daily brought to a table in the yard, where their kind friends had taken care to place a plentiful supply of food.

With the very first snow-storm, the little bird again came to the conservatory, with her pleading tap on the window-pane for admittance to her old warm quarters. Her friends, finding she had concluded to be their guest for the winter, obtained a bird-cage and hung it up among the flowers for her accommodation, where, during the cold winter, she often warbled out sweet notes of pleasure, while her happy, graceful flights added an additional charm to the floral beauties among which her sober-colored wings were quickly waving.

Spring came again, and one day was heard the same loud note which had aroused Bessie the previous year; and now again, after hearing it, there was no rest or happiness for her until the sash was opened, and she had joined her mate. Very pleasant it was to mark the positive joy which seemed mutually to animate the reunited pair. Seven winters, including the first, Bessie passed in the conservatory, and the reunions of the periodically parted couple were never-failing sources of enjoyment to the sympathizing beholders. During all that time, she never left the immediate neighborhood of this pleasant residence, either in winter or summer.

The last spring of her life, the reunion was so marked by loud tokens of joy, that passers-by stopped to notice their actions. About ten days after this she suddenly died. She was found in a convulsion in the food basin, and on being picked up by one of her watchful care-takers, she nestled down into the warm hand as if glad to feel it was around her. She looked up to her protector with an evident expression of pleasure. No kindness or skill could, however, save her life,— a succession of spasms came on, in one of which she died.

Her mate, after her death, seemed evidently conscious that something sorrowful had occurred. He had been one of the most joyful of birds, whose gush of song had often delighted the family and its friends, but he now became a mournful and drooping thing, creeping about through the shrubbery in apparent distress, uttering a low moaning note which deeply touched the sympathy of those who heard him. In a few days he disappeared, and was never again seen in his old summer haunts.

We have seen how kindness tamed this little bird, and some of us know how kindness has tamed wild members of the human family. Many a revolting son and daughter of Adam — a wilful wanderer from the paths of virtue and goodness — has been tamed by the sensible feeling of the mercy of God in Christ Jesus. Dead to appearance in trespasses and sins, and giving no evidence of any spiritual life within them, they have been as it were taken up by Jesus, and warmed by the blessed influence of his Holy Spirit, until there has been a quickening within them and, through saving grace, a new birth unto holiness, the end whereof is everlasting life.

Many a poor outcast, who, feeling that he is despised of the world, has cast away all hope for himself and lost all love for others, has had a great and happy change wrought in him by words of kindness and deeds of love when he had thought that no man cared for his soul. Wild wanderers, scornful and careless of what others thought of them, have been so tamed by kindness, that the company of the pure, and those they once, in the sinful instinct of an unrenewed nature, turned from with dislike, has become pleasant and very comforting. Thus have some been in a measure prepared to seek the Lord Jesus, the fountain of all purity, for the cleansing operations of his Spirit, which produces in the renewed soul an instinctive love for all that is good, elevated, and holy.

Kindness and love are powerful levers to operate

with in our intercourse with mankind. If we habitually use them, we shall be more and more convinced that the exercise of them is as beneficial to others as it is necessary to our own growth and establishment in the Truth. Try it, dear readers, try it, and see whether it does not add comfort to our own home happiness; whether it does not increase the pleasure we derive from our purest earthly enjoyments, the very conservatory where the brightest and richest of the blessings granted us below, bloom even in the wintry season of outward desolation and storm.

KINDNESS TO CHILDREN.

To be really kind to children, one must be capable of entering into sympathy with them. If we cannot feel as they feel, we shall be continually in danger of causing them sadness of heart, even when we are doing them substantial kindness. Ah! if we would minister to their comfort, let us endeavor to look back to the days of our own childhood, and remember how our feelings often suffered from the harshness of those who surrounded us. Let us look on them with tenderness and love, endeavoring to feel something of the spirit which dictated the words, " Suffer little children to come unto me, for of such is the kingdom of heaven."

Professor James Marsh, of Burlington, Vermont, was one whose mind ever prompted him to acts which would give pleasure to those about him,— the humblest as well as the highest. When he lay in his last illness, only a few days before his death, a person travelling in a stage-coach, spoke of his situation to an acquaintance. A woman, whose dress bespoke her to be one in humble life, listened earnestly to what was said, and then inquired if they meant Professor Marsh, of Burlington. She was answered, "Yes." She then said, "When he dies, a great man will leave us." She was then asked if she knew him; to which she answered, "Yes. I was bringing two motherless grand-children in the stage from St. Albans, in April, and the roads were horrible. The horses walked all the way, and the children were tired, and cried; and don't you think Dr. Marsh made the driver stop, and got out, took the children out, and walked on with them by the roadside, showing them stones, and plucking little flowers for them, and talking with them by the way. They were refreshed and perfectly delighted, and said he was the kindest and best man in the world. And to think he should have done all this for two poor, strange, orphan children! Ah! he was a good man, and so kind; I shall never forget him."

Sir William Napier, a man of fine talents and great descriptive powers as an author, although a military man, and of a hasty temper, was very good-natured, and noted for his kindness to children. One instance narrated in his biography, illustrates this as well as his scrupulous honesty in fulfilling his promises, even when made to a little child. The account informs us, that as he was one day taking a long walk in the country, near Freshford, he met a little girl, about five years old, sobbing over a broken bowl. She had let it fall in returning home from a field to which she had taken her father's dinner in it, and she said she would be beaten for breaking it; then, with a sudden gleam of hope, she innocently looked up into his face and said, "But yee can mend it, can't ee?" William explained to her that he could not mend the bowl, but he could mend her trouble by giving her a sixpence to buy another. On opening his purse, he found, to her and his own disappointment, that there was no silver in it; and to fulfil his promise to his little friend, he told her to come to the same spot at the same hour the next day, and he would be there and have the sixpence with him. To save her from the punishment, he bade her tell her mother that she had seen a gentleman who would bring her money to pay for the bowl the next day. The child, entirely trusting him, went on her way comforted. On his return home he found an invitation awaiting him to dine in Bath the following evening, where he would meet with one whom he specially wished to see. He hesitated for some time, trying to calculate the possibility of meeting his little friend of the broken bowl, and of being in time for the dinner-party in Bath. Finding this could not be done, he wrote declining to accept the invitation to the dinner on the plea of a pre-engagement; saying to his children, respecting the child, " I cannot disappoint her; she trusted me so implicitly!"

OUR LITTLE TREASURES.

We almost all of us possess some little thing or other to which we attach a value far above its intrinsic worth. Or perhaps it would be more correct to say, which has a value to us far beyond the value it possesses to others. It may be some little legacy of love, some little memento of a departed friend, something closely connected with important events in our own lives, or with the lives of those we have loved. An authoress mentions that, being in the house of a skilful physician, she saw a poor, withered, shrivelled apple, which, from the care taken to preserve it, she felt convinced had some history connected with it making it precious to the owner. On inquiring respecting it, the physician replied, "That poor apple I shall never part with while it is possible to keep it. It is one of the few offerings of gratitude, through a great many years of practice, I have ever received. I was attending the death-bed of a dear child, and just as his life was about to close, when his last kiss had been given to all around, he turned to me, and in faltering accents, in the sweet lisping tones of infancy, said, 'Doctor, you have been very kind to me when I was naughty, and would not take my medicine, and I have nothing to give you but this beautiful apple dear grandmother sent me,— will you take it?' I did take it, and I am not ashamed to say, shed tears as I did so. There are few things in this house that I set such a value on as that dear child's little apple."

The apple, which to the child seemed so beautiful in its fresh condition, when, as a loving token of gratitude, he presented it to his physician, had lost all its outward fulness and fairness to the eye, — yet never did it lose its moral beauty,— the sweetness and loveliness which the dear child's affectionate feelings imparted to it, in the view of the physician. To him it still spoke of the dear, patient sufferer just about to part with all things earthly, and to enter on the joys of that blessed state, where the spirits of the redeemed children, the lambs of Christ's fold, do always behold the face of their heavenly Father, yet gratefully remembering and acknowledging the kindness shown him by his medical attendant and friend.

WANT OF PROPER THOUGHT.

"Time to me this truth hath taught,—
'Tis a truth that's worth revealing,—
More offend from want of thought
Than from any want of feeling."

" Why, Charles, how many vegetables have gone to waste in thy garden which would have been a great comfort to thy poor neighbors over the road!" "True enough, cousin, and they would have been very welcome to them, but I never thought of making them the offer." "Ah, Charles, if we only had thoughtfulness enough, we might relieve many a one with things which we permit to go to waste. Remember the surplus produce of thy garden next year. A sick neighbor might be benefited by a few of the fine Lawton blackberries, beside being comforted and cheered by thinking that thou had a kindly feeling for him. A few of the spare bunches from those long trellises might, in their season, be messengers of pleasure to others. Thou dost not need to sell it; let thy surplus produce, then, be for the sick and the poor."

"What did the little girl give thee, Ann?" "Oh, nothing but this bunch of common field flowers?" "Didst thou tell her thou felt obliged to her for the kind thought which prompted her to gather them for thee?" "Why, no, to confess the truth, I never thought of it!" "I supposed it was so, for I saw a tear in her eye, which showed that her feelings had been hurt. The poor little thing felt love for thee; and, as she loved flowers, she thought that which pleased her must please thee, and therefore gathered these. She had no hot-house to go to for a fine bouquet. She could but give those her own toil could gather. Remember, my friend, never receive any intended kindness from the young or poor without an acknowledgment. This is often neglected for want of thought, and want of true kindly thought often occasions great sorrow, and is the source of much of the distress with which this world abounds."

"John, I understand that our old friend and school-mate, after a long illness, has been released from his sufferings. He was very much resigned to his situation, yet he often felt lonely, having no near relatives about him, and he did very much enjoy the visits of his friends. Didst thou often call upon him?" "I am sorry to say, I never thought of it. I knew he had sufficient pecuniary means to pay for the necessary nursing; and although I at times regretted that such a valuable man should be called away from us so early in life, somehow I did not think of visiting him." "Well, it is a pity. He would have been rejoiced to have seen thee, and thou might have derived both comfort and instruction from his quiet, resigned state of mind, and the cheerful piety which seemed the constant clothing of his spirit. Ah, John, I sometimes fear this want of Christian thoughtfulness is one of the greatest causes of hardness of heart. Our friends are sick and in trouble; we sometimes, amid the bustle of business, give them a passing thought, but few think of what they can do to alleviate their suffering or sorrow by a visit of love, a letter of friendship, or such other kind act as lies in their power."

POLITENESS.

On an occasion in which many children were gathered together, there was among them a bashful, timid little girl. She was rendered awkward by her bashfulness, and her embarrassment was not diminished to hear herself called silly by some who had never suffered from timidity, or had forgotten how they had felt when enduring the pains of bashfulness. In the company there was one kind-hearted, really polite boy. He felt for her in her distress, and, without appearing to notice her fright, he took a book to her, showed her the pictures, talked to her very pleasantly, and took care not to ask questions which would render it necessary for her to answer. Her fear soon passed away, and the intelligence of her mind was soon manifest on her countenance, showing that the term silly did not rightfully belong to her. When fruit was handed round, he selected a fine apple, and whilst the others were busy in ministering to their own appetites, he carried it to the little girl, called her by an endearing appellation, and told her he had selected it for her. A smile of gratitude spread over her face, and in a low voice she found courage to thank him for his kindness, whilst she gladly accepted the fruit.

Some one has said that politeness is "kindness kindly expressed." The boy, though he could not probably have given a good definition of it, had an instinctive perception of what it was, and practised it. A recent writer says some people think politeness can only wear fine clothes and live in grand houses. Never was there a greater mistake. The

KINDNESS. 27

best teacher is kindness, and she is a teacher who keeps a free school. All may come and learn.

The same writer, in speaking of Christian politeness, after quoting the saying of our blessed Saviour, " Whosoever shall give to drink unto one of these little ones a cup of cold water only in the name of a disciple, verily I say unto you, he shall in nowise lose his reward," adds these remarks: "*Christian* politeness? Yes. Politeness is showing kindness for kindness' sake. Christian politeness is showing kindness for *Christ's* sake, doing kind acts from the love you bear your Saviour, and a desire to honor him, whose whole life on earth was a life of love. Such a value does he set upon 'little deeds of kindness,' that the giving of a cup of cold water is not overlooked or forgotten by him."

INDIVIDUAL INFLUENCE.

NO ONE WITHOUT INFLUENCE.

WE all exert an influence for good or ill on those around us, and it behooves us to see that such as we have, is exercised for the benefit, not the injury, of others. Some do not, apparently, understand that their conduct and conversation have any effect on others, and do not perceive the responsibility that attaches to them for the example they set. An incident is related as having occurred a few years since in England, which illustrates the influence exerted by mere children. At a temperance meeting, a lecturer, in speaking of the influence which might be exerted against intemperance by individual faithfulness, said, "Every one has influence; even that child in her father's arms has influence." As he said this he pointed to where a man stood with his child. "That is true!" said the father, with fervent emphasis. When the meeting was over, the man came to the lecturer, and apologized for his unseasonable speaking, which was occasioned by a sudden outburst of feeling, overpowering his sense of the proprieties of time and place. He then said, "I was a drunkard; but as I did not like to go to a public house alone, I used to carry this child. As I approached the public house one night, hearing a great noise inside, she said, 'Don't go, father!' 'Hold your tongue, child!' 'Please, father, don't go!' 'Hold your tongue, I say!' Presently, I felt a big tear fall on my cheek. I could not go a step further. I turned round and went home, and have never been at a public house since; thank God for it. I am now a happy man, and this little girl has done it all; and when you said that even she had influence, I could not help saying, 'That's true.'"

Without doubt, every one who has mingled in society, has at times, through heedless words or inconsiderate and improper actions, evilly affected others. Who of us but, in looking back over our own lives, can remember cases in which we feel convinced such must have been the effect of things said or done by ourselves. In some of these we may perhaps have the consoling reflection that Divine grace has preserved those most liable to have been affected thereby from permanent injury; but in others, having lost sight of the parties, we cannot tell what their conduct since has been.

Sometimes, in after-life, we have very afflicting evidence given us of sad consequences which have resulted from the actions of our unregenerate days, and sometimes from the missteps we have made even after a spiritual awakening, and when we were in the main desirous of doing the will of our heavenly Father. A case of the former kind comes to mind. An individual who, in the day of his youth, had lived according to the leadings of the prince of the power of the air, the spirit which rules in the children of disobedience, who had been a frequenter of theatres, and had given free course to his unregenerate nature, having, through the quickening, heart-changing visitations of Divine grace, witnessed the work of regeneration cleansing his heart, believed himself called to be a minister of the gospel of life and purity. On a certain occasion, long after this, he was at the bedside of a dying impenitent sinner, one who had been an acquaintance of his in the days of his wicked career, who at that awful moment, when he was about closing his earthly existence, told the terror-struck preacher that his soul was forever lost; but that it was his evil example which had led him to destruction. It was, it is believed, principally in his going to the theatre, that his example had encouraged this person, then a youth, in breaking through the hedge of Christian restraint which had before kept him from that place. The attendance there led almost unavoidably to base companionship;

his course of degradation was rapid, and he now felt heaven was lost to him forever. Despair was his portion even on this side of the grave, and as he passed through the valley of the shadow of death, he could feel no hope, he could see no light.

Such was the death-bed of this poor misled man, who, in the midst of remorse, knew not even to taste the sweet sorrow of repentance. The agony was not alone on his part. Bitter were the feelings of the man whose example had given him an impetus down the pathway of ruin. He clung to his bedside; he agonized for his poor lost soul; and when death closed up the last avenue of hope, his own anguish was of a character to be mitigated only by a fresh feeling of that boundless love which, in Christ Jesus, can save the lost; yea, can make the very unclean white as snow.

Samuel Fothergill, looking over the crimes of his youth, the injuries his evil course of conduct had produced to others, declared that for this it seemed the sword would not pass from his house forever. He had witnessed, through heartfelt repentance and faith in the Lord Jesus, a free pardon for all his sins; yet anguish at times came upon him, when he thought of those whom his example may have contributed to centre where the worm dieth not, and the fire is not quenched.

No true Christian, however deep the anguish of soul he has already experienced for the evil he has committed, however well assured he has been that, in the unutterable love of God through Christ Jesus, all has been forgiven, could look upon one who, through the influence of his example, had been led into and continues in sin, without experiencing renewed sorrow of soul. Some influence for evil may be exerted by us, unless on the watch, even after the main bent of our minds is towards holiness, and when the earnest desire of our hearts is the promotion of purity, and the increase of the Redeemer's kingdom.

LIGHTS IN THE WORLD.

The apostle exhorts the Philippian converts after this manner: "Do all things without murmurings and disputings: that ye may be blameless and harmless, the sons of God, without rebuke, in the midst of a crooked and perverse nation, among whom ye shine as lights in the world; holding forth the word of life." A true Christian, wherever his lot is cast among men, is, and must necessarily be, as a light in the world. There must be, if the love of God dwell richly in him, some outflow of it to others. If he is walking in the light, there will be seen some radiance around his pathway which, others beholding, may, through the merciful visitation of Divine grace operating thereby, be quickened to endeavor also to become children of the light and of the day.

How often has a solitary traveller been encouraged and animated in his lonely journey at night, by the lights which he observes flashing from the windows of the houses he passes by. It is a silent testimony to his mind of home and happiness; the quiet industry and social enjoyments of the home circle, its love and peace; and he is comforted, even although storms and tempests beat upon him. So, when the Christian traveller beholds the light of a consistent life shining forth from those he passes by in his weary worldly journey, he is cheered thereby. It speaks to him of the restraining, directing, illuminating influence of Divine grace in the soul, of the inward work of the Spirit going on, of quietude and comfort, of heavenly love and peace, even though there may be storms and tempest around him.

Some one narrates his grateful feelings, when, on a journey in a dark night, a lad, not knowing he was near, passed on before him, carrying a lantern which gave forth a bright light. The boy had taken the light for his own guidance on a dreary walk through darkness, and, whilst carefully carrying it, thinking only how thereby he should be able to go safely on his own path of duty, was giving unwittingly great aid and comfort to another. Every humble, careful, Christian traveller, through the dark paths of this earth, carries with him, more or less conspicuously, a light, which may, in some hour of gloom, illuminate and cheer a brother or sister pilgrim, as they are enabled thereby to pass on their way in greater safety. Let all then, by giving close heed to the good Master, and the inward working of his grace, seek for ability to let their lights shine more and more brightly as they move on their heavenly journey. Then others, seeing the good works which, by faithful obedience, they are enabled to bring forth, may be strengthened and incited to glorify their Father who is in heaven.

BE YE NOT CONFORMED TO THIS WORLD.

Ko-san-lone, a convert to Christianity from among the Chinese, some years since visited America. He was much surprised at observing the fashionable style in which many professing Christians lived, and the little difference to be observed between them and the people of the world, in manners, customs, and mode of life. He was distressed and perplexed at it; and one day, alluding to it, he made a wide sweep with his arms, to give greater emphasis to his language, and said, "When the disciples in my country come out from the world, *they come clear out.*"

How is it with thee, reader? Hast thou come clear out of the world, its ways, its fashions, its honors, its compliments? Dost thou seek for the approbation of thy Divine Master in thy walk among men, not esteeming in comparison therewith the condemnation or praise of the worldly-minded as of any moment? The inquiry is worthy of thy most serious consideration.

INFLUENCE OF EXAMPLE.

The influence of example is much greater than we are willing to believe. In a narrative of a religious man, it is related that in conversing with his two brothers, who also were cross-bearing Christians, they acknowledged to each other that the uniformly "consistent and upright conduct" of an uncle with whom they dwelt, had been the means, under Divine Providence, of leading "each of them to think seriously about the salvation of his own soul." What a happy and effective preacher was that uncle.

Well, if a good example is often productive of good, the tendency of an evil one is as great towards evil. Not only are the openly depraved sowing the seeds of sin along the path of life they are treading, but the lukewarm, the indifferent, the inconsistent professors of religion are doing the same thing. Often individuals who have been met with by the visitations of the Lord's Holy Spirit, who have in humility submitted thereto, and have attained to some degree of Christian consistency in their walking, have stumbled at the sight of the actions of those they have esteemed religious, and have been turned aside from their high calling in Christ Jesus. Ah! how often do we find individuals who, through inward exercise and the powerful baptisms of the Holy Spirit, have had the outward contaminations of corrupt nature washed away, instead of going onward towards perfection, have settled down into sober, moral men, in whom the living virtue of Truth seems to have died out, or at most to be very far from being in dominion in their hearts. Such men are always weak in the faith; their conversation, although it may be clear from anything openly corrupt, is yet not such as becometh the gospel of Christ Jesus. These are great stumbling-blocks to the newly-awakened, earnest inquirers after Truth.

Reader, art thou a professing member of the church of Christ? Then see that thy walking is consistent with thy profession. Art thou, by thy personal appearance, thy conduct, thy conversation, placing a stumbling-block in the way of others?

It is important for every one to mark his own doings — to consider the influence he is exerting on those around him. In every portion of our earth-travel we are leaving a trace — some impression for good or for evil. One morning, looking from his parlor-window, the writer saw on the brick pavement in his yard the plainly visible record of the night wanderings of a snail. Every turn he had made, from a direct onward course,— and they were very many,— was there written down in silver slime. Whilst musing on it, he was reminded that we, also, leave a record of our devious wanderings. Our sins and transgressions, unless blotted out through mercy, will stand as an awful record against us; and some traces of the good or evil influence of our example may perhaps be found written in the faithfulness or unfaithfulness of those among whom we have walked. Oh, how happy will it be at the last for the humble Christian who, having no might nor strength in himself, yet through submission to the sanctifying power of the Lord Jesus and the holy, preserving influence which he has vouchsafed, has been kept a living example of true Christian purity and perfection on his heavenward course. Such are ministers of the gospel in life and conversation, if not in word, and have a large influence for good wherever their lot is cast. The Lord, who accepts their obedience, will number them among those who, having turned many to righteousness, " shine as the stars forever and ever."

SETTING GOOD GRAFTS.

It is narrated that a person, in riding in the country, observed an acquaintance, some distance from his own residence, grafting a thrifty young apple-tree which had sprung up on the public highway, and which extended some branches quite over the road. On speaking with the person about his employment there, he said that, being engaged in grafting in his own garden, he had remembered this thrifty young tree, which had a situation favorable for good bearing, and he thought he would set some grafts in it. He said, "I thought I would graft some good, early apples, the best kind; perhaps they will do somebody some good." The grafts grew thriftily, and the fruit has without doubt, long before this time, administered satisfaction to many a passer-by, and perhaps to none more than to the kind grafter himself.

What a pleasant world, amidst all its necessary trials, sufferings, and bereavements, this would be, if every one was not only seeking to put good grafts into the sources of enjoyments for the poor, doing them good in every way he finds open, but, by an ever watchful promptness in the exercise of the Christian graces, be setting, by example, the grafts of better fruit into some of the poor, neglected human trees in the highways and hedges, as well as into some who, though in the hot-house, forcing beds of prosperity, yet being still in their natural states, are producing no good fruits.

Beside the ever active influence for good of a religious life, there are many opportunities, dear reader, for thee to benefit, or at least to impart comfort to, somebody or other. Just pause and consider, as thou art perusing this. Look around thee; is there no apple-tree by the way-side to be grafted? Are there none to whom, by a little exercise of Christian charity, thou canst cause as pleasant a gratification as the gift of sweet fruit? Remember, a cup of cold water rightly given has its reward, and few men, women, or children walk in so circumscribed a path that they cannot, if their hearts are in the work, do more than that. A smile bestowed on some humble one, a kindly word spoken, a mite in love handed, may be as good grafts set in their hearts, producing sweet fruits of kindly affection.

Good grafts of kindness and Christian love may

often be readily set, but it is quite as easy to set the grafts which produce bad fruits. How evil disposed should we deem that man who, cutting off the branches of a tree bearing good fruit, should engraft in all of them scions producing fruit bitter, worthless, or injurious. Such, as far as evil example can go, is the result of a lukewarm, ungodly, or wicked condition of spirit manifesting itself in our intercourse with the world. Such is the effect of the influence of those who, by conduct or conversation, are putting stumbling-blocks in the way of others. It will be well for us all to consider seriously, Am I, in my daily walk, in all my intercourse with my fellow-men, setting such an example as may, with the Lord's blessing, prove as good grafts, producing fruits to his praise? Or am I manifesting so much of unsubdued nature—so much of the spirit of the god of this world—so much coldness and apathy towards good—that if any one, influenced by me, should, so to speak, take grafts from my tree, no fruit of holiness or Christian dedication can possibly spring therefrom!

PROFANITY CHECKED.

More than six hundred years ago, the porters of the city of Florence were in the habit of taking refuge in times of rain, or in cold and chilly weather, in a cellar which, from having been at times flooded by the waters of the Arno, had ceased to be occupied by regular tenants. Here the porters found shelter from the sudden summer shower and the winter chill, when not employed during times when business was slack, or whilst waiting for a transient job in more active seasons. Much profanity and corrupt language were uttered among those that congregated there, which caused great distress of mind to one of them, a pious man named Piero di Lucca Borsi. He was advanced in years, and feeling himself religiously restrained from participating in the evil practice, he was anxious to lead away his companions from a habit debasing to the intellect and endangering the future well-being of the soul. To aid him in his labors with his fellows to induce them to abandon this old, depraved custom, he proposed to them to enter into an agreement that for every curse, blasphemous expression, or wicked word they uttered, they would pay a *crazia*, a small coin, as a fine, into the funds of the company meeting there. This by kindly importunity he brought them to agree to, and a box was procured to hold the fines which should be paid. The evil habit was not easily broken; and though somewhat abated, yet fines came in fast, and very soon there was quite a considerable sum of money in the treasury. Piero, whose heart was expanded in love to his fellow-creatures, soon saw a way in which this money might be employed to the lasting benefit of the citizens of Florence. Having matured his plan, he suggested to his companions that a sufficient amount should be appropriated to purchase six litters, one for each ward of their city, to be constantly ready for the carrying of sick people, and such as might meet with accidents in the streets, to the public hospitals. He induced his companions to embrace his plan, and carry it into effect. Under his persuasive eloquence, they also agreed to appoint weekly two of their number whose duty it should be, during the period of their appointment, to be always in readiness to attend to the litters as carriers in time of need. Great good resulted from his thoughtfulness. A sin was publicly condemned and in some degree abated, and a great public benefit was brought about in the establishment of an institution which has continued in healthy activity down to the present day. Such have been the results of the faithful occupancy of his one talent by an illiterate laborer who depended on the work of his own hands for his daily support.

EVIL PREVENTED.

A colored barber in Philadelphia relates that, in the fall of the year 1870, he was once strongly tempted to take the lives of three men, on account of ill treatment received from them. The temptation was presented several times, and at length he actually left his shop intending to commit the foul deed. The pleadings of the inward monitor against the commission of this sin were, however, now heard in the secret of his soul with such power as to induce him to abandon his design; and having thus yielded to the convictions of Divine grace, he began from this time to experience a change in his feeling towards the men, until it became so different from what it had been, that he could regard them as brethren instead of enemies. He now looks back with horror to the awful destruction which threatened to overwhelm his soul, mingled with feelings of gratitude for the great mercy that had been extended for his preservation. The fruit of his repentance is shown by an interesting occurrence that has since taken place. A customer at his shop made a remark which led to the discovery, on the part of the barber, of the man's intention to engage in an act from which he anticipated much satisfaction, although great injury to others as well as himself would result. He reasoned with him for some time. The man departed, and when next seen he stated that he had taken the advice given him, and abstained from committing the sin. Truly, "he that is in you is greater than he that is in the world."

SHORTNESS AND UNCERTAINTY OF LIFE.

HUMAN LIFE SOON OVER.

HOW soon will the hour of death come, even to those who have the longest term of existence granted them in these mortal bodies. A merchant, who had passed his life in the possession of all the comforts which wealth and a loving household could bestow, some years since sank, by a not very painful disease, to the grave before reaching a period much beyond what is called middle age. He was not resigned to death; and a few minutes before his close, turning to his beloved wife, he ejaculated, " Is life so soon over,— *is it so soon over?* " He would willingly have given everything he possessed in the world, if, as his young children testified, "he could only get well." But death may not be bribed to depart from us, and neither will medicine protect us from his dart. Life seems brief to all! Jacob could say," The days of the years of my pilgrimage are a hundred and thirty years; few and evil have the days of the years of my life been." How happy will it be for those who, through the mercies of God in Christ Jesus, are permitted, as this brief period of existence terminates, to feel the assurance that a life of glory and happiness, which shall never be over, is opening before them.

LONG LIFE UNDESIRABLE.

It is the duty of a Christian to be contented to remain on earth, toiling in the service allotted him by his heavenly Father, just so long as his all-merciful and all-wise caretaker shall see meet to continue him in the church militant; yet certainly, to those who have known the washing of regeneration, the forgiveness of past sins, and the adoption that maketh children of God and heirs of eternal life, a long lingering here in probation cannot be very desirable. It is no wonder that the natural man, who hath not known a preparation for participating in the glories of the kingdom of perfect purity hereafter, craves the continuance of this life, embodying all the joys that he can understand. From this point of view, we can see how that wishing our friends long lives,— a common form of blessing in use among certain classes,— should have had its origin. Yet to the Christian the realization of such a wish might be far from a blessing.

The following remark was made by the late William Wilberforce to a friend of his in the year

1807, at a time in which he was quite unwell, yet not confined to his dwelling. "A man in the castle-yard this morning, in the honest ardor of his heart, seized my hand, and with peculiar emphasis wished me a *long life*. I was obliged to him for his kindness; but he forced on me the reflection how *unchristian* are our common feelings and sentiments — that we should be ready to regard a long life as one of the greatest of blessings. Did we really keep Christian principles and Christian views before us, we should assuredly think that 'to depart and be with Christ' was, for ourselves at least, 'far better.'"

Many years ago, I was told by a friend, whose benevolent heart often led her into scenes of suffering, that she had just visited a very aged woman, who had forgotten all the events of her past life, and even that she had ever been married. Her friends to her had become as though they were not, and all that was going on around her — the love, the care, the turmoil — reached her not. Yet upon being asked if she knew Jesus Christ, she brightened up as she replied, "Yes; he is my Saviour." Religion is the only effectual comfort of old age. Kind friends may minister to the wants of the body, and may see that everything is done that can be done to alleviate the hours of weariness and suffering; yet, unless there is a large share of Divine grace afforded in the decline of the powers of mind, fretfulness and impatience may get in. These often render the closing hours of the aged, even of some who have passed reputable and apparently religious lives, less pleasant to the witnesses at the time, and less comfortable to reflect upon, than might have been the case if they had been taken away at an earlier period.

The frailties of flesh and spirit manifested by some, as the mental powers have failed, have been cause at times of great trial to their near friends, and have occasioned some stumbling to the evil judging world. We cannot tell, in the progress of second childhood, when mental accountability ceases, but we know that God is rich in mercy, and that he will judge all things in righteous, loving kindness, through him who hath ever loved his own, and will love them even to the end.

Now and then, as though to exemplify the true meaning of the blessing, "With long life will I satisfy him, and show him my salvation," the Lord sustains some of his servants to a very green old age. Yea, in the weakness of the earthly tabernacle, he grants them to retain the mental powers in great vigor, whilst the spiritual seem even to strengthen, so that with holy alacrity they continue filling up a blessed sphere of usefulness in the church militant long after the friends of their childhood, the fellow-laborers in the Lord's cause, through the meridian of their days, have been gathered into rest. Such are indeed an ornament to the truth, an exemplification of the sustaining power of Divine grace, and of the love and mercy of our Lord Jesus Christ.

Wilberforce spoke of our common feelings and sentiments being *unchristian;* and although he dwelt particularly on wishing long life, without doubt other things had place in his thoughts. Wishing one's friends uninterrupted temporal blessings a real true-hearted Christian would feel some misgivings about uttering. Afflictions are so often ministers of mercy, and prosperity so often tends to deaden religious sensibility, and to alienate the soul from that humility and dependence upon God, which is the soul's only safety, that if a truly conscientious mind dared to give utterance to such a desire, it must be coupled with the hope that it might be granted only so far as it would tend to the everlasting well-being of the beloved one.

The celebrated religious writer, Cecil, called to see a friend, one day, and told him he heard that he was in a dangerous condition. His friend expressed his unconsciousness of any cause of alarm;

on which Cecil told him that he supposed such was the case, and had therefore called on him. The danger to which he was desirous of awakening the attention of the earnest listener was, that he was attaining wealth,— prospering in the world,— increasing that which would necessarily require more and more attention, and which, without a special blessing from above, would be likely seriously to interfere with his eternal well-being.

HEAVEN—HOME.

There is much of interest in a remark made by a young daughter of a rich man. Her father being ill, and likely soon to die, was apportioning his estate among his children by word of mouth, which perhaps he had neglected to do in a proper manner by will. As she heard him saying that he gave this house to one, and that house to another, she inquired of him, if he had any house where he was going? Perhaps she did not fully herself feel the tremendous importance of the query. But it is one that the rich and the poor of this world are alike interested in asking themselves. Hast thou, dear reader, a sure and certain inheritance in heaven — a mansion of glory which ever endureth, made thine through faith in the Lord Jesus, and that new birth unto holiness by which thou hast become an heir of God, and a joint heir with Christ?

When Baxter was dying, to an inquiry as to his condition he could joyfully say, "Almost well! and nearly at home!" One who was made a martyr for the word of God and the testimony of the Lord Jesus, on being asked, as he approached the stake, how he felt, answered, "Never better; for now I know that I am almost at home." Another religious man, near his close, said, "I am going home as fast as I can; and I bless God that I have a good home to go to."

Oh, to feel heaven is our home! that a mansion has been prepared for us therein! what happiness, what inexpressible peace and thankful love, it must beget in the soul. The return to our earthly homes, if we are blessed with sociable feelings, and a loving circle of dear ones there await us, is a cause of happiness to the heart. In the life of the late Patrick Tytler, this passage relative to his father is introduced. "In those days when we knew my father was to be detained in town till late in the evening, we always placed a candle in this window. Often did he remark that he never gained sight of this twinkling light through the trees of the avenue, without feeling his heart raised in gratitude to heaven for the many blessings by which he was surrounded, and the happy home to which he was returning." Such feelings would be likely to arise spontaneously in the heart of every religious, home-loving traveller as he drew near the termination of his journey; and how much stronger should the emotions be in the bosom of the Christian who feels himself rapidly drawing near to the blessed home prepared for him in heaven! Ah! he may see with the eye of faith, not indeed the twinkle of a feeble light through a solitary window, welcoming him to the endearments of his household, but the love of Christ giving forth such a brightness to his everlasting home, that it needs no light of the sun to lighten it, whilst, in the depth of his humble heart, he can catch some whispers of the cheering welcome, "Come, ye blessed of my Father, inherit the kingdom prepared for you."

OUR PAST LIVES.

The experience of an individual is recorded who, in imminent danger of what appeared a certain death, seemed to see at a glance, spread before his mind as on a map, his whole life from his youth up. He lived to record the fact, which may be regarded as an instance of the extreme rapidity of thought in moments of peril. What a succession of scenes of sin and weakness, dear reader, would some of our lives present, were they spread before us in their true character. If a bright spot appeared, it would be where Divine grace had been manifested for our deliverance from sin, enabling us to take up the cross and to follow the Saviour, in some degree of faithful dedication.

" A few years ago," says a writer, "I was travelling in South America. As I approached the base of a mountain which lay in my route, I found it covered with what I supposed to be an undergrowth of weeds. But I pressed my way onward, and climbed up its sides till I had reached the summit. When I had gained the top, I gazed around me with delight, and happened to look back upon the winding way in which I had ascended, and lo! my whole path was clearly marked out to the very foot of the mountain. I found it was caused by my having walked through a growth of the sensitive plant, as it is familiarly known to us, which grows indigenous there. It had left all my way plain before me, so that I could trace my footsteps in all their curves and deviations, as I had struggled up the sides of that beautiful mountain."

Our every action has left an enduring impression more tangible to Omniscience than the sensitive plant record to the eye of the traveller of his every turn in his upward path. How many curves have we made, dear reader, through weakness or faltering, from the straightforward, upward track. Look back over thy past life! Was there not often a turning to the left or right? Time is yet allowed us for amendment of life. The record of our sins may be blotted out, if, through faith in the Lord Jesus, and a patient submission to his purifying baptisms, we are washed and made clean in the laver of regeneration. Blessed are they whose sins go beforehand to judgment. Against such, whatever the darkness of their past lives, whatever the wandering, serpentine course of their earlier days may have been, there stands no record of guilt, but the words of glad welcome await them, "Come, ye blessed of my Father, inherit the kingdom prepared for you."

No matter how high our profession has been, no matter how pure the doctrine we may have advocated, or the precepts we may have inculcated, if we have not witnessed that real change of heart which our Saviour terms "being born again," we are not in a state of acceptance, and our sins of omission and commission stand in terrible distinctness against us. If, in this condition, our past lives should be brought before us, through all their courses, great would be our horror and anguish of spirit. We may have led moral lives, we may have borne excellent characters among men, yet if our path has been trodden in the natural will of man, which is ever opposed to God, and we have not experienced reconciliation through the blood of Christ, which subdues the old enmity, we are aliens from the covenant of promise, and cannot inherit the kingdom of heaven. Let us see to it whilst time is allotted us. Let us look over the paths of our lives, and, whilst in deep sorrow of heart, lamenting our wasted years, let us seek the Lord Jesus for purity, pardon, and peace. These may yet be our portion, if, in unreserved sincerity of heart, we turn to the Lord, and let him rule and work in us that which is well pleasing in his sight. Then will the retrospect of our past lives, whilst humbling us to the dust, cease to bring horror and remorse, for we shall feel that though less than the least of all saints, yet grace has been given us to draw near to him who has said, "He that cometh unto me I will in nowise cast out."

HE IS DEAD!

An incident took place some years ago at Belfast, of solemn interest. Two thoughtless, irreligious young men met. One invited the other to go with him that night to the theatre. The invitation was declined, not from a want of inclination, but because he had promised his parents to go with them that evening to a religious meeting. They parted, the one to the scene of vicious dissipation, the other to a place where, through the mercy of God, a word spoken in season was blessed to the awakening of his thoughtless soul. A time of sore conflict came on him, and having been brought to see that, through the Lord Jesus Christ, a way was opened for his salvation, he felt his mind impressed with the desire that his friend, his companion in many a wrong deed, might also be favored to seek and find that mercy which he thankfully believed was offered to him. On the second morning he called at the residence of his friend, and when the door was opened, he passed in and was going quickly up to the chamber of his friend, as he was accustomed to do, when a woman with a very serious countenance inquired where he was going. He replied, "To see John." "Stop, stop," she said, "he is dead!" He had been taken ill during the night, and before the morning he was no more.

How touching to the feelings of the survivor must have been this announcement. Himself not only spared, but called to seek repentance and amendment of life, while his companion was cut off, it was to be feared, in the midst of his sins.

What a lesson, to take fast hold of that instruction which is the way of life.

Reader, canst thou not gain a lesson here also? Has not the mercy of a long-forbearing God spared thee, when many around thee have been called to give an account of the deeds done in the body? Suddenly it may have been in some cases. Art thou ready? "for in such an hour as ye think not the Son of man cometh." Happy shall that servant be whom his Lord, when he cometh, shall find watching.

RICHES.

IT COSTS TOO MUCH.

OUR blessed Saviour has said, "What shall it profit a man if he gain the whole world and lose his own soul?" This whole world, with all its riches, its honors, its comforts, its enjoyments, would be a bad bargain to him who should give his immortal soul in exchange for it. Yet all around us we see instances in which this soul, in comparison with which in real value all earthly possessions are as nothing, bartered away for a mere trifle.

A striking account has been preserved of an individual who had been piously educated and brought up to industrious habits. Whilst in an humble condition in a mercantile establishment, into which he was introduced after his maturity, he was a professor of religion, and his reputation was good. In time, from his faithful attention to business, he was taken as a partner into the firm. After this his mind was occupied more entirely with his worldly concerns, whilst religion, even in the outward form of it, had less and less time and attention given to it. Whilst yet in the meridian of his days he became very wealthy, and with his increasing store his love of riches increased. He grew covetous and miserly, and from his conduct and conversation, no one would have supposed that he had ever been even a professor of religion. The dew of his youth was dried up; the religious principles received from education were dissipated; the tendering visitations of the love of God once known, were no longer experienced. He then purchased a large estate, reared a costly edifice upon it, and settled down to enjoy himself, as far as one in his situation could know enjoyment, and then came the summons of death. In the prospect of an opening eternity, the folly of his career in life pressed upon him. No doubt the days of his innocent childhood came before him, when, with poverty, some degree of religious peace was his portion. The sad change which had taken place since in his feelings and in his hopes, wrung from him the exclamation, just before death, "my prosperity has been my ruin."

His wealth cost too much. His grand house and immense riches all remained this side of the grave, and, without spiritual hope or inheritance, he was about to enter into the everlasting state. Thousands in our country have bartered away their souls for still meaner things than an earthly estate. For the intoxicating cup; for the gratification of sensual indulgence; for pride, vanity, the love of glory, the applause of men, and the fear of their reproach, countless multitudes have given away their souls, and with them all well-grounded hope of an heavenly inheritance in unfading, unending blessedness.

THE LOVE OF MONEY THE ROOT OF EVIL.

When Baron Rothschild, on a certain occasion, was dining at the house of Fowell Buxton, his whole discourse was of money, of the art of making or preserving and increasing an estate, and the manner in which he had trained up his children to follow his footsteps in this respect. His hostess ventured to express a hope that *he did not allow them to forget that never-ending life so soon to begin, for which also preparation must be made.* He replied, that he could not allow them to think of such a thing. It would divert their minds from business. It would be fatal to their success. To get and keep a fortune is a very difficult thing, and *requires all one's time and thoughts.*

The fruit of these teachings of the father is shown in the biography of the son. Nathan Rothschild, who was called the high-priest of the exchange, was so fearful of being assassinated, the latter part of his life, that he never went out alone after dark, never entered an unlighted room, had servants within call of his bed-chamber, and slept with loaded pistols under his pillow. A Frankforter, dining with him one evening, and observing the luxury of his household, remarked: "You must be happy, baron, with the power to gratify every wish." "Happy, indeed!" was the response. "Do you think it happiness, to be haunted always with the dread of murder, to have your appetite for breakfast sharpened by a threat to stab you to the heart, unless you enclose a thousand guineas to some unknown villain?"

What a contrast does the condition of mind of this millionnaire present, when compared with that of the late Hannah Carson. As regards the possession of the things of this life, she was in a state of abject poverty, entirely dependent, during the last thirteen years of her life, upon the charity of others. This was in consequence of her loss of the use of all her limbs by disease; and she was even unable to take a mouthful of nourishment without being fed. She was, in addition to these deprivations, a great sufferer from acute bodily pain; yet such was her faith that her blessed Saviour would provide for all her needs, that, during the whole period of her confinement, she never doubted he would make provision for her; and she was never disappointed. The streams of Divine consolation so abounded that she testified, "I forgot my poor suffering body altogether. No matter how afflicted I am; no ability to eat or sleep; still I have this peace, this comfort that seems to subdue my bodily affliction all to silence. If every hair on my head were a tongue, I would employ them all in praising Almighty God." This poor colored woman had employed herself in laying up treasure in heaven; Nathan Rothschild employed himself in seeking the riches of this world. Both were successful.

AN AWAKENING INQUIRY.

It is narrated that a young man of good natural talents, and very ambitious to become of eminence and distinction in the world, had, after long craving, obtained permission of his parents to study law, by which he hoped and expected to win fame and fortune. Flushed with enthusiasm, and eager to commence the studies which were the necessary stepping stones in the path he had determined to tread, he entered one of the Italian universities, at which, at that time, resided Filippo Neri, a man noted for his piety and wisdom. The young man had, when a boy, known Filippo, and he now eagerly sought an opportunity of telling him his hopes and his expectations. He spoke of his intentions to spare no pains or labor in his studies, that he might thoroughly qualify himself for becoming an eminent lawyer. The old man listened with kindly interest, as the young one poured out his thoughts and intentions, and when the fluent, buoyant-hearted harangue was ended, quietly inquired what he intended to do after his studies were finished.

"Then I shall take my doctor's degree."

"And then?" said his aged friend.

"Then I shall have a number of difficult and knotty cases to manage; shall catch people's notice by my eloquence, my zeal, my learning, my acuteness, and gain a great reputation."

"And then?"

"Why, then, there cannot be a question I shall be promoted to some high office or other; besides, I shall make money and grow rich."

"And then?"

"Then I shall live comfortably and honorably, in health and dignity, and shall be able to look forward quietly to a happy old age."

"And then?"

"Then," said the young man, "why then,—then,—then I shall die."

Once more the old man uttered the query, "And then?"

The youthful aspirant after earthly honor and riches cast down his eyes, and made no answer. The question sent home to his heart by the awakening visitations of the Holy Spirit, produced a great change there. The pomp and glories of this fleeting world lost their lustre and attractive force to him. Soon he forsook the study of the law, and sought, by devoting himself to the Lord's service, to become humble and useful rather than exalted and popular. He wished to be a faithful servant of Christ and of his church rather than, through riches, qualifications, and station, to be a ruler, a commander, and controller of mankind.

How many of us there are, who, if we would follow out the query, "and then?" to the end, would find, if we allowed the unflattering witness to speak, that our pursuits and intentions are not such as would be desirable in the prospect of a certain and speedy death.

THE UNDUE PURSUIT OF RICHES.

A religious man, who deceased in Philadelphia not many years since, was so anxious that his children should not regard worldly business, and the pecuniary profits thereof, as the most important object of life, that he studiously avoided in the family circle talking about money transactions. Doubtless his concern on behalf of his children in this, as well as other matters, was blessed. Were some of the busy toilers after earthly riches, who from morning to night are seeking to extend their sales and increase their profits, to withdraw for a few minutes occasionally from the bustle, tumult, and strife of business competition, and seek in quiet introversion for the mind of Truth, they would feel the eager spirit of gain in them restrained. Seek ye first the kingdom of God and his righteousness, and all things needful shall be added unto you. If any are neglecting religious duties under the plea of being too much occupied in worldly business, they have need closely to scrutinize their actions and their motives. With them the things of time are getting into undue importance.

WAR.

THOU SHALT NOT KILL.

"What hast thou done? the voice of thy brother's blood crieth unto me from the ground."—GEN. iv. 10.

THE consideration of the state into which an accountable being passes when set free from this earthly existence by the touch of death is that which makes the prospect of the change so awful. An eternity of agony, where "the worm dieth not, and the fire is not quenched," is the portion of those who die in their sins. On this earth is our season of probation, and if, through the mercy of God in Christ Jesus, we have witnessed the washing of regeneration and the renewing of the Holy Ghost, and have received a good hope through grace, we shall obtain "life eternal" with the righteous; otherwise we must take our portion with those who go into "everlasting punishment." How should such considerations influence every one to be faithful in the support of the Christian testimony against war. Every great battle occasions the death of many, of whom, judging with the utmost charity, we must believe that a large portion have never known what it was to submit to the regenerating, soul-cleansing operations of the Holy Spirit. To be in any way accessory to cutting off the life of a human being who is in a state of sin and alienation from God, must ever be abhorrent to the feelings of a Christian; and where he has, through momentary excitement, through what he has deemed a necessary obedience to the laws of the land, or a supposed duty to his country, or through accident, been a participator in that which has occasioned the death of such a one, we can readily feel that the remembrance thereof will prove to him a gnawing worm of bitterness at times to the end of his days. These thoughts have arisen from reading a passage in the life of the late Bird Wilson.

Bird Wilson, son of James Wilson, (one of the signers of the Declaration of Independence, and one of the Judges of the Supreme Court of the United States,) was born at Carlisle, in Pennsylvania, in 1777. He was of a quiet, home-loving disposition from early childhood; and his reputation for prudence and stability of character was so fully established, that even in childhood his father never deemed it necessary to send him out of his office when he had the great men of the times with him there, or other persons on public or private business. Bird was brought up to the profession of the law, and was admitted to the bar at twenty-one. At twenty-five years of age he was appointed President Judge of the Court of Common Pleas, in a circuit comprising Chester, Delaware, Montgomery, and Bucks counties, Pennsylvania. He was religious as a man, conscientious as a judge, and well versed in legal as well as general knowledge. Some years after this appointment, through his love for books and his efforts to obtain them, the writer became, though then quite a boy, somewhat acquainted with him, and can remember the wonder excited when, by a letter from himself, we received the information that he intended to leave the Bench and the bar, and to devote himself to the ministry of the gospel. He probably had, during a considerable period, contemplated such a change; but the exciting cause of his making it at that time appears to have been the distress of mind he experienced in condemning, as a judge, a poor murderer to death. The proof of the prisoner's guilt was complete; and as the jury returned a verdict of "wilful murder," the judge had no escape, if he fulfilled the duties of the station he occupied, but to pronounce the sentence of death upon him. This act he performed. It was soon done, but a life-long penalty of secret suffering for his participation in this young man's death was paid by the judge.

He left the bar. For years he was actively engaged as a clergyman in ministering to his flock; then for a long period he labored as a Professor in a Theological Seminary, and during the whole time various other occupations of a religious and literary character filled up his chosen sphere of life-work; but during more than forty years which he lived after passing sentence on that prisoner, no change of occupation, no labor for the good of others, seemed to weaken or efface the painful effect it left on his mind.

Towards the close of his life, his mind became seriously disordered; and one night, when no person except a beloved niece, and the friend who subsequently drew the sketch of his life, were sitting by his bedside, his mind evidently was agonizing over that most awful act of his life. What followed, we will give in the words of that biographer. "As we narrowly watched every changing expression of his countenance, and listened, in breathless silence, to catch whatever might escape his lips, he turned his straining eyes heavenward, and the most indescribable expression of intense, fearful agony settled darkly on his features. Then clasping his forehead violently with both hands, he exclaimed, in tones of the deepest bitterness, 'He was launched into eternity unprepared; but, O

God! impute it not to me!' The whole scene has made an indelible impression upon the two who witnessed it, and who were at no loss in realizing that he had gone back in imagination to what had been, in all probability, the closing scene in his judicial career. The emotions which then agitated his soul, as he looked down upon the poor, doomed culprit, again wrung his heart with an agony embittered by the fearful reflection that he had been hurried into the presence of his God before his sins had been done away by his mercy.

"Perfectly unmanned by a scene so harrowing to us, and knowing not which way to turn, I can only remember having clasped his trembling hands, entreating him to forget what had transpired so long ago. 'All this, Doctor,' said I, 'occurred years ago, while you were a judge; but, remember, now you are a clergyman.' Turning upon me with the quickness of thought, he exclaimed, 'What of that? Do you suppose that I am not to answer for what I did as a judge?'"

Although his mind was then much shattered, he could still feel his accountability, and despised the sophistry which was kindly intended by allusion to the length of time which had elapsed since the deed was done, and the different circumstances in which he had since been placed, to lessen it in his eyes. His mind never regained the possession of its faculties, and the last glimpse we have of this really conscientious and worthy man is that of one sinking into his grave under the burden of a soul-harrowing dread, in a feeling of awful responsibility for having in his official capacity, and whilst enforcing the laws of his country, which he had been sworn to maintain, condemned an impenitent sinner to death, and precluded all hope of his reformation or preparation, through the cleansing mercy of God, for happiness hereafter: for having hurried one into that place of awful punishment, from which, cut off in his sins, there could be no escape forever.

FROM WHENCE COME WARS AND FIGHTINGS?

No one can calculate the effect which an action, or even a word, may produce. This thought should incite us to watchfulness, that our utterance and our actions should be all of a kind to produce good rather than evil results. A work upon Florence shows the origin of one of the innumerable wars for which that commonwealth was so noted.

At the time of the coronation of the Emperor Frederick II., the Florentines and the Pisans each sent a deputation to Rome to attend that ceremony. Whilst there, the Florentines were invited, one day, to dine with one of the rich men of that city, and being much pleased with a lap-dog belonging to their host, they begged it of him, and he promised that they should have it. The next day the Pisans dining there, made a similar request, and received a similar promise. The Florentines calling first, secured the dog; but the Pisans, finding them conveying the prize to their quarters, with the aid of fifty soldiers fell upon the unprepared company, and took it from them by force. The Florentines, in turn, fell upon the Pisans and took full revenge. The Pisans returning to their city, by their representations inflamed the passions of its inhabitants, who confiscated such property of the Florentines as they could find within that place. As soon as the news of this reached Florence, that commonwealth, ever ready for aught that might weaken a neighbor, or open a prospect of enlarging its own power, declared war against Pisa. The armies met, the battle lasted the whole of a day, and at its close the Pisan army was thoroughly routed, many of its useful and industrious citizens were slaughtered, and thirteen hundred of the members of its principal families were carried captive to Florence. And all about a dog. In considering this awful affair, may we not ask, with the apostle, "From whence come wars and fightings among you? come they not hence, even of your lusts that war in your members?"

THE MARKS OF THE LORD JESUS.

What a blessed thing it is for any one to receive, and to be enabled, through the renewings of preserving grace, to retain and to bear about daily before the world the marks of the Lord Jesus. The Apostle Paul, writing to the Galatians, says: "God forbid that I should glory, save in the cross of our Lord Jesus Christ, by whom the world is crucified unto me, and I unto the world. For in Christ Jesus neither circumcision availeth anything, nor uncircumcision, but a new creature. And as many as walk according to this rule, peace be on them, and mercy, and upon the Israel of God. From henceforth let no man trouble me: for I bear in my body the marks of the Lord Jesus. Brethren, the grace of our Lord Jesus Christ be with your spirit." The marks of the Lord Jesus — blessed are they who bear them! Now, as in the days of Ezekiel, there are marks set upon those who, faithful in their measure to the Lord's requirings as respects themselves, do yet sigh and cry for the abominations that are done by nominal Christians around them. Of these marks, that of a faithful bearing of the cross is a prominent one, and it is surrounded by many others most attractive — gentleness, humility, purity, charity, love! Indeed, all the graces of the Holy Spirit leave their sweet markings there. John Woolman has very characteristically said, "Some glances of real beauty may be seen in their faces who dwell in true meekness. There is a harmony in the sound of that voice to which Divine love gives utterance, and some appearance of right order in their temper and conduct whose passions are regulated; yet all these do not fully show forth that inward life to such who have not felt it; but this white stone and new name are known rightly to such only who have them."

The evangelical prophet Isaiah very beautifully typifies the peaceable glory, the loving harmony, the heavenly brightness, of the Christian dispensation; and the early writers among the Christians appeal to their heathen neighbors to bear witness, whether it did not plainly appear, from the meek, holy, innocent forbearing and forgiving conduct of the Christians, that these prophecies were fulfilled in them. They felt the necessity of a daily watch over all their actions, that, by their circumspect demeanor, their vigilant enemies should have no cause given them even to harbor a suspicion against the purity and holiness of their lives. Tertullian, who wrote one hundred years after the apostles, says, "It is not enough that a Christian be chaste and modest, but he must *appear* to be so: a virtue of which he should have so great a store, that it should flow from his mind upon his habit, and break from the retirements of his conscience into the superficies of his life." Truly, here were unmistakably the marks of Christ. Again, arguing that war, with its harsh, proud, vindictive passions, could have no part in the gospel dispensation, the same writer says, "Can a soldier's employment be lawful, when Christ has pronounced that he that uses the sword shall perish by the sword? Can one who professes the peaceable doctrine of the gospel be a warrior? He who must not so much as strive or contend? And shall he who is not to revenge his own wrongs, be instrumental to bring others into chains, imprisonment, torments, and death?" Tertullian well knew that all the marks of war were those of the Beast. There could be no retaliation for wrong inflicted among the consistent disciples of him who had forbidden his followers even to resist. As to the spirit of patient submission which is one of the marks of a true disciple, he says, "Christ truly teacheth a new patience, even forbidding the revenging of an injury."

The marks of Christ are often seen in the humble, the suffering, the despised among men. In the midst of the scoff and scorn of those around them, such faithful cross-bearing disciples are upholding a testimony for Truth which the enemies thereof often find too powerful for them to resist. Nay, it at times is the case, in the good Providence of a long-suffering Saviour, that an arrow of conviction is shot from the bow of their consistency, which, entering in at the joints of the harness of their wicked or thoughtless opposers, inflicts a spiritual wound, which, by its agonizing sharpness, drives them to the Lord Jesus Christ, the true Physician, for cure. Yea! the innocent faithfulness, the humble, yet firm standing, the unresisting submission to the rod of persecution, whilst bearing an unflinching testimony for the Truth, make a powerful appeal to the consciences of oppressors, and has an efficient tendency to awaken serious and spirit-stirring reflections. In the early days of Christianity, it was said, "the blood of the martyrs is the seed of the Church," and those who now, through many sufferings, through scorn and reviling, faithfully maintain in life and conversation the testimonies of the gospel, do not suffer in vain.

The efficacy of an unwavering testimony to the

Truth, of an open and unfaltering bearing the "marks of the Lord Jesus," is strongly set forth in an occurrence of the late war. A sick prisoner, observing a person passing by him, whose attire he thought proclaimed him a member of the Society of Friends, called him to his side. He told the Friend that in the regiment he belonged to, there were some Quakers, who, because they would neither fight nor perform any military service, suffered harshness and abuse and much ridicule. The repentant invalid acknowledged that he had joined with others in thus heaping contumely and scorn upon them, and had wondered at the meekness and patience with which they bore it all. He knew that he could not have done so, and, on thoughtfully considering the matter, he was convinced that they had attained a condition of mind to which he was a stranger. As his memory recurred to the days of his youth, he felt that he had once known something of such an influence as he supposed strengthened and supported them in their tribulations, and he had been incited by what he beheld in them to seek after a renewed acquaintance therewith. His earnest wrestling after the fresh visitations of Grace appeared to be, through the favor of his dear Saviour, mercifully blessed, and he could add thankfully, "And now, if I die, I shall not die without hope!"

Thus it was apparent that these persecuted, scoffed, and ridiculed confessors of Christ had borne a convincing testimony for the Truth. In simple obedience to the requiring of duty, from day to day they faithfully carried the cross for their Divine Master, without flinching from the suffering, or manifesting ill-will to those who afflicted them. They bore all from love and dedication to their Saviour, for the sake of their own souls' present peace and eternal salvation; but they knew not that their heavenly Father had a purpose of grace towards any one which was to be effected through their faithfulness. What bodily suffering! what mental anxiety! what scorn and contempt ought not a faithful follower of Christ to be willing to endure, if thereby one soul is so awakened from the sleep of carnal security and sin as to be induced so to seek as to obtain of the blessed Saviour repentance for the past, sanctification for the present, and an humble hope of everlasting salvation for the future. Whilst mentioning this incident, to encourage all to a faithful bearing before the world the "marks of the Lord Jesus," we know that all the praise is due to that grace through which they were instructed in the Lord's will, and enabled to walk in humble obedience thereto.

EXAMPLE OF THE EARLY CHRISTIANS.

In the reign of the Emperor Diocletian, who boasted that he had stamped out the Christian religion, Maximilian, a youth of twenty years of age, suffered death, because, being a Christian, he knew that it was unlawful for him to fight. He had, through the new birth unto holiness, received therewith the "marks of the Lord Jesus,"— the spirit to forgive injuries; to love enemies; to do good to those who hated, and to pray for those who despitefully used and persecuted him; and he would not suffer himself to be enrolled in the army, to wear the outward mark of a warrior, which was typical of the inward marks of the Beast,—anger, wrath, revenge, and a spirit not only to return injury for injury, but to render merciless slaughter and destruction to those who, although they had never offended, were yet citizens of another government, and politically enemies. On the inquiry of Dion, the proconsul, as to his name, he came at once to his conscientious testimony against war: "I must not fight, for I am a Christian." An officer being commanded to *mark* him, he earnestly exclaimed, "I cannot fight." "Bear arms, or thou shalt die," said the proconsul. "I cannot fight, if I die! I fight not for this world." Being questioned as to who had persuaded him not to fight, he answered, "My own mind, and he who called me." Yes, Christ, the Prince of Peace, who had called him out of darkness into his marvellous light, through his Holy Spirit, had begotten in him a new heart, which felt and could breathe the language, "Glory to God in the highest! peace on earth, good-will to men!" The Spirit within him bore testimony against all war, all ill will to others, and it was in accordance with the New Testament record of the heavenly doctrines, the pure, loving, meek, forgiving utterances of our Lord Jesus Christ. Dion, finding that he could not intimidate the young Christian, turned to Victor, the boy's father, and urged him to prevail on his son to bear arms. The father had not so learned Christ. Although deeply feeling, no doubt, because of the sufferings his son must endure, if faithful; yet he would not do anything, or say anything, to weaken his confession of the Truth, but would rather incite him to faithfulness to the inward manifestations of duty, and to the outward testimony of Scripture to the peaceable nature of the gospel dispensation. "He knows his own mind, and what is best for him to do," he said. He knew the mind of his child. He knew what that faithful disciple of a crucified Saviour thought it best to do, and he felt no wish to see his beloved son escape death, if it must be by sacrificing principle. Dion, failing to influence the father, once more addressed the son: "Take thy arms, and receive the mark." One portion of the mark was a ring of lead, which, as a visible military badge, was placed around the neck. To the command, the undaunted youth answered, "I can receive no such mark. I have already the mark of Christ." Dion threatened that he would quickly send him to his Christ, and then again directed an officer to mark him. This occasioned Maximilian to say, "I cannot receive the mark of this world; and if thou shouldst mark me, I shall break it, for it will avail nothing. I am a Christian; and it is not lawful for me to wear such a mark about my neck, when I have received the saving mark of my Lord Jesus Christ, the Son of the living God, — whom thou art ignorant of, — who died to give us life, and whom God gave for our sins. Him we Christians obey. Him we follow as the Restorer of our life and the Author of our salvation." Being told to take the mark, or he would perish miserably, he said, "I shall not perish: my name is already enrolled with my Lord. I cannot fight." On the proconsul asserting that to bear arms was becoming to a young man, he observed, "My arms are with my Lord. I cannot fight for this world. I am now a Christian." Being told that some professors of Christianity were in the army, he declined answering for their acts, but said, "I am a Christian, and cannot do evil." The proconsul then said, "Take thy arms; despise not the business of a soldier, lest thou perish miserably." With holy confidence in the mercy of God, through his blessed Son, the young man answered, "I shall not perish; and if I leave this world, my soul shall live with Christ, my Lord."

His name was stricken off the roll, and his sentence was read, that, because he had refused to bear arms, he was to die by the sword. As he was led to the place of execution, he endeavored to encourage his Christian brethren to be faithful unto death, that they also might receive the crown of life. Thus bearing openly, in the sight of others, the marks of the Lord Jesus, he passed along with a pleasant countenance. After requesting his father to give a coat, prepared for his own use, to the executioner, he cheerfully submitted to death. The whole family appear to have received, and to have openly borne, plain "marks of the Lord Jesus." In an ancient narrative of this remarkable transaction, it is said, "Victor, his father, returned to his habitation rejoicing and praising God that he had sent before such a gift unto the

Lord, himself expecting to follow after." His mother obtaining the dead body, had it conveyed to Carthage for burial, and in thirteen days after the martyrdom of her son, she was herself released by death from bearing the cross for her Lord on earth, and was taken to receive the crown in heaven.

The marks of the Lord Jesus! How desirable it is that we should all bear them openly and fully. When the apostles were brought before the council, the rulers took notice " that they had been with Jesus." Acts iv. 14. They bore marks which even the heathen could recognize.

THE HEART OF MAN IS DECEITFUL ABOVE ALL THINGS, AND DESPERATELY WICKED; WHO CAN KNOW IT?

When Timour Beg, often called Tamerlane, or Timour the Tartar, was about eighteen years of age, it is recorded that he went through some severe struggles of mind on account of the sins of his earlier youth. It is probable that the convictions which then came upon him were dispensed, by Infinite mercy, for his everlasting good, and that, if he had continued obedient to the light then unfolded, he might have been a benefactor instead of a scourge of the human family. As it was, a great change for the better came over him. His habits of thought and of action were altered. He made profession of repentance for the follies and the wickedness of his past life. As an act of duty, he abstained from playing at chess, to which he had been greatly addicted; and, in view of the kindness which he deemed the due of every living creature from man, he made a vow that he would never wilfully injure any one of them. So tender, indeed, at that time were his feelings for the comfort of the smallest created object endued with life and sensation, that he was greatly grieved on finding that he had inadvertently set his foot upon an emmet, extinguishing life; causing at least momentary suffering, and preventing whatever future amount of pleasure that insect might otherwise have enjoyed. It is recorded that, through the shock his mind endured from having been the occasion of this accidental destruction of life, a nervous debility affected the foot which had crushed the animal, and he felt for a time as though it had lost all muscular power. Such was Timour under the influence, without doubt, of some holy impressions, yet filled with fanaticism, engendered by a false religious faith, tending to exaggeration in feeling and hypocrisy in profession. Time passed on. This man, so deeply affected at the destruction of an ant, under the teachings of ambition, learned to turn a deaf ear to the cry of suffering humanity; to gaze unmoved at the massacre of thousands, and, in his march of desolation, to leave as famous a name as a destroyer of his fellow-creatures, as any one with whose career as a conqueror history has made us acquainted. Ambition prompted him to the destruction of kindred, and led him on to aggressive war; success increased his delight in the fierce carnage of the battle-field, whilst he conjured up pretended principles of justice to soothe his own conscience, to enable him to stifle its convictions, and to offer some sort of a plea by which he hoped to obtain a favorable verdict from those who should undertake to judge of his actions. The principles he avowed, and under which he sought to screen his own course of rapine and blood, were to this effect. First, " from regard to justice, a prince should assault every kingdom wherein tyranny, oppression, and iniquity predominated, and extirpate the authors of these national calamities;" and again, "It is the duty of a victorious king to bring under his authority every kingdom where the people are oppressed by their rulers."

Had any one told Timour, in the period of his tender-hearted feeling for the lower animals, that he would one day, without hesitation, in cold blood, order the destruction of myriads of his fellow-men, with multitudes of helpless women and children, slaying some with the sword, burning others in the dwellings wherein they had witnessed the pleasures and comforts of domestic life, he would have felt, probably, as Hazael did, when, on being told of the enormities he should commit as a conquering prince, he exclaimed, " Is thy servant a dog, that he should do this great thing?" No one knows, when he departs from the convictions of truth, to what degree of wickedness he may debase himself. No one can tell, when he stifles the pleadings of mercy in his bosom in ever so small a degree, be it under whatever plea it may, how far the one act of inhumanity may open the way for others. Little by little does the heart become hardened; little by little do mankind in a general way lose the tenderness and innocency of youth. We should turn from sin in every shape; nay, the apostle exhorts to avoid even the appearance of evil. Thus only shall we, can we, be preserved from participating in wickedness.

Leslie, the noted English artist, would not look at pictures painted with bad taste, lest inadvertently his pencil should, as he expressed it, take a hint from them, or, in other words, lest his own style of painting should be debased. It is well for Christians to feel a great jealousy over themselves, lest, dwelling on the evil actions going on around them, they become more or less leavened into the prevailing spirit actuating the many to wrong; lest, in other words, they in their actions show that they have "taken a hint" from sin, instead of keeping to the soul-preserving instructions of grace. At a time when the spirit of war strongly actuates the community around us, if we do not watch over our spirits with great care, if we do not seek for preserving grace from the only Fountain thereof, we shall be almost certain to "take a hint" from the actions, the conversation, the prevailing war-tone of our neighbors, and shall find ourselves losing ground as respects a faithful support in our thoughts and feelings of the spirit of the gospel, the spirit that breathes and craves nothing but peace on earth and good-will to all men.

LOVE YOUR ENEMIES.

Basil Patras Zulu was born in Greece, in the year 1804. He was a chief by birth, and when only eleven years old, his father being deceased, he was taken from under the care of his mother, by the chiefs of his tribe, and placed at their head. The Greeks were then in active rebellion against their old masters, the Turks; and Basil was not only educated as a warrior, but with the most intense hatred of those who were then oppressing, and had for centuries tyrannized over, his nation. The boy-warrior was active, bold, and energetic; and, being beloved by his tribe, whom he led to bloody victories, he was as cordially hated by the Turks, who offered a reward for his head before he was sixteen years of age. He was one of that band who, having defended Missolonghi against the army of Turkey and the Egyptian fleet until it was no longer defensible, cut its way through the Turkish camp, leaving the pathway covered with fallen enemies and stricken friends. One-half the band fell in the attempt, and Basil was himself severely wounded. He, however, was one that effected the passage. He was sick of the horrible scenes he beheld; for although he had a passion for war and victory, and on the battle-field showed no compunction for the slaughter of multitudes, yet he loathed the terrible acts of revenge and retaliation which he witnessed. At last, having in vain remonstrated with his countrymen against the cold-blooded murder of a band of captive Turks, he retired from the Greek army with disgust.

His character and actions had won him the respect and admiration of many, and he found active and faithful friends, under whose auspices he continued until the year 1828, when he was awakened to a serious consideration of the condition of his own soul, under the ministry of the Moravians. In a hotel in Dublin, a Moravian woman in his presence offered up a prayer so different from anything he had ever heard, that it immediately drew his attention. As a Greek, he had in times of danger called upon the Virgin for aid; but he knew nothing of a heart-cleansing, heart-changing religion, and of that faith and love which animated the utterances of this woman. He inquired to what community of Christians the woman belonged; he read the history of the Moravians; he attended at their place of worship, and having, through submission to the inward work of the Spirit, been thoroughly roused, he very naturally entered into communion with that body of Christians through whom, or with whom, he had been spiritually blessed. The chief, proud of his birth and station; the accomplished man, whose society had been courted by the best circles where he had travelled; the fierce soldier, was soon found mingling in Christian union among the simple-hearted Moravians. He had deemed that to fight for one's country was a glorious privilege, and, whilst ever gentle and courteous to his friends, he had thought himself bound, as a good citizen, to hate the enemies of Greece. He had often declared his belief that the Lord Jesus Christ and his apostles would have had no mercy on the Turks, the bloody tyrants, the insatiable plunderers of Greece; but he now soon found that the gospel of our Lord Jesus Christ laid the axe to the evil root in man's nature, from which alone war, revenge, and angry feelings can spring. One of the Moravians who had been specially delegated to answer his inquiries, and to instruct him in needful things, was surprised, one day, by Basil's entering into his room, and in great agitation exclaiming: " Come, now! come! I see it now!" Hastily leading his instructor to his own apartment, the late soldier pointed to the text, Matthew v. 44, " Love your enemies! Love your enemies!" " I see it now!—even the Turks! It bids us love our enemies, *even the Turks! even the Turks!*"

The spirit of the gospel was more and more opened to him, and, through the grace of our Lord Jesus, it more and more ruled in him. He became a devoted Christian, a lover of peace, desiring the good of all men, even of the Turks. The tumults, the fears, the bloody strifes which had been abundantly his portion during his childhood and youth, had given place to a quiet retirement in

Ireland; to the humble yet heart-cheering comforts of domestic life; to loving labors for the good of others, and for the spreading of the dear Redeemer's kingdom of righteousness and peace. In a few years he married that sister whose earnest prayer first led him to feel what true communion and worship was. They were prepared, by supreme love to the Saviour, for abounding love to each other, and they trod this world of much sorrow and comfort in sweet union until the year 1844, when death, coming at a few days' warning, found him ready with joy to render up his stewardship. With grateful resignation he exclaimed, "O Lord, my trust is in thee. I am thine, do with me as seemeth right in thy sight." His time was come, and the Prince of Peace, his blessed Saviour, gathered him to that city of love where all is harmony, and not a discordant thought can enter.

The proud Greek chief, the fierce enemy-hating warrior, had, through the grace of the Lord Jesus, been transformed into a loving, peaceable, forgiving Christian, even into an humble cross-bearing disciple of Him who prayed for his murderers, and who has left as a standing injunction on his faithful followers to do good to those who hate, and to pray for those who despitefully use and persecute. Near his humble home in Ireland his mortal remains were interred, his loss lamented by a bereaved family and a sorrowing church. The world took little note of his death; but a far higher, far more heavenly glory attends his memory than if he had been stricken down in some of his scenes of mortal conflict, and had been chronicled in stirring poesy with the Marco Bozzaris of his fatherland.

ROBERT BARCLAY AND THE HIGHWAYMEN.

When Robert Barclay's principles were put to the test, he did not forsake them to avoid persecution or imprisonment, which was often his lot; nor did he let them fall to the ground, as is the policy of some, in cases of imminent danger.

In one of his journeys from London, a circumstance occurred which strongly manifested his adherence to the principle of Christians being precluded from retaliating violence, even in self-defence. He was attacked by highwaymen on the road, one of whom levelled a pistol at him, and made a determined demand for his purse. Calm and self-possessed, Robert Barclay looked the robber in the face with a firm, but meek benignity; assured him he was *his* and every man's friend; that he was willing and ready to relieve his wants; that he was free from the fear of death through a

Divine hope in immortality, and therefore was not to be intimidated by a deadly weapon. He then appealed to him whether he could find it in his heart to shed the blood of one who had no other feeling or purpose but to do him good.

The robber was confounded: his eye quailed; his brawny arm trembled; his pistol dropped out of his hand to the ground, and he fled from the presence of the non-resistant hero, whom he could no longer confront.

It was observed the morning before he was attacked, Robert Barclay was more pensive than usual, and he expressed an opinion that some unusual trial or exercise would occur that day; but when it occurred, he enjoyed a remarkable serenity.

RETRIBUTION.

The underhanded way in which a few Cherokee Indians were induced to sign a pretended treaty, fraudulently conveying away the lands of the nation, which had never committed any power to them so to do, and the high-handed manner in which the provisions of that illegal and unjust agreement were carried into effect, are doubtless in the recollection of many. Before the Indians were removed, Georgia had sold portions of the land by lottery, and those who by these wicked means became claimants of such a title as that State could give, entered into possession of some parts of the lands, and turned the poor Indian out of his own house.

As an example of the manner in which many of them were used, we will give an extract from a " Memorial and Protest of the Cherokee Nation." It describes the process used in the case of John Ross, principal chief of the Cherokees. " He was at Washington city, on the business of his nation. When he returned, he travelled till about ten o'clock at night, to reach his family; rode up to the gate; saw a servant believed to be his own; dismounted, ordered his horse taken; went in, and, to his utter astonishment, found himself a stranger in his own house, his family having been, some days before, driven out to seek a new home. A thought then flitted across his mind that he could not, under all the circumstances of his situation, reconcile it to himself to tarry all night under the roof of his own house as a stranger, the new host of that house being the tenant of that mercenary band of Georgia speculators at whose instance his helpless family had been turned out and made homeless. Upon reflecting, however, that 'man is born unto trouble,' John Ross at once concluded to take up lodgings there for the night, and to console himself under the conviction of having met his afflictions and trials in a manner consistent with every principle of moral obligation towards himself and family, his country and his God. On the next morning he arose early, and went out into the yard, and saw some straggling herds of his cattle and sheep browsing about the place: his crop of corn undisposed of. In casting a look up into the wide-spreading branches of a majestic oak standing within the enclosure of the garden, and which overshadows the spot where lie the remains of his dear babe, and most beloved and affectionate father, he there saw, perched upon its boughs, that flock of beautiful peafowls once the matron's care and delight, but now left to destruction, and never more to be seen. He ordered his horse, paid his bill, and departed in search of his family; after travelling amid heavy rains, he had the happiness of overtaking them on the road, bound for some place of refuge within the State of Tennessee. Thus have his houses, farm, public ferries, and other property been seized and wrested from him."

It will be useless to our present purpose to narrate the manner in which the Cherokees and Creeks were removed west of the Mississippi, and there settled on wild lands. We will here, therefore, introduce a portion of a letter from John

Ross, dated "May 6th, 1837," relative to their great wrongs, and then show how desolating judgments have fallen on those who occupy the Cherokee and Creek's rightful homes.

"We distinctly disavow all thought, all desire, to gratify any feelings of resentment. That possessions acquired and objects attained by unjust and unrighteous means will, sooner or later, prove a curse to those who have thus sought them, is a truth we have been taught by that holy religion which was brought to us by our white brethren. Years, nay centuries, may elapse before the punishment may follow the offence, but the volume of history and the sacred Bible assure us that the period will certainly arrive. We would with Christian sympathy labor to avert the wrath of Heaven from the United States, by imploring your government to be just. The first of your ancestors who visited as strangers the land of the Indian professed to be apostles of Christ, and to be attracted by a desire to extend the blessings of His religion to the ignorant native. Thousands among you still proclaim the same noble and generous interest in our welfare; but will the untutored savage believe the white man's *professions*, when he feels that by his *practices* he has become an outcast and an exile? Can he repose with confidence in the declarations of philanthropy and universal charity, when he sees the professors of the religion which he is invited to embrace, the foremost in acts of oppression and of outrage? Most sincerely and ardently do we pray that the noble example of William Penn may be more generally followed, and that the rich rewards which attended his exertions may be showered upon the heads of those who, like him, never outraged the rights nor despoiled the property of the Indian. To such, among their highest earthly comforts, and among the assurances of still higher enjoyments hereafter, will be the blessing and prayer of the friendless native."

About twenty-five years after the poor Indians had been forced beyond the Mississippi, came the time of retribution. When the great conflicting armies were at Chattanooga, in the State of Tennessee, they were contending on old Cherokee ground, and the destruction of the property of the inhabitants was immense. When, from Chattanooga, Sherman commenced his pursuit of Johnston, every battle fought, and every farm-house plundered for the wants of either army, until the victor reached Atlanta, stood on ground from which that tribe had been driven. So perfect was the destruction, that the inhabitants had to seek of the Union army that nourishment which would keep them from perishing with hunger. Very beautiful and luxuriant the appearance of the country around Atlanta is reported to have been when the desolating plague of the contending armies came upon it. The inhabitants of that flourishing place were driven from their homes as the poor Cherokees had been. Their houses were burned, their mills, factories, bridges, railroads, were all destroyed, and a retribution most terrible came upon them. When the rebel authorities appealed to General Sherman against his driving the inhabitants from their homes, after giving the reason why he thought it was needful, he adds this honest confession, " War is cruelty, and you cannot refine it."

On the first start from Atlanta to the coast, Sherman was on land from which the Creek Indians had been driven, and the destruction of property continued; mills and cotton-gins, etc., were everywhere destroyed, and the horses, mules, and provisions of the inhabitants taken without stint. The whole State of Georgia had been engaged in the wicked act towards the Indians, and in oppressing the negroes, and the whole State suffered terribly on Sherman's way to Milledgeville, and on to Savannah.

Does it not seem as though the hand of Divine Providence had allowed the late wicked rebellion to be entered into by cruel men, that the punishment for national crime might be openly and intelligibly inflicted?

PREVENTION OF WAR.

A recent writer remarks, that if a nation could but attain to such high wisdom as to abjure war, and proclaim to all the earth, "we will not fight under any provocation; if other nations have aught against us, we will settle the question by umpires mutually chosen;" think you that any nation would *dare* to make war upon such a people? Nay, verily, they would be instinctively ashamed of such an act, as men are now ashamed to attack a woman or a child. Even if any were found mean enough to pursue such a course, the civilized world would cry "fie upon them!" and by universal consent brand them as poltroons and assassins; and assassins they would be, even in the common acceptation of the term. It is related that a regiment was once ordered to march into a small town (it is believed in the Tyrol) and take it. The place was settled by a colony who believed the gospel of Christ, and proved their faith by their works. A courier from a neighboring village informed them that troops were advancing to take the town. They quietly answered, "If they *will* take it, they must." Soldiers soon came riding in with colors flying, fifes piping their shrill defiance. They looked round for an enemy, and saw the farmer at his plough, the blacksmith at his anvil, and the women at their churns and spinning-wheels. Babies crowed to hear the music, and boys ran out to see the pretty trainers, with feathers and bright buttons. Of course, none of these were in a proper position to be shot at. "Where are your soldiers?" they asked. "We have none," was the brief reply. "But we have come to take the town." "Well, friends, it lies before you." "But is there nobody here to fight?" "No; we are all Christians." Here was an emergency altogether unprovided for by the military schools. This was a sort of resistance which no bullet could hit — a fortress perfectly bomb-proof. The commander was perplexed. "If there is nobody to fight with, of course we cannot fight," said he; "it is impossible to take such a town as this." So he ordered his horses' heads to be turned about, and they carried their riders out of the village as guiltless as they entered, and perhaps somewhat wiser.

This experiment, on a small scale, indicates how easy it would be to dispense with armies and navies.

if men only had faith in the religion they profess to believe. When France reduced her army, England immediately did the same; for the existence of one army creates the supposed necessity of another, unless men are safely ensconced in the bomb-proof fortress above mentioned.

RELIGIOUS DUTIES.

RETIREMENT ESSENTIAL TO THE CHRISTIAN.

A MEMBER of the writer's family, on one occasion, brought home a cactus; a poor, eccentric-looking little thing, with no beauty to recommend it. It was one of a small species, which appear like a collection of leaves joined together, each new one springing from the extremity of the one of a previous growth. There was little grace or symmetry about it, and yet, in despite of its want of beauty, it drew attention more than some lovelier plants, from the very peculiarity of its ugliness. It seemed like one of those stubborn cases of the human species we sometimes meet with,—rough, jagged, and ungainly in individual and self-reliant characteristics, to whom we are apt to manifest greater deference and respect, if less love, than to those of gentle amiability and soft, yielding manners.

This awkward-looking plant was placed up-stairs, out of sight of visitors, for its interesting ugliness was not thought a sufficient qualification to entitle it to a prominent position. Time rolled on; and one day, by a passing glance, little points were observed, of real rose-hued beauty, projecting from the edges of the leaves. From day to day those points enlarged and unfolded, increasing in depth of color and elegance of form, until they drew forth exclamations of admiration from all who saw them. Soon the plant, rendered, by its large, splendidly hued flowers, " a thing of beauty," was drawn from its position of obscurity, and transferred as an ornament to the parlor, where it was examined and praised by every one who beheld it. It had been as a diamond hidden in the deformity of its matrix, — now, by the kindly operations of nature, its internal beauty and brilliancy were opened out to view. It had been as a poor, unknown man of genius encrusted with awkward habits, but who, by the force of innate character, had risen from obscurity, and, throwing off the deformity appertaining to his early position in life, had shone forth, adding lustre to the polished, elevated society to which he had raised himself.

Often, in the annals of religious society, have instances occurred of persons uncouth in manners, and depraved in practice, who, by giving way to the visitations of Divine grace, have been made to experience an inward flow of heavenly instruction which has given purity to the thought, polish to the manners, and occasioned a rich bloom of heavenly graces, which none who came near them could witness without admiration.

The dry warmth of the furnace-heated parlor was too great, and, exposed to its atmosphere, the exquisite beauty of the cactus flowers could not long continue in their original freshness. The blossoms, already fully blown when introduced to the increased temperature, soon manifested symptoms of decay — those nearly out, hurried rapidly to a brief perfection, and a few of the more feeble buds, just starting in the career of beauty, withered without fully expanding. It is thus, at times, we see that individuals, who in obscurity have begun to bloom, through grace, and to give hopeful promise of future excellency, when elevated in position, or brought to obtain the hot, dry breath of popular applause or injudicious praise, have sadly withered as to present attainments, and disappointed our reasonable expectations of the future.

After the flowers on the cactus had generally manifested some tokens of decay, it was banished again to the cooler, more healthful obscurity of its first position. There it will without doubt remain, receiving no admiration, and no more attention than is requisite to furnish it with the necessary portion of warmth and moisture. With this care, it will in time, probably, be prepared once more to minister to the pleasure of beholders, and to cover its deformity with a fresh and abundant bloom.

How strange it seems that in that rough, ungainly plant there should be shut up powers which, at the season of their appropriate exercise, are able to produce such beautiful results. In the works of the Creator, we often see great results springing out of the comparatively insignificant, unsightly, and unpromising. Look at yon peach-tree; the branches already begin to grow ruddy with the returning sap, whilst as yet there is no putting forth of green leaves. Mark those buds! Their dark-brown wrappers fold up from sight all beauty. No one, who had not for himself watched the process of vegetation in similar plants, or profited by the observations of others, would suppose that contained in those buds were blossoms preparing to expand into exquisite loveliness, and germs which should grow and ripen into luscious fruit. Almost everything of value in this world seems nourished in quiet insignificance, and out of sight. It is so in the world of matter; it is so in mental, moral, and religious things. Luther declared "that for the most part, when God set him upon any special service for the good of the church, he was brought low by some fit of sickness or other." God saw fit to separate him from dependence on others,— to loosen him from all trust in himself. Thus in quiet nothingness of self, and withdrawn from self-working, he was prepared, as is the peach-bud in the silent repose of winter, for the bringing forth blossoms of beauty and fruits of excellence in due season.

It requires time and changing seasons to prepare a plant to bloom, and it requires time and baptisms of various kinds to qualify Christian laborers to bring forth fruit to the praise of the Great Husbandman.

TRUST IN THE LORD.

Paul Gerhardt, a religious man and poet, was born in Saxony, in the year 1606. He occupied a station in Berlin; but, being honest in the expression of his religious opinion, he was deprived of his appointment, and was ordered to quit the country. He had not accumulated property, and, when obliged to leave the home wherein peace and happiness had been his portion, it was with a helpless family, and destitute of the means of subsistence. His faith, however, in his Divine Master was unshaken, and in full confidence that all his afflictions had been meted to him in wisdom and mercy, he determined to take refuge in Saxony, where he hoped he might find friends and some means of subsistence. The family had no means of performing the journey save on foot, and when night came, Gerhardt felt his heart almost fail, as he looked on his weary, worn-out wife and children. They entered a little village inn; and then his wife, unable any longer to restrain her sorrowful emotions, gave vent to a flood of tears. Concealing his own feelings, he endeavored to comfort her with the passage from the Scriptures, "Trust in the Lord with all thine heart, and lean not to thine own understanding; in all thy ways acknowledge him, and he shall direct thy paths." These words, spoken by him for the comfort of his wife, took hold of his own feelings powerfully, and retiring to a little garden belonging to the inn, he composed some lines expressive of faith similar to that exhibited in the passage quoted. A part of this composition has been thus translated.

"Commend thy ways, O mortal!
   And humbly raise thy sighs
To Him who, in his wisdom,
   Rules earth, and sea, and skies.

All means and ways possessing,
   Whate'er He does is right:
His every deed a blessing,
   His steps one path of light!

To thee it is not given
   The tempest's rage to quell;
God reigns supreme in heaven,
   And all He does is well.

True, it may seem a moment,
   As though thou wert forgot,
As though He were unmindful
   Of thine unhappy lot;

> As though thy grief and anguish
>   Reached not his glorious throne,
> And thou wert left to languish
>   In sorrow and alone.
>
> Yet if, though much should grieve thee,
>   Thy faith shall ne'er have ceased,
> Be sure He will relieve thee,
>   When thou expects it least."

This little poetic effusion ends with the ascription of heart-felt praise to his heavenly Father. Returning to the parlor of the inn, he was sitting there with his sorrowful wife, when two men entered, and soon commenced conversation with him. One of them said they were on their way to Berlin, to seek Paul Gerhardt, a deposed clergyman, by order of Duke Christian, of Merseburg. The poor wife, hearing this, was more overwhelmed than ever, expecting some greater calamity was about to befall them. Paul, however, was calm; and full of confidence in the preserving power of his God and Father, although he knew not for what cause he was sought, told them he was the person they were in search of. The strangers then presented a letter from the Duke to Gerhardt, informing him that, in consideration of the injustice which had been shown him, he had settled a considerable pension upon him. Great was the thankfulness of the pious couple. Paul, turning to his wife, handed her the little poem he had just composed in the garden, and said, "See how God provides! Did I not bid thee confide in him, and all would be well?"

DUE ATTENDANCE OF RELIGIOUS MEETINGS.

The late Robert Scotton being asked, on a certain occasion, if he remembered James Simpson, replied that he had cause to remember him. He then stated that when he was young, he was not diligent in the attendance of religious meetings, but that one day being at the one he belonged to, James Simpson and Peter Andrews came in. The meeting held for a long time in silence; but at last James arose, saying, he thought there was some one present who did not attend meetings as frequently as he should, and who was trying to make excuses for himself to satisfy his conscience, by pleading the necessity of being diligent in his work. "Here," Robert said, "he looked right at me, and went on telling just how I had been making excuses, so that I had to put my hands over my face. Every now and then I looked between my fingers, and found he was still gazing right at me. When he had done, I concluded, 'Well, I will come regularly to First-day meetings, and when I *can*, to those held on week-days; but I must attend to my work.' Then Peter arose, and began to tell of a man he knew, who made no reserves, but went to *all meetings*, and found he lost nothing by it. So, between them, I was knocked out of all my hiding-places. After meeting, James came right up to me, asked who I was, and had something to say to me. Yes, I think I do remember James Simpson, for I have cause."

It is probable that the labor of those two ministers that day were of essential benefit to Robert Scotton, and that from that period he was strengthened to consider his duty to his heavenly Father as of paramount importance, and to be attended to, let his earthly prospects suffer or not therefrom.

James Thornton, of Byberry, Pa., during his last illness, which was in 1794, was drawn to dwell much on the peace afforded at that time, by his persevering attendance of religious meetings throughout a long life. He was early afflicted with bodily infirmities, and remarked that many times in his youth, while walking to them, he had been forced to stop and lean his head against a tree to rest; and that since he had arrived at years of maturity, storms, nor tempests, nor any other consideration, had hindered him from going his Master's errands when able; nor did he remember ever attending meeting without receiving some satisfaction, believing, when people complained of poor meetings, the fault was mostly with themselves; that if we did our part towards attaining a right state of mind, nothing was to be doubted of. He also remarked, that overrating others, and underrating ourselves, should be avoided, as our conditions are best known to the Lord.

FORGIVENESS OF INJURIES.

A recent writer says that under his window there were, one day, two little girls talking, whose conversation he overheard. One had evidently received an injury or insult from a companion, and the other was inciting her to be very much offended about it. She said, "I would never speak to her again. I would be angry with her as long as I lived." The little sufferer was, however, of a different mind; and although the tone of her voice showed that she was grieved at what had occurred, yet promptly and heartily she answered, "No; I would not do so for anything. I shall 'forgive and forget' just as soon as I can." Ah, "forgiving and forgetting" is the proper way for the Christian who has been hardly dealt with; and, indeed, it is the only way to get rid of an insult or wrong without suffering any injury from it. This is the right way for the injured. The injurer has, however, no right to forget until, by a hearty acknowledgment of the wrong done, he has obtained forgiveness therefor. Reader, hast thou a quarrel, or, if thou wouldst rather call it so, a misunderstanding with any one; or dost thou think any one has, in his or her intercourse with thee, done thee wrong? If the quarrel, or whatever thou mayst call it, has taken much hold of thy feelings, remember, it is almost a certainty that there is some fault on thy part; and if, with true Christian magnanimity, thou art prepared openly to acknowledge that, and then, as thou art in duty bound as a follower of the Lord Jesus Christ, to forgive and forget all that thou thinks mayst have been done or said against thee, it is probable that thy faithfulness in taking up the cross to thy own self-sufficiency, in asking forgiveness, may prove a life-long benefit to others. It is recorded in the biography of a certain pious man, that he was always willing to acknowledge when he had been wrong. He remarked on one occasion, "He is a poor man who cannot afford to give away a sixpence; and he is a *poor soul*, a very *poor soul*, who cannot afford to acknowledge an error, lest perchance some one should charge him with inconsistency." Have we not been wrong in some of our actions or sayings? If so, a prompt and full acknowledgment is due from us, whether we conscientiously believe that our antagonist has been as much or more to blame. We must make amends, unless, indeed, we intend to give up all claim to Christian consistency, and hold that we are not bound to manifest the gospel order and spirit towards those who have offended us. If such is our conclusion, we are not Christians in conduct, whatever we may be in profession.

It is recorded that two individuals, one of whom was a pious man and the other was not, having married sisters, met at the house of their father-in-law. During an evening conversation there, they fell into a dispute; and the contest waxing warm, some sharp and severe things were uttered by each. The man who made no claim to religion was of a very fierce and determined spirit, and his peculiar harshness no doubt had excited his brother, until he was induced to give utterance to language which he bitterly lamented over after he had retired to rest. In the morning when he arose, he was in his *right mind*, for in his sorrowful communings in the night, he had been with his blessed Master, who had cooled the fever of his spirit, but showed him his duty, and gave him the needful grace to perform it. He called the whole family together, and before them all he acknowledged his sin in suffering himself to be heated up in his controversy with his brother, and speaking so harshly to him, and he begged his brother to forgive him. The effect was powerful. His brother, who became a religious man, in after years, writing of this occurrence, says, "Then I felt that he had got his foot upon my neck, and that taught me the *first* decisive lesson of the superior excellence of Christianity." This occurrence probably did more than anything earthly, in preparing the way for this fierce unbeliever's reception of the Truth. He could see the beautiful propriety of his brother's conduct, and being led into a submissive acquaintance with the Holy Spirit, he came to experience in himself a measure of that power which subdues the proud spirit of man, and brings it into a willingness to confess as well as forsake errors and sins.

Two brothers, residents of Westport, Conn., who had lived on bad terms with each other several years, finally came to blows. Both made complaint before a trial justice, and both were convicted of breach of the peace. Dissatisfied with this, they appealed; and at the next session of the Supreme Court the jury failed to agree in the case of one, but found the other guilty. The judge, grieved at the spectacle of two warring brothers, and humanely anxious to stop further litigation between them in the future, called the men before him, and talked to them in a strain of serious but kind reproof. He briefly reviewed their difficulty; showed the absurdity of their quarrel, and then appealed to their self-respect, their relationship, and their sense of moral responsibility, not to let this unnatural enmity go on longer; solemnly charging them never to *go to law* in any difference again, and urged them then and there to pledge friendship and brotherly kindness for the future. His efforts were not without effect, and in reply to the question of the judge, each promised henceforth to be friendly to his brother.

"Then shake hands!" said the judge; and as the softened brothers grasped each other's hand, the spectators and members of the bar felt their eyes moisten and their hearts swell.

The judge himself was deeply affected when the offenders both audibly invoked a blessing on their reconciliation, and his voice trembled as he imposed on them a small fine as the lightest sentence of the law. Of all present at this unusual scene, it is probable that none went away without some sense of the sweetness of forgiveness and the beauty of harmony and peace.

BE NOT ASHAMED OF THE CROSS.

How many who desire to be true lovers and faithful followers of the Lord Jesus Christ are yet manifesting by their actions in some things that they are ashamed of the cross, or unwilling to endure the odium which a consistent bearing of it brings upon them. Sometimes these feeble-minded Christians receive rebukes for their weakness and inconsistencies from quarters where they least expected it. We have an anecdote narrated of John Berridge, one of the indefatigable laborers for the good of others during the last century in England, which is in point. His honest zeal and open reproofs of evil brought upon him many scoffs and taunts from the ungodly and profane, in his travels to promulgate Christian principles and Christian practices. One day, in approaching a town in which, on former occasions, he had received much abuse, he felt a spirit of weakness come over him, and instead of passing along the main street, he turned into a by-way to escape the obloquy which, if he were observed by the inhabitants, would, without fail, come upon him. As he passed along the less frequented way in which he hoped to escape detection, he met a pig driver, who immediately recognized him, and fathoming the reason of his being in such an unusual place, cried out,

"You cowardly John Berridge; you are ashamed of your Master, and therefore you skulk along here to avoid the cross." The pig driver's rebuke did him, as he often afterwards said, incalculable benefit, being stirred up and incited thereby to a willingness more faithfully, under all circumstances, to stand boldly as a confessor of Christ; and which, through the grace of God, he never afterwards flinched from. Having, during life, borne a faithful testimony to his Divine Master, and having been taught and strengthened unflinchingly to bear his cross, he was enabled in a good old age to put off the shackles of mortality, blessing the Holy One that he had been enabled to fight the good fight, and to finish his course with joy.

FAITHFULNESS TO CONVICTIONS.

The late Christopher Healy narrated the following incident. Shortly after he had been received into membership among Friends, his brother requested that he would introduce him to Elias Potter, with whom he had some business to transact, connected with a public station the latter held. Elias Potter was a man standing high in the political world, and, from the civil position he occupied, was frequently addressed with titles of honor.

As the two brothers rode to his dwelling, a deep concern came upon Christopher that he might not, in the interview about to take place, shrink in anywise from bearing a faithful testimony for the Truth. This language was powerfully impressed on his mind, "Whosoever shall deny me before men, him will I also deny before my Father who is in heaven." He had been convinced of the impropriety of hat-honor, as offered to men; of all titles of mere compliment; and he had seen the necessity of plainness of speech and honest truthfulness in all his intercourse with others. When he entered the presence of this "great man," he approached him with the salutation, "Elias, how art thou?" The brothers were courteously, nay, kindly received, and the business which occasioned their calling promptly attended to. Some time after this, Christopher's brother being with Elias, he said to him, "Some of the Quakers baulk their testimonies respecting giving titles of honor, but your brother is not one of these."

Years afterwards, when Christopher was on a religious visit in the neighborhood where Elias lived, he appointed a meeting for worship to be held there, which Elias Potter was active in furthering, attended it himself, and whilst in it behaved with great solidity.

WATCHFULNESS OVER SELF.

"OUT OF SORTS."

IN a company of children met on one occasion, all seemed happy, and were pleasantly employed, except one, who sat by herself, neither partaking of the labor nor joyfulness of the busy group. One of the company remarked she was "out of sorts," rendering this as the reason why she was sullenly sitting alone, instead of participating with them in their employment. After doing an act which forced the other children to seek elsewhere for the pleasure she had interrupted, and refusing to accompany them, she was left to mope and distress herself as much as she pleased. After a time she grew tired of being out of humor, and seeking an aunt of hers, she sat down by her, crying, and acknowledged, to an inquiry from her kind relative, " I am all out of sorts." Conscience began to stir in the little girl, and at last she said, " Is out of sorts one of the sins mentioned in the Bible, aunty?" "Not by that name," was the reply. The work of self-examination and condemnation was going on in the heart of the child, and at last she spoke out, "I know what it is; it is getting on the side of the heart that is turned from God." The aunt was much struck with the child's definition, and thought it the best one for the sad distemper she had ever heard. For if the heart is turned from our heavenly Father, who is the fountain of love and the God of all consolation, the spirit of contradiction, malicious mischief, dislike, and gloom, which is so apt to govern those "out of sorts," may readily enter. Her aunt accordingly told the little girl she did not know but she was right in her view of it, and that the only thing for her to do was to leave the wrong side, and jump over to the right, as soon as she could. The advice was followed; the child joined the other children in the spirit of love, and a happy time they had of it.

We may all have had to do with people who were "out of sorts," disposed to complain of those around them, and making themselves and others unhappy by their unreasonable conduct. If we were strictly to scrutinize our own conduct, many of us might remember times when we were, at least to a certain extent, "out of sorts,"—times when we have been improperly exacting in our demands upon the attention and submission to our views of others, and have been wrong in showing our resentment for not receiving what we claimed.

Whenever we allow ourselves to show temper because our own views do not obtain place with others, we are getting "out of sorts," and the only remedy is to get back into a spirit of submission and love as soon as we can. Grown persons have been known very much "out of sorts," who were too wise to show it forth, as the little girl did, and not honest enough to confess it, who would yet manifest a wrong feeling to a careful observer by a stinging word, a remark which carried bitterness with it, incidentally dropped. These, too, in the sight of Him who looketh at the heart, must have been seen to have got all on the wrong side there.

LITTLE WON'TS.

We sometimes meet, in our social intercourse, individuals with whom we find great difficulty in getting on harmoniously. They seem constitutionally, or at least habitually, to act in a manner contrary to the wishes and desires of those they mingle with. Such are very serious obstacles to the comfort of their friends. They seem to see so many causes of fault-finding with the actions and remarks of those around them, and are so bent on having their own way, that it is often quite a relief to a company when such retire from it. This disposition is frequently met with in children, and a simple narrative fully exhibits it, as acting in a little boy.

A little girl named Jessy, who expected two of her young friends to pay her a visit, had put her baby-house in nice order for their entertainment, and had swept the barn-floor clean, where a swing had been put up; and, in short, had exerted herself to prepare everything so that they might have a very pleasant time together. She had a little brother, Harry, who sometimes was very pleasant, but at other times was hard to manage. The two visitors came at last, and Jessy asked them which they would see first, her baby-house or the barn. "The baby-house," said the strangers; but that did not please Harry, who shouted out "barn." His sister told him they must do as the company wished. They went out together, and probably the good-natured visitors submitted to Harry. After a time, however, Jessy came dragging Harry in to their mother, and requesting she would keep him, saying they could not have a good time where he was.

The mother, of course, was sorry; but Jessy said she could not help it, and added, "I tried to love him, and coax him, and please him, and we all did, but it is of no use; he does not fall in with us, and he spoils all our comfort." To the mother's inquiry as to the difficulty he made, Jessy said,

"He is so full of *little won'ts*. He won't swing or let us swing. He won't play school. Then we play horse to please him, but he won't let us be three horses; and he won't drive us on the gravel, but into the thorn-bushes, and is so all the time. We are pleased with him, but he will not be with anything we do."

Many people have *little won'ts* about them who do not know how uncomfortable some of their disagreeable ways render them to those among whom they mingle. In our intercourse with others, Christian politeness does not by any means constrain us to unite with all the sentiments expressed, but we should offer our dissent with a mild tone and a courteous manner. Let there be nothing manifest of the disposition which prompts *little won'ts*, in what we say in opposition to the sentiments of others.

Those who only manifest this disposition towards particular individuals, are far from having attained Christian perfection. There have been cases where a mutual feeling of this kind existed between individuals, which led to public rebukes from either side in respect to matters not in themselves of much consequence; increased mutual jealousy and dislike, until it spread almost to the destroying of the Christian usefulness of individuals. Some have let it go so far as to cause them to condemn all who felt and expressed a friendly interest in those against whom they have let in this dislike. Some have nourished it until it is to be feared that their own spiritual condition has been sadly injured, until they could hardly, from the great growth of prejudice, give an impartial judgment in regard to any one.

Men and women who feel themselves disposed to act and to speak crossly, and contrary to the judgment of those among whom they move, if they have not sufficient self-control to enable them to restrain the public exhibition of this disposition, had better retire. The universal fault-finders — the persons determined to have their own way in everything — have no right to mingle in social society, the comfort and enjoyment of which they seriously disturb, even when they do not wholly destroy it. The disposition they manifest is contrary to Christianity, and, however great their profession may be, they are not living in the spirit it inculcates.

HUMILITY.

How often do we meet with professedly religious characters who can talk very beautifully on the necessity of meekness of temper and humility of mind, as never-failing marks and characteristics of the Christian, but who yet are evidently far from maintaining, in their daily intercourse among men, the gentleness of Christ, and the humility which recognizes no good in themselves. True humility is hard to attain, and it is harder to retain. Especially is it difficult to one who has been much favored in religious labors, and has thereby won the confidence of the wise, and has obtained popularity as an eloquent speaker among the hearers generally. The following anecdote is fraught with instruction, and has a point calculated to make itself felt. A young minister had been engaged in certain services in which he had been most remarkably favored, so much so that some of his religious friends felt a fear lest, being lifted up thereby, he should fall into the snare of the wicked one. They therefore took an opportunity to press upon him the necessity of cherishing a spirit of humility. In reply, he said, "He constantly prayed to be *kept humble.*" One of his friends, a minister of greater age and experience, wishing to deepen the hint which others had given the young man, and perhaps fearing his prayer did not go deep enough, told him of a circumstance he had recently been a witness to. He had attended a meeting which had been held by some pious poor persons, and one John, a thresher by occupation, appeared in it in prayer. At the close of the meeting, the old minister said he heard "Mary," a washerwoman, say to the thresher, "John, you made a sad mistake in your prayer to-night." "Did I?" he replied. "In what way?" "Why, you prayed that the Lord would *keep* you humble. Now I thought it would have been better if you had prayed that God would *make* you so." The hint intended by the old minister was properly received by the young one, who acknowledged long afterwards that it had been of singular service to him, placed as he was in the dangerous position of a popular preacher.

Whatever our station in society or in the church may be, we are always in danger from the soaring, cross-shunning influence of self. If we have done that which was right in the circumstances under which we were placed, under the promptings of the Lord's Holy Spirit, the praise belongs solely to him. If we did it to gain the applause of men, no credit is due to us. Yes, the experience of every day confirms us in this truth, *Humility* is a difficult attainment. Is not our self-sufficiency, our want of true humility, proven by our sensitiveness when we are blamed by others for what they deem some improper action or unguarded word? Are we not far readier warmly to justify ourselves, than meekly to hear what others think, and then, in the depth of true humility, to seek to the Lord for instruction, being as ready to receive it, if it comes *condemning*, as if it brings our acquittal?

Humility is the Christian's best condition in living and in dying. When the eminent Du Plessis was near the close of his earthly career, one who was with him at that solemn time, spoke to him of the great service he had done the church by his writings. Feeling the inconsistency of such consolation offered the dying believer in Christ Jesus, and unwilling to have it thought that at that awful moment he was trusting to aught of his own righteousness, or on any works which, through the grace of God, he had done, he exclaimed, " Alas! what was there of mine in that work? Say not it was I, but God by me." Then raising his hands and looking upward, as if anxious to forget the untimely suggestion, he exclaimed, " Mercy, mercy, mercy!" He then declared that it was the mercy of God to which only he had recourse. His faith and hope rested altogether on the mercy of God in Christ Jesus, who had been made to him, he said, as to all other sincere believers, " Wisdom, righteousness, sanctification, and redemption." " Away," he exclaimed, "away with all merit: I call for nothing but mercy, free mercy!" One standing by expressing his thanks that God had given his servant such peace and comfort, he said, "I feel, I feel what I speak." As to the truths of Christianity, he declared, "He was entirely persuaded thereof by the demonstrations of God's Holy Spirit, which was more powerful, more clear, and more certain than all the demonstrations of Euclid." So, in humility of soul, feeling the nothingness of self, yet in holy dependence on the grace of God in Christ Jesus, which had wrought mightily in him in the work of regeneration, he departed in great peace, his spirit longing to be set free and to be with his blessed Saviour.

How deep was the humility of Augustine, who, when near his close, feeling that the Lord alone could preserve him, cried out, "Lord, *perfect that which thou hast begun*, that I suffer not shipwreck in the haven." A worthy, favored minister being near his close, was told of his eminent gifts and faithful services in the ministry, to which he replied, "I dare not think of any such thing for comfort; only Jesus Christ, and what he hath done and endured, is the ground of my comfort." When one told Knox, on his death-bed, that he was going to receive the reward of all his labors, he replied with this gentle rebuke, "Brother, I am going to receive mercy." When Rutherford, whose dying hours were wonderfully favored with comfort and enjoyment, heard one speak of his former painfulness and faithfulness in the work of God, he said, "I disclaim all that; the port I would be in at is redemption, and forgiveness of sins through his blood."

THE LEAKY ROOF.

Some years since, in a house newly finished, a large spot was observed on the ceiling of part of the upper entry, where the plaster was moistened, evidently from a leak; on examination, it was discovered that through carelessness, probably from dropping an edged tool by one of the workmen on the roof, a small hole, not more than one-quarter of an inch in diameter, had been made in the tin gutter, just at a point where the water descended from the upper part of the roof; the consequence was, that during every shower a stream of water entered the building at that point, wetting the timbers, rotting the lath, destroying the tenacity of the mortar, loosening it from the ceiling, and producing an unsightly stain. A few drops of solder promptly applied by the tinman, put a stop to the train of evil consequences that had commenced to flow from this tiny leak. If the remedy had not been applied, the injury to the building would have gone on increasing in extent; the edge of the tin exposed to the weather would have rusted away, and thus enlarged the aperture; the alternate wetting and drying of the timbers would have caused them to decay, and the ultimate damage to the building, resulting from this apparently trifling cause, would have been serious.

How small an opening in our defensive protection is sometimes sufficient to introduce fatal decay in our spiritual buildings. In the relaxed and debilitated state of the physical system, which is a frequent attendant upon the sultry weather of the latter part of summer, we may pass the closet where the wine-decanter stands, and find a refreshing stimulant in a glass of its contents: in a day or two we may pass the same spot, and, remembering the comfort we derived from its previous use, may repeat the potion: in a little while we may, from day to day, find a recurrence of the desire; and as it continues to be gratified, the tendency to the use of the stimulant becomes stronger and stronger, and the apparent need of our system for it becomes greater and greater. The rust is rapidly enlarging the opening through which the element destructive to our spiritual edifice is entering; and

I

if we do not soon apply the remedy, the unsightly evidences of decay will become apparent. Our heavenly Father, who is ever watching over us for good, does not suffer us to fall into evil, without giving us due warning. There will be impressed on the mind a feeling of caution — an impression to abstain from that which may injure us; but this gentle warning may be easily set aside and disregarded, especially when the cry of appetite is loud and imperative; and when, in other things, we have not been careful reverently to listen for and honestly to obey the teachings of the Holy Spirit within us.

It is related that a minister, in the course of a religious visit, advised his hearers to beware of closet tipplings. A valuable woman who was present, felt uneasy with the communication, as she did not see that it was applicable to any who were present. Sometime after, feeling exhausted with her household labors, and perhaps with the heat of the weather, she thought a glass of wine would be helpful, and accordingly drank one. In a day or two she again thought she felt the like need, and again partook of it. A third time she approached the closet where the wine was kept, with the same intention, when the language of the preacher flashed across her mind: Beware of closet tippling. Convinced now that his arrows had not been shot at random, she turned away, leaving the tempting liquid untouched.

The late Samuel Cope was riding one day in company with one who was an eminently gifted minister. Possessed of remarkable powers of eloquence, and the faculty of controlling large bodies of people, he was greatly admired and followed; but he had probably at that time begun to give way to a taste for spirituous liquors, which afterwards increased to a mournful extent. The leak had been made in his roof, and he had not the moral resolution and self-denial to close it. In the course of their ride, he said to Samuel, that a report had been raised affecting his reputation for temperance. Samuel replied, in substance, Thou knowest whether it is true or not. If it is true, and thou dost not quit the practice, there is no help for thee but to go down. The individual referred to ultimately fell away, and became impoverished. This narrative is a striking proof of the truth, that however spacious and splendid in the eyes of others may be our spiritual building, it is liable to decay and ruin if we do not carefully watch over it to keep it in order, and apply to the great Master Mechanic for his help to repair the injuries which it may meet with.

When the late Amos Lawrence, so widely and favorably known as a merchant and citizen, was a lad, he was placed in a store, in one of the interior towns of Massachusetts, to receive his business training. It was the custom of the store, for one of the young men about eleven o'clock in every forenoon, to prepare a beverage in which whiskey or brandy was mixed with water, sugar, and other ingredients, to give it a palatable taste; of this the employees and customers of the store were at liberty to partake. Amos shared with his companions in the pleasant draught; but as time passed on, he became conscious of a longing for his accustomed stimulant when the usual hour arrived. Aroused to reflection by this feeling, he at once resolved to repair *the leak in his roof*, and never again drank of the tempting liquid. His own success in life was, no doubt, to a large extent, due to the moral firmness and self-denial which he practised, of which the above incident is an illustration. The peril to which he was exposed may be estimated from the fact which he relates, that every one of the young men employed with him in the store, contracted a fondness for strong drink, and became habitual drunkards.

It is not in the indulgence of the appetites alone, that small beginnings often lead to great results.

The first deviations from the right path in anything are often so small that the mind is not fully awakened to the danger of the departure. Almost insensibly the path diverges, turning more and more rapidly in the wrong direction, till the poor wanderer at last finds himself plunging into ruin, and in such a state that nothing but the powerful interposition of the Divine arm can rescue him from destruction. Recent occurrences in business communities have disclosed several cases where persons of hitherto unblemished reputation, highly esteemed in the circles where they were known, holding official positions in the religious bodies to which they belonged, and occupying places of trust, have been found to have made use of the funds of institutions under their control for their own purposes, in an unwarrantable manner, and thus to have caused serious loss to innocent parties.

In well meaning persons, such things generally commence in a very small way. Feeling the need of a little money, a man may anticipate his salary, and draw a few hundred dollars some weeks before it becomes due. As a matter of convenience, he may keep a private debtor and creditor account with the institution over which he presides, borrowing occasionally small sums for his personal use, which he returns at his own convenience, and of which no entry is made in the official books. These things seem to him harmless in themselves. When he has become accustomed to this, an opportunity may present of making a purchase which he thinks will be largely to his pecuniary advantage, and which will require more funds than he has of his own. It is but a slight extension of his debtor and creditor account to borrow a few thousand dollars of the company he is connected with, and to do this without notice to the directors, or giving that kind of security which the rules of the institution require. One speculation often leads to another; the amounts required become larger and larger, till finally the transactions grow to such an amount that they can no longer be concealed, and the poor man finds himself the victim of public censure and private self-reproach, and that he has become a ruined man.

May we all learn to avoid the beginnings of evil, and if we discover an opening, however small, in the roof of our house, figuratively speaking, may we lose no time in having it repaired. We will undoubtedly find it a task too great for our own skill and ability, to repair the injuries which our spiritual edifices have received; but if we become thoroughly humbled under a sense of our transgressions, and in sincerity and earnestness beg for help of our compassionate heavenly Father, he will, in his own time and way, extend such relief as he sees to be best for us. For as one who had large experience of his goodness says: "He is a God of mercies, and delighteth in pardoning and forgiving much, and very often. What tender mother can be more ready to forgive and embrace the child that appears broken and afflicted with her sore displeasure! Yea, he gives brokenness, he melteth the heart, that he may be tender towards it, and embrace it in his arms of reconciliation, and in the peace of his Spirit."

BE FAITHFUL TO THE IMPRESSIONS OF DUTY.

Richard Williams the surgeon, who is noted as a devoted missionary in Patagonia, had a very severe struggle to encounter in giving up the use of tobacco, which sacrifice he believed was required of him. He knew that a profession of religion, without so dwelling under its power as to be willing to give up, for the sake of peace of mind, all gratifications which he felt to be wrong for him to indulge in, would be unavailing. Yet he found it no easy thing to give up one practice which had enslaved him; and he describes in his journal his struggles in the conflict, and the final breaking of the fetters. He says, "For more than a month before leaving England, I had given up the practice of smoking. At various times I have been under strong impressions that I ought to leave it off, and have felt dissatisfied with myself for the self-indulgence. But the cravings after it had become so strong, and the will of the flesh so urgently demanded it, that it was no easy task to overcome the propensity.

"At length I resolved to leave it off, and happily succeeded, without experiencing any uncomfortable effects. This was six weeks before leaving England. During that time I kept my firm resolution, though, in lieu of smoking, I had recourse to snuff. Some of my friends, who thought I was going to unnecessary lengths of self-denial, would put up for me, among the equipments for my voyage, tobacco, cigars, and a canister of snuff, and they made me promise to purchase a meerschaum. 'Well,' I thought, 'circumstances may possibly be such as to render it desirable to have them;' so I yielded to their wish. On board, I could not resist the temptation of taking a cigar, such was my weakness. Giving them freely away, and smoking them daily, my stock was soon exhausted; but all the cravings for tobacco were reacquired. I took to the meerschaum, but with the indulgence came the condemnation. My conscience would not allow me to continue; so I gave the canister of snuff to the captain of the ship, and reserved only a small quantity. Captain Cooper, likewise, had my meerschaum, on condition of my not requiring it again. Three or four days passed without having recourse to him for it, but never did I suffer such cravings after it; my stomach became affected, and my spirits so depressed, that I was compelled to ask for it again. With a sense of bodily relief and comfort, I smoked it; but, alas! my condemnation was great. Hurriedly opening a book in my hand, the question of the Psalmist was presented to my eye, 'Lord, who shall abide in thy tabernacle? who shall dwell in thy holy hill? He that sweareth to his own hurt, and changeth not.' These words were applied to my mind most forcibly. I was condemned. But now I knew my duty, and, suffer what I might, I resolved to give up the practice in all its forms. Having sought mercy and forgiveness with the Lord, and his grace to help me, I gave away, in good earnest, all my tobacco, my pipe, and my snuff-box, and I threw overboard the small quantity of snuff I had reserved. Thus a clear riddance was effected."

Richard Williams was comforted in thus giving up to what he believed was required of him; and well will it be for all who, whenever they are conscious that any of their ways are not well pleasing in the Divine sight, do turn therefrom, and stand firmly in their duty, humbly relying on the Lord's sustaining strength.

TEARING DOWN A WALL.

In watching the proceedings of a workman who was engaged in cutting a doorway through a stone wall, it was observed that when he had by blows of his pick on the softer mortar effected a slight entrance, so as to obtain a foothold for his implement, he endeavored to pry out one of the stones, using all the force the implement would bear. But his effort was unsuccessful; the stone was too massive and too firmly fixed into its place to be moved. Finding this to be the case, he soon desisted from the attempt, and proceeded to pick at the mortar, gradually detaching pieces of it, and loosening the smaller pieces of stone that had been wedged in the crevices between the larger ones. In this way, he soon removed the supports from the large stone, so that it readily yielded to the blows and prying of the pick, and fell to the ground. An opening having once been made in the wall, the work of destruction proceeded more rapidly. The other stones, thus left with only a partial support, were easily displaced, and the whole process was soon accomplished.

How apt an emblem is this workman, with his pick, of Satan assaulting with his temptations those whom he is seeking to delude and destroy. He does not begin by persuading his intended victim to do some gross or outrageous action, the mere mention of which would alarm and put him on his guard. He attacks the weak points, and attempts to get a foothold there first. Are we naturally persons of strong appetites? He leads us to an undue indulgence of these; an indulgence which leads us beyond the limits which a proper attention to the checks and restraints of the Spirit of Christ in the heart would impose. The advantage thus gained over us, he follows up by stimulating us to take greater liberties, and indulge in more lavish expenditures in gratifying the corrupted wishes of the heart. The further steps by which he leads us to ruin may accord with our physical and mental constitution, and with the outward position in which we are placed. Many a young man, who has thus entered on the downward course, has been led to appropriate to his own use the funds of others without their knowledge and consent. The principles of his education, and the convictions of Grace, show him the wickedness of dishonesty, and at first he attempts to quiet the pleadings of these by resolving to return the money to its rightful owner at a convenient time. But that convenient time too often never comes; the devil, to whose service he is submitting, leads him on from one step to another, until disgrace and ruin are his portion.

Some who have thus entered the broad way that leads to destruction, have been aroused to a sense of their lapsed condition, and of the danger that overhung them, by the renewed and merciful visitations of the Spirit of Christ; and by submitting their hearts to its awakening call, and suffering the Divine judgments to have their full effect, have been brought into true repentance, and enabled, with the poor publican of old, to cry out from the bottom of their hearts, "God be merciful to me a sinner." Such have been so humbled, that they have felt that they could not obtain that peace of mind they longed for, without making confession of their guilt to those they had wronged. When the poor sinner has been brought to the situation in which he makes no reserves, but is willing in all things to obey the Divine requiring, if he may but know the return of peace to his soul, surely then is verified the language, "He that covereth his sins shall not prosper; but whoso confesseth and forsaketh them shall have mercy."

THE LOST CHILD.

A person passing along the streets of our city was startled by the sudden outcry of a little child. The tones indicated that the heart was filled with terror. Instinctively turning to see who it was, and what was the cause of its alarm, it was found that its older care-taker had turned the corner of a street, so as to be out of sight of the infant; and the sense of desertion and the feeling of being without a protector, had nearly overpowered the feelings of the little one, and brought forth the passionate cry which was at once the expression of its fright and the appeal for relief.

How vividly does the course of this little one recall our own spiritual steps. Like it we are sent out into the world with a Guide and Companion ever near to help and direct us. That Holy Spirit, which our Saviour promised to send to his disciples, and which should lead them into all truth, is indeed, as Wm. Penn describes it, "God's gift for man's salvation." It raises the warning voice when we are in danger of being led astray by any temptation, exciting a feeling of uneasiness in the mind, which, if heeded, would preserve us from evil. The more watchfully we observe its monitions, and the more faithfully we heed them, the more fully will our lives be under its influence, and the more safely will we move through the varied snares and dangers that may await us. But it too often happens that, like a child following its caretaker, we are diverted by some of the pleasing things that life presents; our eye is withdrawn from our Leader; the gentle warnings given us are unheeded amid the loud calls of the world that surrounds us; we stop in our onward path to partake of the amusements and excitements that abound, until we seem entirely to have lost sight of our heavenly Guide, and our thoughts are absorbed in our temporal matters, and we come to live almost as if there was nothing beyond this present world. We recognize in words the claims of religion, but it has no ruling power in our hearts. We do not daily and hourly bring our thoughts, words, and actions to be tried by the test: "Is it well-pleasing to my heavenly Father?" That most precious language of the Psalmist, "May the words of my mouth, and the meditations of my heart, be acceptable in thy sight, O Lord, my strength and my Redeemer," is no longer the breathing of our spirits. Thus we sometimes go on for a long time, really walking in the "Broad Way" that leads to destruction, though we may be unwilling to admit it even to ourselves, and wandering far from that path which leads Zionward. It is in the infinite mercy of God who willeth not the death of the sinner, but that all men should return, repent, and live, that his love reaches to us even in this state of wandering and forgetfulness of him. Sometimes he permits heavy outward calamities to assail us; our business prospects may be blasted; disease may invade our powers, or the dearest of our earthly companions may be taken away. At other times his judgments may be more in the secret of our own hearts. Our sins may be set in order before us, and the awful consciousness that we have been rejecting the proffered mercies of our God, may press heavily upon us. We are awakened to a sense of our condition; we feel that we have lost our Guide, and that there is no other who can help us or save us from the consequences of our own foolish ways. What then is left for us but, like the lost child, to cry out from the depth of the heart for the return of our Guide, and to say, "God be merciful to me a sinner"?

So great is the Divine goodness, that such a cry, uttered in sincerity, is never unheard; but he who puts the prayer into the heart, is ready to answer it in his own way and time. For "joy shall be in heaven over one sinner that repenteth, more than over ninety and nine just persons which need no repentance."

A STRAWBERRY-BED.

A strawberry-bed which yields a bountiful supply of fruit has furnished a full illustration of the truth of the common remark, that nothing valuable is to be obtained without corresponding labor and pains. The proper preparation of the ground, the selection and setting out of the plants, and their subsequent cultivation, till they had overspread the plot assigned them, and had obtained the age and vigor requisite to enable them to produce a large amount of luscious berries, are not the only things that experience has shown to be needful. After the first full crop was borne, and the plants were left to throw out their runners, and renew their strength for the production of fruit in the following year, it soon became apparent that various unwelcome intruders had established themselves in the bed, and, if not removed, would overshadow the rightful occupants of the soil, hinder their growth, and rob them of their proper nourishment. The slender spears of grass of several varieties, the heads of clover, and the stems of weeds of many kinds, were to be seen thickly projecting above the leaves of the strawberry plants. Some of these were easily removed; others clung so tenaciously to the earth, and were so deeply rooted, that unskilful force merely detached the part above ground, and left the subterranean portions still alive. One of the most troublesome was the common sheep-sorrel, which throws out, just under the surface of the earth, long roots, which wander over the bed, and send up at intervals leaves and stems.

The sacred writings often compare the church and its members to outward and visible things. "A garden enclosed is my sister, my spouse." "The daughter of Zion is left as a cottage in a vineyard, as a lodge in a garden of cucumbers." "Thou shalt be like a watered garden." The Prophet Isaiah, in figurative language, speaks of the church as a vineyard, of which he says, "I the Lord do keep it; I will water it every moment: lest any hurt it, I will keep it night and day," and continuing the same metaphor, he adds, "He shall cause them that come of Jacob to take root: Israel shall blossom and bud, and fill the face of the world with fruit."

This strawberry-bed might be compared to an individual who had experienced the operations of the Lord's hand. The fallow ground has been broken up; the rampant growth of evil propensities, words, and actions has been cut down; and good seed has been sown in the heart, which, under the fostering care of the heavenly Gardener, has taken root and grown. Through the aid of his Holy Spirit, and the renewed visitations thereof, which descend on the soul as the dew and the rain, the plant of heavenly origin has borne fruit,—it may be of humility as shown in a meek and humble behavior, of kindness to all, of quiet submission to severe trials, or of more conspicuous, because public, labor for the religious welfare of others.

Those who are thus exercised, especially those engaged in the great work of proclaiming the gospel of light and salvation, are exposed to some trials of a peculiar nature; and it is wise for such to prize and improve the intervals of rest from active service which are granted by the Lord of the vineyard. Let them, as well as all others, examine the gardens of their own hearts. They will find young weeds coming into view here and there among the good plants which must be removed, or they will soon grow, and destroy the beauty and lessen the fruitfulness of their fruit-beds. They may discover that the kindness and sympathy of their friends, and the favor with which their ministrations have been received, have nourished a disposition to appropriate to themselves the honor which belongs only to the Giver of all our gifts; and that, like the sorrel, this hurtful weed has been secretly insinuating its fibres into their hearts, until it has so developed that its acid leaves are being shot up into sight. They may find that they have relaxed in that tenderness of conscience and watchful care to avoid the first approach to evil, into which they were led in the day of their espousals; when, yielding themselves fully into the Divine hand, they followed him into the wilderness, and "Israel was holiness unto the Lord, and the first-fruits of his increase." From this neglect may have followed too much indulgence to the appetites of the body, too much latitude in the range of the thoughts, and too little restraint on the expressions of the tongue. The danger of this is especially great, if in earlier years they have yielded to corrupting influences. Through submission to Grace, they may have been enabled to remove all visible signs, and faithfully to reject all temptations to indulge in the sins which, at one time, so easily beset them. But these roots remain long in the ground, and in an unguarded hour often manifest their presence. What sad examples have we seen of persons who, for a series of years, had maintained an unblemished reputation, and yet have afterwards yielded to temptations which at one time they probably thought they had fully mastered! Let him that thinketh he standeth, take heed lest he fall; and let us all feel the importance of the apostolic injunction, to work out our salvation with fear and trembling — a fear lest by any means we should come short of that heavenly rest which has been set before us.

The evil seeds which grow in the heart of man are as multifold in number and form as the weeds which spring up in our gardens. Some make their appearance in the early spring-time of life; others flourish more luxuriantly in the meridian of our strength and vigor; and others again find a congenial climate in the autumnal period. There is no way in which our gardens can be kept clean, but by heeding the injunction which our Saviour has so emphatically given as of universal application, "What I say unto you, I say unto all, Watch." As this holy watch is maintained, our eyes will be anointed to see, and strength will be given to remove those things which are of evil tendency.

CHILDREN.

PROMPT OBEDIENCE.

OH the value, the inestimable value to youth, of a habit of prompt obedience to parental commands! An anecdote strikingly illustrating this, as well as setting forth Christian heroism of an exalted character, some years ago occurred in Prussia. On one of the railroads in that country, a switch-tender was once taking his place in order to turn a coming train, then in sight, upon a different track, in order to prevent a collision with a train approaching in a contrary direction. Just at this moment, on turning his head, he discerned his little son playing on the track of the advancing engine. What could he do? Thought was quick at such a moment of peril! He might spring to his child and rescue him, but he could not do this in time to turn the switch, and for want of that, hundreds of lives might be lost. Although in sore trouble, he could not neglect his greater duty, but exclaiming with a loud voice to his son, "Lie down!" he laid hold of the switch, and saw the train safely turned upon its proper track. His boy, accustomed to obedience, did as his father commanded him, and the fearful heavy train thundered over him. Little did the passengers think, as they found themselves quietly resting on that turnout, what terrible anguish their approach had that day caused to one noble heart. The father rushed forward to where his boy lay, fearful lest he should find only a mangled corpse, but to his great joy and thankful gratitude, he found him alive and unharmed. Prompt obedience had saved him. Had he paused to argue, to reason whether it were best, death and fearful mutilation of body would in all probability have resulted. The circumstances connected with this event were made known to the king of Prussia, who the next day sent for the man, and presented him with a medal of honor for his heroism.

This is a striking case of highest duty triumphing over warm, parental feelings. Dear reader, couldst thou have done as this switch-tender did? Consider. Thy darling—the delight of thy eyes, the joy of thy heart—about to be crushed and mangled by that coming train, and thou couldst save him by neglecting the switch! The momentary contest in the bosom of this noble man must have been intensely agonizing. . We can all rejoice with him when he found his obedient child uninjured by the mighty hurricane of power that had whirled over his head; but let us pause and consider, Could we have done as he did? And then another question may well claim the serious thoughtfulness of parents: Have we brought up our children in such habits of prompt, unhesitating obedience as characterized his little boy?

Prompt obedience to the commands of our Christian parents is a duty, and tends to our safety. We may not be in danger of being crushed by engines of power if we hesitate, but we are always liable, if we wilfully pause, of falling into temptation and the snares of the evil one, and of being more and more leavened into the spirit of disobedience, which ever tends to our spiritual destruction.

Prompt obedience to parents in the Lord's leadings, seems to pave the way for obedience unto him. His commands come to us by day and by night, and there is always soul-saving efficacy in obedience thereto. Are we running on in a course of vanity and folly? hearken to his inward voice bidding us touch not, taste not, handle not. Seek to become more and more acquainted with his voice; and the easiest way to that knowledge is by rendering prompt obedience to all its commands which we do know. "He that doeth the will shall know of the doctrine," said our blessed Saviour, and this certainly implies that all his obedient children shall be more and more taught of him. "Thy children shall be all taught of the Lord, and great shall be the peace of thy children."

"OUT OF THE MOUTH OF BABES AND SUCKLINGS THOU HAST PERFECTED PRAISE."

In the year 1819, Stephen Grellet and William Allen were in St. Petersburg, the capital of the Russian empire, engaged in the prosecution of religious service. In his journal, S. G. says, "At one of our late visits to the Prince Alexander Galitzin, he stated to us an interesting circumstance that occurred lately in Finland. Some children, from seven to nine years of age, were so brought under the sensible influences of the Spirit of God, convincing them of their sins, that, on their going to or from school, they retired into the woods, and there put up their prayers to the Lord with many tears. By degrees their number increased. The parents of some of them found them thus engaged, and with rebukes and stripes dispersed them; but the parents of others, who had noticed the increased sobriety and good behavior of their children, encouraged them to meet together in their houses, and not to go out into the woods. The children did so; and some of their parents, observing their religious tenderness, and hearing their solemn prayers to the Lord, the Redeemer and Saviour of sinners, felt in themselves strong convictions of sin. They joined their children in their devotions, and a great reform took place in that part of the country. This excited the angry feelings of the priest, who was a bad man and a drunkard. He went to the magistrates to enter his complaints against both children and parents.

"The prosecution ended in their all being sent to prison. They had been some months in confinement, when Prince Alexander Galitzin heard that *children* were in prison on account of religion. He thought it so strange an occurrence, that he sent confidential persons to inquire into it. They found so much religious sensibility and tenderness in the children, that they were greatly surprised, especially at the simplicity with which they related how they had been brought into trouble because of their sinful hearts, and how they felt they must pray to the Lord Jesus Christ, who alone could forgive them, and enable them to live in a state of acceptance before God.

"Being inquired of, if their parents or others had not put them on doing this, they said that, so far from that, they were afraid their parents or any one else should know how it was with them; that they retired privately in the woods to pray and cry with tears unto the Lord. The parents also stated that the children had been the instruments of bringing them to a sense of their sinful lives, and to seek to the Lord that he might give them a new heart, and pour forth his Spirit upon them. Moreover, it was found that the conduct of these people and children had been such, during their imprisonment, as to comport with their Christian profession. The Prince ordered them released, and had the priest and magistrates severely reprimanded, and removed from their offices. The Emperor having heard of all this, and the great suffering to which these families were reduced in consequence of their long confinement, which took place last year before harvest, ordered that all their losses should be liberally made up to them, making ample provision also for their present support."

CHILDREN ARE AN HERITAGE OF THE LORD.

A pious mother related to Ann Mifflin, wife of Warner Mifflin, that on one occasion, when in company with two of her children,—a son of seven years and a daughter four years old,—she requested them to remain silent while she was engaged in reading a religious book, and, as an inducement to them, proposed that they should think for half an hour, and then tell her their thoughts.

After a pause, the little boy replied that "It was impossible to tell his thoughts; they were the same that had been in his mind more than one year; and that they were so delightful the more he thought, the more he wished to continue in that sweet meditation; and if all the world would get into the same feeling, it would be impossible for any to be damned."

The mother, startled at such an unexpected reply from so young a child, inquired of him if he could recollect the first time he felt these serious impressions. He said, "They came on by degrees from a desire to be good and serve God." He was then asked if he was willing to die and go to heaven. He said, "He had heaven already in his own heart; therefore he believed, if he should be called from this world, his spirit would unite with God his Father; but he wanted to live to pray for those who were wicked; and that many times he burst into tears for the sins of the world, and wished it was in his power to bring them into the same feeling with himself." He also said to his mother, "He could not speak of these things to his companions at school, knowing he should be ridiculed; and if she knew all he suffered in mind among such a set of wicked boys, she would weep for him continually." He further said that he grieved for them, "lest they should continue hardened in wickedness,— sorry that they should offend so good a God; and distressed for himself in struggling against the temptations before him, and afraid he should do something wrong; but that these thoughts, which were continually before him, were his comfort." On inquiry from his mother if he knew whence these thoughts proceeded, he answered, "Yes; from God; and that it was God's Spirit in him, and that he sometimes enjoyed heaven without waiting for death."

After the child had left the room, the eldest daughter, aged twelve years, who was present, burst into tears, and said, "What but the Spirit of God could make a child like this speak in this manner?"

HONOR THY FATHER AND MOTHER.

It is the duty of parents to bestow a religiously guarded education upon their children,— to endeavor, as ability may be afforded, to bring them up in the nurture and admonition of the Lord; seeking daily, by prayer and reverent waiting upon the alone Helper of his people, for wisdom to advise, encourage, and restrain. Where true heart-changing religion rules in the parents, the family circle must necessarily be a privileged place. Parents cannot bestow grace upon their children; but if they are guided by wisdom from above,— if fervent earnestness for their spiritual welfare is mellowed by the meekness and gentleness of Christ, —if their natural affection for their offspring is tempered by a holy zeal for their best welfare, it can scarcely be but that some spiritual benefit will be gathered by the children. How often have we seen the earnest concern, the living exercise and travail of the parents for the eternal well-being of the children eminently blessed. Sometimes spiritual graces seem to rest, through the Divine blessing, on whole families of such dedicated ones, and in children and grand-children we find reproduced preachers of righteousness and standard-bearers in life and conversation.

The temptations of the evil one are many, and at times even the children of really concerned Christians are caught in his snares. How sorrowful is it to observe those who have been educated under Christian discipline,— who have been conscious of the religious concern of pious parents for their eternal happiness,— who have known the prayers and tears which have been poured forth in secret and in public on their account, break out into open immoralities, or throw off all appearance of being under the cross of Christ. What greater anguish of mind can we conceive pious parents could suffer, than to see one of the lambs committed to their charge, thus rushing into the spirit of the world, and into its fashions and wickedness.

Can there be anything more touching than the parting of John Fothergill, that eminent minister of the Gospel of Christ, with his reprobate son Samuel, when, after years of painful labor with him,—all hope of his restoration seeming closed up,—he took leave of him, for an absence of some years on a religious visit to America, with these words: "And now, son Samuel, farewell! farewell! and unless it be as a changed man, I cannot say that I have any wish ever to see thee again." What a farewell! The son was of bright talents; he could appreciate the anguish his conduct had given to a tenderly concerned father; he could see what a stumbling-block his evil course was to others; he knew how it stood in the way of his father's usefulness as a minister of Christ; all these thoughts were doubtless, at that moment of parting, struggling within him. His father left him; soon the Atlantic Ocean rolled between them;

but his heavenly Father was still watching over him for good, and still granting the reproofs of his Holy Spirit, which awakened in him repentance unto life. Yes, even to this son of revolt, who had rushed into great wickedness, who had strayed until he had no hope of obtaining peace, who wandered until life became a burden, and he wished he had never been born, even to him there was granted repentance unto life. On returning to England, his father rejoiced to find that in him a thorough change had taken place, and he afterwards became an eminent minister of the gospel.

Many individuals who have not fallen into such open immorality as Samuel Fothergill did, are yet as far estranged from a willingness to take up the cross. Children, whose parents are constrained openly to uphold the testimonies of Truth, are sometimes found running with the world in its customs, its manners, and its language, and yet do not seem to consider that they are thus laying waste the religious exercises of their dear parents.

The late William Evans related that on one occasion, in his youth, being about to engage in something that his godly father would have condemned as evil, he seemed to see the face of that father between him and the accomplishment of his purpose. He dared not pass on. His honest love and regard for his father, and the secret conviction of his mind that his intended action was wrong, might have had something to do with producing the vision; but doubtless it was in the permission of Divine Providence, and to save him from sin.

The remembrance of family gatherings for religious retirement, and if it should so prove for Divine worship, has sometimes been blessed. An incident is related of a religious man who had been favored with many such opportunities in his father's family, who was in the habit of gathering all the members of his household at a stated hour every evening. The young man had left his father's house, and engaged in business in another place; was tempted to go to a place, perhaps it was to the theatre, which he knew was wrong. He had put down the pleadings of conscience against the act, and was drawing near the place when the clock struck. In a moment he remembered that at that hour his honored parents, his beloved brothers and sisters, had sat down with the intention of drawing near to the Holy One, and to offer, if enabled, supplication, adoration, and praise. The striking difference between their engagement and that he was about entering on, so forcibly took hold of his mind, that he turned away from the scene of sin. He could not at *that* hour so dishonor his father. As he waited on the Lord Jesus, who by this powerful remembrance had enabled him to resist the temptation, he gained strength, and through the washing of regeneration and the renewings of the Holy Ghost, became a consistent Christian.

It is sometimes the case that apparently religious parents, whose children have grown out of their control, and have refused to submit to their authority, attempt to buy, as it were, the love they have lost in order to prevent a still greater alienation, and allow the introduction of things in the furniture and embellishments of their houses, and in the company invited there, which are inconsistent with their profession, and which occasion, or should occasion, much uneasiness to their minds. They do not attempt to justify themselves save on the one ground of retaining an affectionate hold on their ungoverned children. Doubtless they are under a mistake. No parent who, in the meekness of true Christian love, and in the firmness of Christian duty, lives up to the requirements of what he knows to be right, ever destroys thereby respect and affection. On the contrary, where he easily gives up his principles, he forfeits the respect, and often loses the affection of the child; whilst the evil example which he tolerates in his family is felt with pernicious consequence by his honest-hearted neighbors. Such yielding parents soon lose the nice appreciation of error which they may once have possessed, and having given way to admit some wrong things, others more manifestly evil easily find entrance.

PROVIDENTIAL DELIVERANCES.

PROVIDENCE DIRECTING.

MANY anecdotes are recorded which illustrate the exercise of providential direction in human affairs, and incidents showing the same overruling influence are not unfrequently brought to our notice. These are always interesting. To feel that, though we are feeble in strength and deficient in understanding, there is an Omnipresent, Omnipotent Being, infinite in wisdom, who is caring for us, preparing the paths for us to walk in, modifying the very dangers which threaten us, and shaping the afflictions which assail us, is indeed comforting and sustaining to the humble Christian.

An instructive incident occurred in the experience of Thomas Lee, formerly of Exeter, Berks County, Pa., who was taken several years ago, after an exemplary life, to receive the recompense of reward for his faithful walking among men. One day, Thomas was suddenly impressed with a belief that he must go quickly to the house of a German neighbor; and though he hesitated at so unexpected and, so far as human reason could fathom, so useless a requiring, he could not with peace of mind refuse to obey the call. As he was hastening in obedience to the inward direction, he perceived that his neighbor and several laborers were at work in a quarry near by, and that the bank above them, heavily laden with rock, was about to fall, and must, if they remained where they were, inevitably crush them. Exerting his voice to the utmost, he succeeded in drawing their attention to the crumbling bank, and they fled from it for their lives. All of them escaped the falling mass but one, who, though he was not caught under the stones, was buried several feet deep in the looser soil from above. His companions being at hand with their tools, he was soon liberated from his premature burial, and though at first insensible, he was not found, on after examination, to be seriously injured.

Thomas Lee, to the end of his days, recurred to this event with grateful emotions, and, indeed, he could not speak of it without tears. His faithfulness, in this instance, was without doubt blessed to his own furtherance in righteousness. For his own spiritual benefit, we may reverently believe this exercise was meted to him by his heavenly Father, as well as for a powerful lesson and an awakening call to those whose lives were saved. Infinite power could have warned them of their danger by other means, or it could have stayed the parting rock until they had voluntarily left the quarry to obtain their meals or needful rest. But a lesson of instruction was to be given, the reward of obedience was to be obtained, and infinite wisdom appointed the way from which those results should certainly follow.

The following incident, which occurred a few years since, also illustrates the necessity of giving heed to the intimations of the heavenly Monitor. An aged farmer asked his son if he would drive him to a neighbor's. "Yes, father," he replied. Instantly, as he said this, an impression was made on the son's mind as though one had said, "Don't go!" He was perplexed at the unusual impression, and as he did not immediately make ready, his father inquired if he did not intend to take him. "Yes, father!" he again said, and then immediately came the inward response, "Don't go!" His evident hesitation induced the father to ask him the third time, and his reply, "Yes, father!" was followed by the "Don't go," as before. He felt ashamed of giving way to these feelings, and so bestirring himself, he prepared his vehicle and drove his father whither he desired to go. They found their neighbor engaged killing a bullock, and the beast, infuriated by a stroke which had but wounded him, ran at the new-comers, and gored the old farmer so dangerously, that he was for years a cripple and sufferer therefrom. Had the young man been faithful to the impression, it might have opened the way, as an act of obedience to the inward guide, to a further acquaintance with that blessed Spirit, which, when faithfully followed, will lead onward to earthly purity and to heavenly blessedness and peace.

THOMAS STORY.

Many Christians of the present day suffer loss, from want of sufficient faith to enjoy some of the privileges partaken of by the saints of old, promised in the Holy Scriptures, and experienced in measure by some of modern times. The skeptical atmosphere in which we live, with its blinding mists, appears to affect them in degree, and prevent them from seeing with clearness, and receiving some of the blessings which are bestowed upon others who have more simple-minded faith.

The efficacy of prayer to procure both spiritual and temporal blessings, the indwelling of the Spirit of Christ and its sensible operations on the heart, the gift of prophecy and of healing the sick, and the extension of Divine Power in a manner out of the ordinary course of nature, are all reali tics confirmed by the records of the past, and which we have Scripture authority for expecting to find in the experience of the present day.

Thomas Story was an intimate friend of William Penn, and held several important offices under him. He was a member of the Council of State, Master of the Rolls, and Commissioner of Property for Pennsylvania. He had received a classical education, and possessed an unusually clear and logical mind; and having early in life yielded his heart to the operations of Divine Grace, he possessed both the intellectual and spiritual qualities which give value to his testimony on religious matters. He left behind him an autobiography in which are recorded the following interesting circumstances.

In 1692, having been absent from home travelling on a religious account, he says: "This journey being finished, I went home to my father's house in the evening, and having taken much cold, so that I was hoarse, I spoke with difficulty when I went into the house; yet, through a very sensible operation of the Divine Truth, and the healing virtue thereof, under which I sat in silence for about half an hour, I was perfectly healed; by which I was forever confirmed in the belief of the miracles of Christ recorded in the Holy Scriptures."

In 1698, on a voyage from England to America, the ship in which he sailed encountered a violent storm, so that, as his narrative relates, "all the yards were brought down on the gunnels, and the helm lashed and made fast, and the ship let drive before the wind: and we being met together in the great cabin and steerage to wait upon the Lord, as at other times, he was pleased to appear in the needful time; for the tempest increased with thunder and lightning and rain to that degree that few there, if any, had ever seen the like.

"And in waiting upon the Lord, I became concerned in prayer; and being in a mighty agony, and wrestling in spirit with the Lord, I received hope that we should not perish; and having concluded for that time, and my concern returning, I prayed again; and then some stout hearts were broken, and the Lord's power was glorified, and we greatly comforted: for I prayed unto the Lord, who is God of the seas as well as of the earth, and of the winds, the Creator of all things visible and invisible, that he would be pleased to send forth his word, and command the winds as of old; and that if there was any opposing spirit that stood in our way to hinder our progress, the Lord would please to drive him away: and then I was easy, having fully overcome; and my companion, and some others, were also greatly tendered; and as soon as I arose I took the Friends by the hands, and some others also, and, in full assurance, told them the worst was over for that time; and the words were scarcely out of my mouth, and I set down in the cabin, till the storm abated, and the weather became moderate for some time after; and we had no more great storms after it to that degree."

In 1698, when in Ireland, at the castle of Shannigary, which was on the estate of William Penn, he met with "a gentlewoman of good sense and character," who gave him the following relation:

"That she, being in the city of Cork, when it was invested by King William's army, and having a little daughter of her's with her, they were sitting together on a squab; and being much concerned in mind about the danger and circumstances they were under, she was seized with sudden fear, and a strong impulse to arise from that seat, which she did in a precipitant manner, and hastened to another part of the room; and then was in the like concern for her child, to whom she called with uncommon earnestness to come to her, which she did; immediately after which came a cannon-ball and struck the seat all in pieces, and drove the parts of it about the room, without any hurt to either of them.

"From this relation, I took occasion to reason with her thus: that Intelligencer which gave her notice, by fear, of the danger they were in, must be a spiritual being, having access to her mind (which is likewise of a spiritual nature) when in that state of humiliation, under those circumstances; and must also be a good and beneficent Intelligencer, willing to preserve them, and furnished also with knowledge and foresight more than human. He must have known that such a piece would be fired at that time, and that the ball would hit that seat, and infallibly destroy you both, if not prevented in due time, by a suitable admonition; which he suggested by the passion fear (the passions being useful when duly subjected), and by that means saved your lives. And seeing that the passions of the mind can be wrought upon for our good by an invisible, beneficent Intelligencer in the mind, in a state of humiliation and stillness, without any exterior medium, is it not reasonable to conclude that an evil intelligencer may have access likewise to the mind, in a state of unwatchfulness, when the passions are moving, and the imagination at liberty to form ideas destructive to the mind, being thereby depraved and wounded? And when so, is it not likewise reasonable to think that the Almighty himself, who is the most pure, merciful, and beneficent Spirit, knowing all events and things, doth sometimes, at his pleasure, visit the minds of mankind through Christ, as through or under a veil, so as to communicate of his goodness and virtue to a humble and silent mind, to heal and instruct him in things pleasing to himself, and proper for the conduct of man in his pilgrimage through this present world, and lead him to the next in safety?"

RELIEF FROM STARVING.

About the commencement of the present century, a number of families removed from the eastern part of Pennsylvania, to form a new settlement in Canada. During their first winter, which was a very severe one, the crops raised the preceding summer became exhausted, and the great depth of snow rendered travelling in search of provisions impracticable. In one household, consisting of a man, his wife, and eight children, great suffering ensued. Their only resource was the bark of the slippery-elm and bass-wood, from which they made a kind of jelly, which sufficed to support life. They earnestly looked for spring,—but the approach of it, at first, increased their affliction.

As soon as the sap began to run in the slippery-elm and bass, the jelly made therefrom caused sickness, and ceased to afford sustenance. In the prospect of death from famine, the family collected together, endeavoring to look to Him who careth for the sparrows, and who much more careth for those of his dear children who put their trust in him. Whilst they were sitting thus gathered, one of the family observed a pigeon alight on a tree by the door. It was taken, and, being cooked by the mother, furnished a scant supply for that day. The next day another pigeon was taken in the same manner, and so for fourteen days in succession. On the fifteenth day, they watched as usual for another, but it did not come. One of the little boys, who, weakened by the want of sufficient nutriment, was lying on the bed, asked his mother, "Is the Great Spirit offended, that he does not send another pigeon?" Death seemed again to threaten the family; but on going out of the house, the father found that the ice had given way on a neighboring stream. This enabled him to catch fish, which, with the sap of the maple-tree, that soon afterwards commenced its annual flow, furnished an adequate supply of nutriment. This account was given in 1830, by one of the members of the family thus preserved.

RELIEF IN EXTREMITY.

An individual who owned some land in the southern part of the city of Philadelphia many years ago, borrowed five thousand dollars to improve it with; of this amount three thousand dollars were loaned him by a rich acquaintance, and two thousand dollars by an Insurance Company. Before his meditated improvement had produced any profitable returns, the financial crisis came on, which closed the war carried on against the Bank of the United States. It was a time of pecuniary losses and bankruptcies, in which many comparatively wealthy firms paid one per cent. a day for money, to redeem notes due, in order that their names should not, in mercantile language, be dishonored. During this season of commercial distress and panic, as this debtor was walking in the street, he saw his principal creditor on the other side of the way, who beckoned him over, and informed him that he should want the three thousand dollars by noon the next day. The poor man was so panic-struck by the sudden announcement, that he scarcely attempted to say anything, although he could perceive no way by which he could possibly raise the money. His real estate, at such a time as that, could scarcely be sold, or if sold, it would not be likely to produce half as much as the borrowed money he had expended on it, and he could see nothing but distress and ruin before him. He went home in distress, and there found an agent from the Insurance Company, requiring the immediate return of the two thousand dollars. This seemed to fill up his cup of affliction. His case seemed hard; he had not entered into extravagant speculations to the hazard of other people's property; he had endeavored to act with caution; but a time had come on the commercial world which could not readily have been foreseen. He passed a sorrowful night, and in his sleepless musings endeavored to think of some plan to suggest to his larger creditor to induce him to give him more time. He drew up a series of notes falling due at short intervals, covering the principal and interest which had and would accrue on them. He felt a hope that, if his creditor would agree to his proposal, he might find some means for raising the varied sums as they would be required to take up each note. He had little expectation that his proposition would be accepted, yet he could see no way by which he could offer one more acceptable to his creditor.

It was now Fifth-day morning, and as noon was the hour fixed on to meet the creditor, he concluded to attend a Friends' Meeting at Fourth and Arch Streets, for he well knew that in seasons of affliction there is no consolation like that derived from the comforting presence of our dear Saviour, who has promised to be with those gathered in his name, as well as to be with his own even to the end of the world. As he sat in silence, his heart heavy with the oppressive weight of his outward troubles, John Letchworth, a valued minister of the Society, arose, and addressing one in peculiar pecuniary difficulties, briefly held forth the language of encouragement, saying: "The money will come before thou needs it." The afflicted man felt the discourse must be intended for him, and he was in measure comforted; yet he hardly dared so in faith to lay hold of it as to derive perfect settlement of mind. After meeting he went to his home, and then taking the notes he had prepared, he went to the house of the rich creditor. On inquiring for him, great was his astonishment to receive the information that he had that morning started for Europe. On being informed who the persons were who had charge of his affairs during his absence, he went immediately to their place of business, where he received a confirmation of his departure. To his inquiry whether he had left any message about him, he was told he had not, but his informant added: "We know you owe him money, but you may take your own time in paying it."

Faith and hope grew stronger within the poor debtor as, with grateful emotions and thankfulness of heart to his Almighty Creator, he turned and retraced his steps to his own residence. Still, he felt some fearful forebodings as he thought of the two thousand dollars called for by the Insurance Company. No doubt he pondered over expedients for raising that amount, but he could find no satisfaction in any that presented themselves to his mind, until during that afternoon the late Thomas Stewardson called on him, and in his brief, plain way said, "Dost thou want to borrow two thousand dollars?" On receiving an affirmative answer, Thomas handed him that amount. Whether this kind friend had learned that the Insurance Company had demanded the return of its loan, and knew that, in the condition of the money market, the poor debtor would be unable to obtain it, we know not; but the thankful receiver could look up gratefully to his heavenly Father and return the praise to him who had thus providentially cared for him, and in his season of distress ministered through another the needed relief. Ah! the true Christian, whilst ever thankful to earthly benefactors, looks over them all to return the chief praise unto him who prompts every kind act and loving-kindness of his children.

GO TO LAUNCESTON.

The following remarkable instance of Divine interposition on behalf of an individual in very humble life, and under circumstances of peculiar trial and difficulty, strikingly illustrates the care of our heavenly Father over his creatures, and the safety and excellence of trust in him. It was related by an esteemed minister in the Society of Friends resident in Cornwall. We are not to expect miracles to be wrought in our behalf, though we sometimes see, as in the present instance, what seems to partake of their character; but in whatever circumstances we may be placed, or however unfavorable and discouraging our situation may appear, we should not despair, but seek for ability calmly to rely upon him who careth for the sparrows, and who said to his disciples, "Even the hairs of your head are all numbered."

A person of respectability and good standing in society, residing in the town of Plymouth, England, was awakened out of sleep, one night, under strong emotions of mind by a voice sounding in his ear, as he thought, and calling him to "*Arise, and go to Launceston.*" Launceston is an ancient town in Cornwall, about twenty-two miles from Plymouth.

Having no acquaintance in the place, nor any

known business that would take him there, he treated the occurrence as the effect of a dream, and again composed himself to sleep. In a very short time he was awakened under stronger feelings by a similar command, which he still treated with neglect, though more reluctantly than before; and after falling asleep, was a third time aroused under sensations which admitted of no further postponement. He therefore arose and mentioned the singular occurrence to his wife, who endeavored to discourage him from attempting so long a journey at such an hour of the night, and especially as he had no apparent object in going. But his uneasiness was so great, that he was not to be turned aside from his purpose, and saddling his riding horse, he set out. After proceeding some miles in the chilly darkness, groping his way as best he could, his resolution began to waver, and he reasoned with himself on the folly of his undertaking. "Surely," said he, "I am going on a fool's errand. I am an entire stranger in Launceston; I have no business there, nor any one on whom I can call." Under the influence of these cogitations he turned his horse towards home and thought of returning, but had retraced only a few steps when his mind became exceedingly distressed, and the words seemed to sound in his ear, with commanding authority, "Go to Launceston — go to Launceston." Yielding to this renewed requisition, he resumed his journey, and reached an inn in the town soon after breakfast-time.

While eating his breakfast, he inquired of the waiter what objects of interest there were in the place. "Oh," said the waiter, "not many: there is the old castle — people sometimes go to look at that. But now everybody is going to the Court of Assizes which is sitting here. The bell is ringing now, and the court assembling." After finishing his meal, he inclined to go to the court-house, and found they were trying a man for his life on a charge of burglary. Two witnesses deposed positively that they saw the prisoner in the house at the time of the robbery; and the evidence being conclusive, the judge asked him if he had any defence to make. The poor man was evidently much distressed, and firmly but earnestly asserted his innocence — declared that he was in Plymouth at the time specified by the witnesses against him, and that there was a gentleman in that town who could prove it if he were here. The judge told him he had heard the evidence against him — that it was full and positive, and that the court could not receive his assertion in the face of such testimony. That if there was any one in Plymouth who could prove him to have been there at the time specified, he ought to have procured his attendance on the trial. The prisoner said he was poor; had been shut up in jail, and had neither the means nor the opportunity to obtain the attendance of witnesses. That he was an innocent man; that it was hard to die for a crime which he had not committed, and that he had no refuge but to trust in that Being who knew his innocence. His bearing and manner of speaking made an impression on the audience, and attracted more than ordinary attention. The judge said he pitied him, but if he had no testimony to adduce, he must instruct the jury to find a verdict of guilty. The poor man again asserted his innocence; spoke of the gentleman in Plymouth who could exculpate him, and closed by again committing his cause into the Divine hand. The judge made some further remarks about the person of Plymouth, and the desirableness of having him produced, when, as the prisoner glanced his anxious eye around the crowd of gazing spectators, he suddenly descried the face of the Plymouth gentleman; and calling to the judge, said, "My lord, there he is now!" The court requested the prisoner to point him out; the traveller appearing to have no idea that he was the individual alluded to. On facing the bench, he was desired to look on the prisoner at the bar, and say whether he knew him. "No, my lord," answered the man, "I never saw him before." This seemed discouraging; but leave being given to the prisoner to ask him some questions, the following interrogatories and replies, in substance, ensued:

Prisoner. Do you not remember a person calling at your office on the day specified, and asking you to give him employment?

Ans. I do not remember such a circumstance.

Prisoner. Do you not recollect his telling you that he had a large family, and was destitute and in great distress?

Ans. No; I have no such recollection.

Prisoner. Do you not remember that you gave him some encouragement to hope you might soon be able to employ him, and gave him permission to call on you again?

Ans. I do not.

Prisoner. Do you not remember expressing sympathy for his distressed situation, and a desire to help him, and, that you might not overlook his case, making a memorandum of his name, and the date, etc., on a note-book with a red morocco cover.

Ans. I cannot recall any such circumstance.

The prisoner seemed distressed at the want of recollection in the witness, and ceased to question him. After a few moments' silence, the witness remarked, "But I believe I have my note-book in my pocket, and will refer to it, and see if there is any such entry." On this, he drew from his pocket the little book with the red morocco cover, and turning over the leaves, suddenly paused, and looking towards the bench with a countenance expressive of strong emotion, said, "Why, here it is,—the name, the date, and all about it. It had all entirely passed from my memory." The excitement throughout the court-room had been increasing in intensity during the questioning, and now seemed at its height. The judge examined the memorandum-book, and by comparing the date with the time at which it was proved that the burglary had been committed, it was obvious the prisoner could not have been there, and consequently could not have been the robber. The judge was so fully satisfied of his innocence, that he directed the jury to find a verdict of acquittal, and thus the life of an innocent man was spared to his needy family.

It is incumbent upon us, whatever may be our privations, to cast our eyes around, and endeavor to discover whether there are not some means yet left us of doing good to ourselves and to others;

that our lights may, in some degree, shine in every situation, and, if possible, be extinguished only with our lives. The amount of good which, under such circumstances, we do ought not to disturb or affect us. If we perform what we are able to perform, how little soever it may be, it is enough; it will be acceptable in the sight of him who knows how to estimate exactly all our actions, by comparing them with our disposition and ability.

LARKS SENT TO THE STARVING.

Thomas Fuller, that quaint, religious writer, relates the following interesting circumstance which occurred at the city of Exeter, in England, in the year 1643. He was himself a witness of the transaction which he records, and we give the narrative in his own words:

"When the city of Exeter was besieged by the Parliamentary forces, so that only the south side thereof towards the sea was open unto it, incredible numbers of larks were found in that open quarter, for multitudes like quails in the wilderness, though, blessed be God, unlike them both in cause and effect, as not desired with man's destruction, nor sent with God's anger, as appeared by their safe digestion into wholesome nourishment: hereof I was an *eye* and *mouth* witness. I will save my credit in not conjecturing any number, knowing that therein, though I should stoop beneath the truth, I should mount above belief. They were as fat as plentiful; so that, being sold for two-pence a dozen and under, the poor, who could have no cheaper, or the rich no better meat, used to make pottage of them, boiling them down therein. Several natural causes were assigned hereof. . . . However, the *cause of causes* was *Divine Providence.*"

There were, without doubt, divers other pious persons besides Fuller shut up in Exeter at that time,— children also, and many persons who, in a spiritual sense, could hardly " discern between their right hand and their left," and he who spared Nineveh of old,— who caused quails and manna to fall around the camp of his hungry Israel in the wilderness,— who bade even ravens minister to the necessity of his prophet Elijah, saw meet, in preserving providence, to cause the famine in Exeter to be stayed by the larks.

DELIVERANCE FROM SHIPWRECK.

Richard Jordan, a minister of the Society of Friends, from America, after having visited those in profession with him who resided in Germany and France, and had religious service in several other places, came to Bordeaux to take shipping for England. The voyage across the Bay of Biscay is often performed in less than a week, but owing to a violent storm which they encountered, and a succession of boisterous weather, they were forty-five days on the passage. The crew of the vessel in which he embarked were principally Danes, and during the first few days of the voyage seemed to vie with each other in wickedness and profanity, neglecting the proper care of the ship, and spending their time in drunkenness or gambling. They treated Richard Jordan with great contumely and contempt, scoffed at his religious life and serious demeanor, and even abused his person. They had not been long at sea, when the sky was overcast with clouds; the atmosphere became dark and hazy, and a tempest arose, during which the fury of contending elements seemed let loose upon them.

Their situation soon became apparently hopeless, and the officers gave their wicked crew the dread warning, "*To prepare for a watery grave.*" Oh! then what a change was seen in their conduct. Terrified at the prospect of the awful fate which awaited them, smitten with remorse for their past wickedness and contempt of God, they gave way to despair, and became almost incapable of managing the ship. The helm was ordered to be lashed, and giving up all hope of safety, they let her drive at the mercy of the winds and waves. Amidst this general consternation, when all around him bespoke distress and terror, Richard Jordan sat peacefully in the cabin, waiting in humble confidence upon the Lord. His mind was calm and collected, securely anchored on that Rock of Ages which no storms can move, no tempests overturn.

The captain, awakened from his sensuality and wickedness, and tremblingly alive to the doom which seemed to be impending, betook himself to the cabin, and, seconded by his anxious crew, besought Richard Jordan to implore for them the mercy and protection of that Being whose power they had so lately contemned, nay, whose very existence they had impiously denied. He informed them in a few words that the spirit of availing prayer was not at his command: but after waiting for a considerable time in solemn silence, he was permitted to approach the throne of grace in reverent vocal supplication.

This religious service seemed to be in some degree blessed to them; they were humbled into contrition, and became more composed; their conduct towards him was now reversed; every one seemed desirous of doing him some kindness; and so sensible were they that the Divine presence was near to preserve and support him, that all were anxious to get as close to him as possible. Their exertions in managing the vessel were renewed; but they had lost their reckoning, and provisions running short, they were put on allowance. The violence of the storm soon after abated; yet the probability of reaching land before their stores were exhausted became very doubtful. The vessel was so much injured that she began to take in water very fast, and the pumps had to be constantly worked to keep her free. Discouraging as the prospect before them appeared, such was the confidence and faith with which Richard Jordan's mind was replenished, that he told the captain it was his full belief they should yet be brought safely into port, without the loss of a life. In a few days after this, when almost the last portions of bread and water were served out, they descried land, and soon after entered the harbor of Dartmouth. His gratitude for this happy deliverance from imminent danger, and his release from long confinement in a vessel which a variety of circumstances rendered extremely unpleasant, may readily be conceived. He appointed a public meeting for Divine worship in the town, to which the captain and some of the crew came, and it proved a memorable and humbling opportunity to many present.

DAILY MERCIES.

"The Lord shall preserve thy going out and thy coming in."—Ps. cxxi. 8.

John Campbell, the noted traveller in Africa, when a young man, lived in Edinburgh. He was warmly interested in the religious welfare of others, and understanding that in a village five miles south of the city in which he resided, the young people were very ignorant, he exerted himself in endeavoring to establish a school there. He soon had nearly two hundred scholars, and as it was held in the evening, he used to hire a horse to ride to it. He was an unskilful rider, and often encountered difficulties occasioned by the badness of the roads. The following brief abstract of one winter night's ride, and the preservations he on that occasion experienced, is interesting.

The darkness was so great that he could not see how his horse stood, and was obliged to feel for his head before he attempted to mount. When starting, he remembered a heap of large stones in the middle of the road near by, and feared that his horse must stumble over them. As he drew towards them, he, with thankfulness, perceived a person with a candle in his hands, looking among them for something which had been dropped.

He then recollected that in a short time he would

come to a sharp turn in the road, whilst straight before, with nothing to guard the traveller from a dangerous fall, the bank fell off precipitously eight to ten feet. The thought of this place gave him considerable uneasiness, from his inability in the darkness to see where he was going. When he reached the spot, he found a woman and a girl there with a lantern. They were on their way home from school, and their light enabled him safely to turn this dangerous corner.

Although, in view of the two helps he had already received in difficult places, he was induced, with the apostle, to thank God and take courage; yet he could not help remembering that a little before him there was an old bridge, which was a very difficult one to pass in the dark. Some cottages were near it; and as he approached, to his great surprise, the door of one of them opened, and a woman stood in it, holding a light so as to shine on the bridge until he had crossed it. He supposed that, hearing the tramp of his horse's feet, she had thought some relative might be returning for whose safety she was concerned; whatever her motive, he felt thankful for the aid afforded him.

There was still one dangerous spot before him, and that was where the road crossed a very narrow bridge, with scarcely any protection at the sides to keep a traveller in the dark from falling off. "It will be most extraordinary," he thought, "if I find a light there too!" But, extraordinary as it seemed to him, it turned out so. A man was crossing the bridge with a lantern, and hearing a horse approaching, he very kindly stood still till John Campbell had passed over.

There is nothing wonderful in any one of these occurrences, yet those who feel that a superintending Providence is indeed about the Lord's devoted children in all their ways, will sympathize with John Campbell in his desire not to forget the preservations of that evening. How many mercies of this kind are received by all of us which we either never note at all, or quickly forget.

A PARTICULAR PROVIDENCE.

George Dillwyn, of Burlington, New Jersey, an eminent minister of the Society of Friends in the early part of the present century, was remarkable for spiritual discernment. Among other anecdotes related of him illustrating his quick perception of the pointing of duty, and his faithful obedience thereto, is the following. On one occasion, when sitting in his parlor with his wife, he suddenly rose from his seat, took his hat, and seemed about to go out for a walk. His wife attempted to detain him, informing him that it was raining, of which he seemed to be unaware, and that it was nearly dinner-time. He replied that he *must* go; his wife accordingly brought him an umbrella, and he left his home without apparently knowing his destination. After walking the street for a time, he came opposite a house into which he felt it right to enter. He opened the door and walked into the front parlor, in which he found two men, who appeared greatly astonished to see him. He sat down by them in silence, and after a time said that he had felt impelled to enter that house, though for what purpose he could not tell, but perhaps they could inform him. They then told him that they had had an earnest discussion on the doctrine of a particular Providence, which one of them had stoutly maintained, and the other as strenuously opposed. At length the latter had said, that if George Dillwyn were to walk into the room at that instant, he would believe the doctrine. He had no sooner said the words, "than," remarked the narrator "you came in." After this remarkable incident, George Dillwyn addressed them in an impressive manner, and took his leave.

THE LORD OUR DEFENCE.

C. G. Steinhofer, formerly of Germany, was a Christian firm in faith, consistent in principle and practice, and, as a clergyman of the Lutheran community, very earnest and zealous in fulfilling what he considered to be the duties of his calling. These were often arduous and unpleasant, but he did not shrink from their performance. On one occasion he was informed that the chief man, the highest public officer in his district, was living in sin, to his own disgrace, to the inexpressible grief of his wife, to the sorrow of every really Christian citizen, and to the great scandal of the Lutheran Church there, of which he was a member. On receiving this information, this faithful guardian of the flock went at once to the offender. After mentioning the occasion of his visit, he said he had come, in the authority of his office, to bid him remove the public scandal he had given rise to, adding, " My Lord will require *clean* sheep of his shepherds, and as I am engaged in keeping this flock, I dare not suffer such doings as this in it." The man was irritated at this honest reproof, and unconditional condemnation of his wickedness, and told him, if he meddled much more with him or his affairs, he would have him removed from the ministerial office. Steinhofer let him know that the fear of such a result would not deter him from the performance of the duty devolving on him from his station. A week passed by, and as the offender had not abated the scandal, Steinhofer called upon him again. After expostulating with him, he plainly told him, that if he did not manifest that he intended to amend his evil ways, he should on the morrow publicly bring the matter before the congregation, when assembled for worship. This would clear him before the people of having any active or passive complicity in this wickedness, and he added, he should then "leave it with the Lord, who would prove that he would not be mocked."

This honest rebuke, and even the prospect of a public exposure, did not induce the man to change his course. But to try to prevent Steinhofer from spreading the case before the congregation, he called upon him, before the meeting, with many threats, seeking to frighten him into silence. The pastor had counted the cost; no fear of pecuniary loss or personal suffering could induce him to draw back from the performance of what he esteemed his duty. He did, as he had promised, spread the case before the congregation, and requested their prayers, that this iniquity should be removed from among them, and that it might not be laid to their charge.

The rage of the public officer was so great that, in the insanity of passion, he determined to kill his faithful reprover. Knowing that on that afternoon Steinhofer would visit a sick member of his congregation, he determined to waylay him and execute his wicked design. The road, from the parsonage to the residence of the sick man, passed through a small wood, in the recesses of which, behind a tree, the intended murderer placed himself with a loaded gun. In due time the clergyman came in sight, but, to the dismay of the watcher, two men appeared to him to be with him, one on either side. This for that time baffled his intention; but being determined to effect it, he concluded to do it when the visit was over, and therefore remained waiting in the wood. Steinhofer after a short period returned, but, to the surprise of his enemy, the two men who had appeared to accompany him as he went, were still apparently beside him; and thus he again passed safely through the wood, not knowing that it concealed an enemy.

Perplexed in mind and uneasy in conscience, the officer felt an earnest desire to know who the men were whose presence had protected his intended victim. To obtain that knowledge, he sent a servant-maid on some trivial errand to the house of the minister, telling her to find out who the strangers were who accompanied him on his afternoon visit. She made the inquiry, and was told that he went out alone, and took nothing with him but his Bible, which he carried under his arm. This return to his question startled the inquirer more than ever. He immediately despatched a messenger to the clergyman, demanding who those two men were who, one on his right and the other on his left side, accompanied him to visit the sick man. The messenger was also instructed to say that his master had seen them with his own eyes.

C. G. Steinhofer, although he knew not what peril he had escaped, yet felt convinced that the Lord's hand was in the thing, and also that he had, by his preserving Providence, been round about him that day. He bade the servant tell his master that he knew of no man having accompanied him; but, he added, "I am never alone; the Lord whom I serve is always with me." This message, faithfully delivered by the servant, produced a powerful effect on the master. His conscience was alarmingly awakened. He immediately complied with the requisitions of duty, and the next morning, as an humble penitent, he called on his faithful reprover, with tears confessed his past crime, and also his wicked intention so providentially frustrated. The work of repentance did not stop here, but through the Lord's assisting grace this evil man amended his ways.

ANN YOUNG'S TEXT.

More than a century ago, a worthy and hard-working couple were struggling through life in a secluded part of Scotland. The country was thinly peopled, employment precarious, and they were sometimes reduced to great necessity for want of food. On some of these occasions, by unexpected interpositions of Providence, help was sent to them in an unlooked for manner.

An excellent woman, called the Lady Kilmarnock, in whose family Ann Young, the cottager's wife, had formerly lived as a servant, resided some miles distant from this humble home, through whose bounty the worthy cottagers had frequently been relieved. But such was the repugnance of Ann Young to appear burdensome to her benefactress, that she seldom, when in want, made her distress known to her.

On one occasion the resources of this poor family entirely failed, and they were reduced to the greatest extremity. Their little store of provisions had gradually diminished, and the children had received the last morsel the mother could furnish. Yet Ann was not cast down, for she was a Christian indeed, and, knowing in whom she had believed, she had learned to trust in the loving-kindness of her God when apparently cut off from human aid.

This day of distress passed, and no prospect of relief appeared; the children were put supperless to bed, where they soon cried themselves to sleep; and the father, much dejected, likewise went to bed, leaving his wife in solitary possession of the room; yet she felt she was not alone. Many precious hours had she spent in that cottage in pouring out her soul to God, and in spreading her trials and her sorrows before him, apart from the world.

Having seen her children safely at rest, she made up the peat fire on the hearth, that she might not be disturbed for the night. She then trimmed and lit the cruisy (a small iron vessel which served as a lamp), and took down a large family Bible from among the six or eight well-worn volumes on the book-shelf. She paused before opening it, when the following text came involuntarily into her mind, "For every beast of the forest is mine, and the cattle upon a thousand hills."

This text she thought was not very applicable to her present condition, and opening the volume, she proceeded to look for some of her favorite passages. Yet "For every beast of the forest is mine, and the cattle upon a thousand hills," was uppermost in her thoughts. She endeavored to commit her case to the hearer and answerer of prayer; then to recall former experiences, and to bring to remembrance those portions of Scripture which used to come home with power to her heart, but without feeling that lively pleasure and comfort she had heretofore found in them. The text, "For every beast of the forest is mine, and the cattle upon a thousand hills," seemed fastened in her memory, and despite every effort she could not banish it from her mind. It was, she reflected, a Divine declaration, and she turned to the fiftieth Psalm, in which it is contained, but on reading the Psalm, thought there were other verses in it more suited to her condition. Several hours were thus passed in reading, meditation, and prayer. Daylight at length appeared through the casement, and a loud, impatient rap was heard at the door.

"Who's there?" said Ann.

A voice from without answered, "A friend."

"But who is a friend?" she replied. "What are you?"

"I'm a drover," said he. "And quick, mistress, and open the door, and come out and help me. And if there's a man in the house, tell him also to come out with all speed, for one of my cattle has fallen down a precipice and broken its leg, and is lying at *your door.*"

On opening the door, a large drove of cattle from the highlands of Scotland met her astonished gaze.

As far as the eye could reach in either direction, the road was black with the moving mass, which were being driven on to the market in the south. And there lay a disabled beast with its leg broken, and the drover standing by, looking ruefully over it, with his faithful *colley* dog by his side, gazing up as if in sympathy with his master.

The worthy couple were concerned for the drover, and evinced entire willingness to assist him, had it been in their power. He, in turn, was at a loss to know what to do with the animal, and paused to consider what course to pursue. To drive the maimed beast on was obviously impossible; to sell it there seemed equally so; for by remaining long enough in that place to find a purchaser, he must detain the whole herd of cattle, and incur more expense than the animal was worth. At length he exclaimed, "I never was more completely brought to my wits' end in my life;" and then turning to Ann, he added, "I must just make you a present of it, for in truth I don't know what else I can do with it; so kill it, and take care of it, for it is a principal beast. I'll answer for it, a mart like that has never come within your door." And without waiting for thanks, he whistled on his dog, and joined the herd, which was soon moving slowly on its weary journey.

The poor cottagers were lost in wonder at this unexpected deliverance from famine by so signal an interposition of Providence. And after they had in some measure recovered from their surprise, the father assembled his little family to give thanks for this new proof of the Lord's condescending kindness towards them. He then proceeded to follow the advice of the drover, and found his gift, as he had told them, to be a "principal" beast.

They now had meat sufficient to serve them for many months, but they had no bread. About six o'clock in the morning, however, another knock was heard at the door, when the "grieve," or bailiff of the benevolent woman in whose family Ann had formerly lived as a servant, presented himself with a load on his back.

He then proceeded to relate that he had been sent for by her the previous morning, who inquired, "If anything had happened to Ann Young." To which he replied, that he was not aware that they had met with any calamity, and when he last heard of her family they were all well. Then replied she, "She must be *in want;* for these few days she has been incessantly in my thoughts, and I am sure she is in distress," further directing him to take her a large sack of meal, and bring back word how she was, adding, "I know she would almost starve before she applied for relief."

Thus these pious cottagers were amply provided for, and Ann Young found the reason that this passage of Scripture had been so impressed upon her mind, and learned to understand more fully the meaning of that old and yet new and true declaration, "For every beast of the forest is mine, and the cattle upon a thousand hills."

GUIDANCE IN GIVING.

The Lord makes use of various means to relieve his suffering children who, in living faith, cry unto him for help. Many are the interesting incidents recorded showing how, in the very moment of extremity, succor has come from unexpected sources, which the Lord, by his controlling providence, has commanded to relieve his faithful ones. Manna may not fall from heaven, ravens may not minister to their necessities; but if the Lord leads one of his children to them with the needful help, by the motion of his Spirit, or if he opens the heart of any to send it, it is as truly from him. John Thorp relates, that meeting a poor beggar, he felt the expression raised in his heart, "The Lord help thee;" and he was passing on, when the query arose, How shall the Lord help but by putting it into the heart of his children to administer the help? on which he felt constrained to return and bestow something. It is often thus that the Lord works. The following, related in "The Christian," is an interesting instance of providential guidance in giving alms. One winter morning, a few years ago, a merchant of Boston, while attending a place of worship, became interested in a middle-aged man, a stranger to him, who took part in the proceedings of the meeting, and felt strongly inclined to go to him and give him some money. He wondered at the strangeness of the impression; the man was better dressed than himself; there were no evidences of want or poverty about him; the gift might be uncalled for, abrupt, and unwelcome; and the query arose whether it was not a temptation of Satan, rather than an admonition of the Lord. The conviction, however, deepened, and the command, "Give him five dollars," was repeated and impressed with such urgency upon his mind that he could not resist the inward call.

He accordingly took out a five-dollar bill, and when the meeting was over, with an embarrassed feeling placed it in the hand of the stranger, to be used as he saw fit, and hastened away without waiting for thanks, but feeling the inward approval known only to those who have "the witness" in themselves.

The next morning the merchant was again at

the meeting, when the stranger arose and spoke substantially as follows: "In days past, I possessed means, and in those days I delighted to do good. Many a five-dollar bill I have given to the poor and distressed; but reverses have overtaken me; and though I am provided with food and raiment, yet it is a great grief to me that I am unable to do for the poor and needy as I formerly could.

"Yesterday morning, on my way to this meeting, I saw a Christian sister in a neighboring town. She was sick, and poor, and friendless, and had neither food nor fire in this cold weather; and I felt in my heart, Oh, if I only had five dollars to give her, how glad I should be; but I did not have it. But I came here yesterday morning, and at the close of the meeting a brother came and put five dollars into my hand, to use as I saw fit, and went away. I went from this meeting to that poor woman's house, gave her the money, and told her the Lord had sent it to her, and she believed he did send it." He further expressed a desire to meet with the person who had given the money. After the meeting the merchant made himself known to him, and they rejoiced together in having been made the instruments of blessing to one of the Lord's little ones in a time of sore distress.

CAPTAIN YONNT'S DREAM.

A striking instance of providential deliverance is narrated by Horace Bushnell in his work on "Nature and the Supernatural, as together constituting the one system of God." "As I sat by the fire," says this writer, "one stormy night, in a hotel parlor in the Napa Valley, California, there came in a most venerable and benignant looking person, with his wife, taking their seats in the circle. The stranger, as I afterwards learned, was Captain Yonnt, a man who came over into California, as a trapper, more than forty years ago. Here he has lived apart from the great world and its questions, acquiring an immense landed estate, and becoming a kind of acknowledged patriarch in the country.

"In the course of conversation, he related the following incident in his experience. About six or seven years previous, in a midwinter's night, he had a dream, in which he saw what appeared to be a company of emigrants arrested by the snows of the mountains, and perishing rapidly by cold and hunger. He noted the very cast of the scenery, marked by a huge perpendicular front of white rock cliff; he saw the men cutting off what appeared to be tree-tops rising out of deep gulfs of snow; he distinguished the very features of the persons and the look of their particular distress.

He awoke profoundly impressed with the distinctness and apparent reality of his dream. At length he fell asleep, and dreamed exactly the same dream again. In the morning he could not expel it from his mind. Falling in shortly with an old hunter comrade, he told him the story, and was only the more deeply impressed, by his recognizing without hesitation the scenery of the dream.

" This comrade came over the Sierra, by the Carson Valley Pass, and declared that a spot in the pass answered exactly to his description. By this the unsophisticated patriarch was decided. He immediately collected a company of men, with mules, and blankets, and all necessary provisions. The neighbors were laughing, meantime, at his credulity. 'No matter,' said he; 'I am able to do this, and I will, for I verily believe that the fact is according to my dream.' The men were sent into the mountains, one hundred and fifty miles distant, directly to the Carson Valley Pass. And there they found the company in exactly the condition of the dream, and brought in the remnant alive.

"A gentleman present said, 'You need have no doubt of this, for we Californians all know the facts, and the names of the families brought in, who now look upon our venerable friend as a kind of saviour.' These names he gave, and the places where they reside, and I found afterwards that the California people were ready everywhere to second his testimony."

REMARKABLE PRESERVATION OF LIFE.

A young Cornish miner, who had been seriously awakened by Divine grace, was on his knees in prayer, in the mine in which he worked, when three large stones fell out of the roof above, striking the floor around him, without touching him. Immediately after, before he had time to rise, a large mass of the rock settled down on the stones which had previously fallen, and which alone prevented his immediate death. The large mass was only about four inches above his head as he knelt, and had he been standing up, he must inevitably have been crushed. He was so closely hemmed in as to be unable to rise from his kneeling position until the mass of rock which rested above him had been removed. This young miner was afterwards, for many years, one of the most effectual laborers among John Wesley's coadjutors throughout Cornwall, Wales, and Oxfordshire, working, through the blessing which attended his labors, a great moral reformation throughout a very benighted region. Labor for the good of others was in store for him, and the Providence which had assigned him further work in his cause, preserved him as effectually and easily amidst the falling of rocks as it would have done had he been threatened by nothing more ponderous than flakes of fleecy snow, or the settling of dew upon him.

Our late friend, Samuel Bettle, during the prevalence of yellow fever in this city in 1793, was taken down with the prevailing disease. His illness was great, and at last, to all appearance, he sank to his last repose. His nurses and physician considered him dead, and the coffin was prepared for his burial. During a few hours in which he lay in apparent death, although incapable of voluntary motion, and all perceptible respiration and circulation had ceased, he was yet perfectly conscious. At last he found ability to speak, which he exercised to the great fright of his attendants, and soon after strength began to return. The coffin which had been brought to the house for him, was needed to contain the body of his father, who died at this time. About twenty years after this event, Samuel Bettle was called to the ministry, in which he was exercised about forty-seven years. He told the writer that many years after the strange event above related had occurred, a hand was laid on his shoulder in passing through a crowded market, and a voice whispered, " I once made your coffin. I thought you were preserved for some good purpose."

We all, dear readers, have been preserved through many dangers to this day. Not of such a striking nature perhaps; yet if we are possessed of sound minds and thankful hearts, we must feel that a preserving hand of Providence has been about us. Well, let us then inquire and consider, For what have I been preserved? For what *good purpose* have I lived in safety to this day? Am I fulfilling the end of my being for which the merciful protection of the God and Father of all goodness has been powerfully and efficiently around me? The query is an important one, and deserves serious and frequent consideration.

LEONARD FELL.

Leonard Fell was attacked, whilst travelling alone, by a highwayman, and gave up without resistance, at his demand, his money and his horse. But his Master laying a concern upon him for the good of the poor thief's soul, he warned him to cease from his evil way. The robber in his rage threatened to blow his brains out if he offered to preach to him. But Leonard, nothing daunted, replied, "Though I would not give my life for my money or my horse, I would give it to save thy soul." Struck with the nobility of this sentiment, the anger of the highwayman departed, and he declared that from such a man he would take neither money nor horse. So he returned all to Leonard, who pursued his way with a thankful heart, and a portion of peace from his Master as a reward for his faithful dedication.

HENRY ERSKINE.

There are many instances recorded in the life of Henry Erskine, of Cornhill, Northumberland, wherein the providence of the Most High, in the time of great extremity, interfered in a remarkable manner for his relief. One evening, when residing at Dryburgh, in Scotland, with his large family, they had eaten the last morsel of food, and he was without a penny to purchase more. Morning came; his children were clamorous for something to eat, but there was none. After a time a knock was heard at the house-door, and a man requested assistance to take from a horse a very heavily loaded sack, which he was to leave there. On a doubt being expressed as to its being intended for them, and that it might be for another of that name, the man very gruffly said, he knew it was to be left there; and if they did not help, he should throw it on the ground and leave it. In the sack was a large supply of provisions. On another occasion, being in Edinburgh without the means of buying food, he was stopped in the streets by an individual, who inquired if he was not Henry Erskine, and being satisfied of his identity, gave him a letter and left him. The letter contained a considerable amount of money, with the words, "From a sympathizing friend." There were but eight words in the letter, and no clew as to the donor. The Lord ministers, when it seemeth him good, to the necessities of his children.

WOMAN THE MESSENGER OF MERCY.

The following incident, illustrating the working of Providence for the salvation of individuals, was narrated by an interesting woman, under whose notice it occurred. Her husband, a clergyman, had employed a laboring man to mow the yard around his dwelling, and in order that her plants and flowers should not be injured, she went out to caution him to be careful. She was thus led to take notice of the stranger. Some months afterwards, a message came for her husband to visit a person who was very ill. He himself was quite unwell; and his wife told him that she would visit the sick man, and, if it was needful, send one of the elders to see him. This was agreed to by her husband, and on visiting the sick man, she found he was the same person who had mown their yard. He was in deep distress, very sensible that death was approaching, and very anxious to witness the great work of preparation for another state of existence to be going on. As she received ability, she directed him to Christ Jesus, the Way the Truth and the Life,—the sinner's only hope. After which one of the elders, at her request, made the sick man a visit.

The next day, on receiving a message from the sick man, she went again. He was still in great anxiety of mind respecting his future condition, and she was once more prepared to speak to him of the Saviour, through whom alone cometh purification and salvation. He seemed to receive the Truth; and when his close came she had a consoling hope that, through the merciful offering upon Calvary, and the inward cleansing of the Holy Spirit, this poor penitent had been permitted to enter into eternal rest.

After his death, the widow told her that her husband had some time previously dreamed that he was very ill, and that a woman had led him in his last extremity to the Saviour. On awaking, he related his dream to his wife. On returning from his labor on the day in which he had mowed the yard, he told her that he had found, in the clergyman's wife, the very woman who had led him in his dream to Christ. This was the reason that he had sent to the clergyman's house when he found himself ill, and likely to die.

It seemed, in this case, that the Saviour, who had a purpose of mercy towards this poor man, had given him this dream to open the way in his dark heart to receive instruction by the mouth of this woman. The Lord's ways are not as our ways, but are perfect in wisdom no less than in mercy and truth.

A SUPERINTENDING PROVIDENCE.

Our heavenly Father sometimes restrains his children from running into dangers to them unforeseen; sometimes he preserves them in the midst of and through dangers. At others he permits accidents, as they are termed, to open a speedy entrance for them into his eternal rest. To those who are faithful to known duties, and who are found constantly waiting on him for his counsel, he more frequently manifests a restraining, directing guidance. To such, a little uneasiness of mind, a slight pointing of the finger of Truth, seems sufficient to cause them to move in the path of safety. In other cases the parties have been, as it were, constrained to be prepared to escape unseen dangers. Several years ago, a Friend, now living in Philadelphia, took his seat in a railroad-car at the depot in Kensington, on his way to Centre Bridge Station, in Bucks County. He had heard of the very low and precarious condition of a cousin, living about a mile and a half from the latter place, who had been ill for some time; and without giving notice of his intentions, he had provided himself with several articles, with which to pay her a visit, in the hope that they would contribute to her relief and comfort. Shortly after sitting down in the car, he felt an impression that he must at once change his seat. Without reasoning, he obeyed at once the intimation of the inward monitor, and moved to another seat, which proved to be less comfortable. The train immediately started, and just as it was leaving the depot, a stone, with ragged edges, about the size of his fist, was hurled through the window near which he had first seated himself, breaking the glass to pieces, and shivering the panel on the opposite side of the car. A fellow-passenger was so impressed with the occurrence, that he asked him the reason why he had moved his seat, adding that he would certainly have been killed had he remained in his former position, as he would have been struck on the temple. The train was stopped, and the man, who, under the influence of passion, had thrown the stone, was arrested.

On arriving at the station in Bucks County, he was surprised to find a brother of his sick relative in waiting with his carriage to take him home. As no intimation of his coming had been sent, he inquired why it was that he had met the train. The man replied, that about four o'clock in the afternoon, his sister had insisted that the Friend was coming, through great peril and with his life in his hand, to see her. She was so fully persuaded that such was the case, that she could not rest satisfied until he started with the conveyance for the station. On conversing with the invalid, relative to her weak condition, he found that she was then prepared to accede to his request to use certain remedies, to which she had previously felt a strong aversion, that he had brought with him, and which, under the Divine blessing, were instrumental in raising her from her low state and prolonging her life.

A MISTAKE PROVIDENTIALLY DIRECTED.

Various are the ways by which an all-wise, all-directing Providence ministers to the necessities of his poor. A recent female writer gives a narrative which strikingly exemplifies one way in which the Lord accomplishes his purposes of mercy and love. She had been attracted by the appearance of an interesting little lame girl who sold candy, and had sometimes bought it of her. The child appeared poor, and her stock was small. One day, the writer, passing along, met the little girl, who was accompanied by her mother, a person of a very sad, anxious countenance, and a bright little baby brother, who could just walk along. Pleased with the appearance of the little one, she took out her purse, and taking out a penny, she gave it to the child, and passed on her way. On reaching her own residence, she found that half a crown which she had in her purse when she started, and which she had not spent, was missing, and with all her thinking, she could not imagine what had become of it. Finally she dismissed the conjecture, where she could have dropped it, from her mind, hoping that whoever found it, it might do him some good.

Two months after her loss, in passing the place where she had seen the little girl, her mother, and little brother, she found the two former standing by a small table, nicely spread with candy, apples, and other eatables. The girl beheld her coming, and recognizing her, ran to welcome her; and the mother warmly expressed her gratitude to her for the help given in "that day of my great trouble." The writer was astonished at the warmth of feeling manifested, until she found that, in taking out the penny, she had, without noticing it, taken out the half-crown, and placed both in the child's hand. The grateful mother, in explaining her condition on the day in which her child had received the gift, said her children had had nothing to eat; that she had left her eldest child at home lying on the floor, and crying with hunger. It was the day of the family's very great want. The half-crown had kept her children from starving, and they had been enabled to procure the little table; and although they did not sell much, yet they had supported themselves, and had been better off since. On hearing these particulars, the unintentional donor said to herself, "This is the way my half-crown went: God needed it to supply the wants of his poor suffering ones." "It was one of these beautiful providences, often unseen and unnoticed by us, of which the world is so full." "The cries of that suffering family had reached his ear, and in Infinite Wisdom he came to their relief."

WARNING BY A DREAM.

Ralph W. Wood, a young English resident in India, returned to his native country about the year 1781. He took with him his eldest daughter, leaving his wife and three youngest children in India, who were to follow him sometime in the next year. When the time had nearly arrived, she expected to take passage in the "Grosvenor," which was announced to sail in the Sixth month, 1782. The children remaining with her,—the oldest being but five years of age,—were an anxious care to their mother to undertake during the voyage, long as it then was from India to England.

While making preparations for her departure, she was troubled by a dream of the shipwreck of the vessel. The impression would probably have faded away, had not the dream occurred a second and a third time before the vessel sailed. She then visited the captain, and informed him of her dream, and of her efforts not to allow herself to be influenced by it, until its repetition so impressed her mind, she had resolved that he must sail without her. The friends who were to have accompanied her on the voyage, endeavored by reasoning and ridicule to induce her to change her mind. The women especially were urgent, but her resolution was not to be changed, and she was left behind.

The "Grosvenor" sailed on the thirteenth of Sixth month, and on the fourth of Eighth month she struck upon the rocks on the coast of Africa, some distance from the Cape of Good Hope. In the attempt to land the crew and passengers, nineteen men lost their lives; the remainder reached the inhospitable coast. The next morning the natives came upon them, and carried off all they could lay their hands on, without actually plundering their persons. They then determined to journey by land to the Cape, and started upon this expedition under the command of Captain Coxon. They were followed by the natives, who continually plundered and insulted them. On one occasion they were attacked by a party of more than three hundred Kaffirs armed for war. A number of them were wounded, but no lives lost. Peace having been made at length, they pursued their journey. A few days later, the natives came upon them again, and robbed them of everything valuable, including flint, steel, and tinder-box, which had been useful kindling fires at night. The distressed party afterwards divided into two bands, half of them travelling inland, and the rest by the sea-shore. Those who took the inland way were soon compelled by hunger to return to the coast where they could procure shell-fish, which were their principal articles of food. After enduring these dreadful privations, at the expiration of one hundred and seventeen days only a small portion of their number succeeded in reaching a settlement near the Cape, where they were kindly cared for by the

Dutch government, although it was then engaged in a war with England.

When the news of the loss of the "Grosvenor" reached England, R. W. Wood gave up his family for lost. At the end of six months, being on a visit to his wife's mother, a carriage drove to the door. It contained his wife and their three children. His joy at thus again beholding them was almost overpowering. The faithful wife, with her usual energy and decision of character, had hastened from the vessel which had brought her safely to her native land, to be the first to communicate to him their safety. She had only waited for the next ship that sailed, a Danish East-Indiaman, and then safely returned to her husband, to unite with him and her children in thanking Him who in mercy had so wonderfully warned and preserved them from impending dangers.

A WIDOW PROTECTED.

In the "Journal of a Missionary in Canada," the following interesting incident is related. "A respectable farmer who had died, had left a widow, a very amiable and pious woman, and three children. She thought herself unequal to the management of the large farm which her husband had occupied, and therefore took a cottage in the village where I lived, and was now selling everything off except a little furniture.

"After the sale was over, I went into the house to see her. I congratulated her upon the plan she had adopted, and remarked that she would be much more comfortable, not only in being relieved from the cares of a business she could not be supposed to understand, but in a feeling of security, which in her unprotected state in that lonely house she could hardly enjoy.

"'Oh, no,' she said; 'not unprotected — far from it! You forget,' she continued, with a mournful smile, 'that I am now under the special protection of Him who careth for the fatherless and the widow; and I feel quite confident that he will protect us.'

"And he did protect them, and that very night, too, in a most extraordinary and wonderful manner. The farm-house was a solitary one — there was not another within half a mile of it. That night there was a good deal of money in the house, the proceeds of the sale. The mother and her three young children, and a maid-servant, were the sole inmates. They had retired to rest some time. The wind was howling fearfully, and shook the wooden house at every blast. This kept the poor mother awake, and she thought she heard, in the pauses of the tempest, some strange and unusual noise, seemingly at the back of the house. While eagerly listening to catch the sound again, she was startled by the violent barking of a dog, apparently in the front of the house, immediately beneath the bed-chamber. This alarmed her still more, as they had no dog of their own.

"She immediately arose, and going to the maid's room, awoke her, and they went down together. They first peeped into the room where they had heard the dog. It was moonlight, at least partially so, for the night was cloudy; still it was light enough to distinguish objects, although but faintly. They saw a large black dog scratching and gnawing furiously at the door leading into the kitchen, whence she thought that the noise she first heard had proceeded.

"She requested the servant to open the door which the dog was attacking so violently. The girl was a resolute creature, and she did so without hesitation, when the dog rushed out, and the widow saw through the door two men at the kitchen-window, which was open. The men instantly retreated, and the dog leaped through the window after them. A violent scuffle ensued, and it was evident, from the occasional yelping of the noble animal, that he sometimes had the worst of it.

"The noise of the contest, however, gradually receded, till the mistress could hear only now and then a faint and distant bark. The would-be robbers, or perhaps murderers, had taken out a pane of glass, which had enabled them to undo the fastenings of the window, when, but for the dog, they would doubtless have accomplished their purpose. The mistress and maid got a light, and secured the window as well as they could.

"They then dressed themselves, for to think of sleeping any more that night was out of the question. They had not, however, got down stairs the second time, before they heard their protector scratching at the outer door for admittance. They immediately opened it, when he came in wagging his bristly tail, and fawning upon each of them in turn to be patted and praised for his prowess.

"He then stretched his huge bulk at full length beside the warm stove, closed his eyes, and went to sleep. The next morning they gave him a breakfast any dog might have envied, after which nothing could induce him to prolong his visit. He stood whining impatiently at the door till it was opened, when he galloped off in a great hurry, and they never saw him afterwards.

"They had never seen the dog before, nor did they ever know to whom he belonged. It was a very singular circumstance, and they could only suppose that he came with some stranger to the sale. The family moved the following day to their new cottage in the village; and when my wife and I called upon them, the widow reminded me that, when I last saw her, she had told me they were not unprotected."

GOOD OUT OF EVIL.

A recent author gives an interesting narrative, in which an intended act of wickedness led, in the overruling Providence of our heavenly Father, to effect his gracious purpose of mercy towards one of his erring and depressed human beings. A young woman being at some distance from her own residence one evening, was stopped by two ruffians with great clubs, who evidently had a murderous intent towards her; seeing this, she turned and fled. They pursued her, but were not able to overtake her, as she had not far to go to the next gate on a turnpike near Sandgate, England. When she entered the gate-house, she was so completely exhausted that she sank down through weakness. After she had somewhat recovered from the fright and the effect of her violent exercise in running, she began to consider what she should do. She dared not attempt that night to travel the road whereon she had been so recently assaulted, and remembering that an old female friend of her family had charge of the mansion of a baronet, which was near by, she concluded to apply to her for accommodation for the night. She knew the owner and his household were absent.

She reached the house safely, knocked at the front door, and then at all the side doors of the house successively, without receiving any intimation that any one was within. At last her old friend appeared at a small door among the stables, and inquired who was there. The young woman was hospitably received, and retired to rest with a thankful heart for her preservation that evening. In the morning she related to her old friend the circumstances of her escape, and also gave utterance to the fervent gratitude stirring within her to her Almighty Care-taker. From that evening, the aged woman treated her young friend with most extraordinary respect and kindness whenever they met, and was so intent on ministering to her comfort, that the recipient of her attentions was often tried that one so much older should take so much trouble for her. The cause of this was not explained for several years. At last, the aged woman, being about to remove from the neighborhood of Sandgate to London, took an opportunity of speaking of this matter to her young friend. At their parting interview, she asked her if she remembered coming to the house of the baronet on such an evening. "Certainly I do; nor can I ever forget the deliverance I was then blessed with." She then asked her "if she remembered finding all the doors bolted and barred, and that she came to her at a door among the stables?" "Oh, yes; I remember it all." The old woman at this point became greatly agitated, but having obtained some relief by giving vent to tears, she went on to say, that previously to the evening referred to, she had been much depressed in spirit, and had been tempted by the evil one to destroy her own life. That evening, there being no one in the house with her, she had given way in spirit to the temptation, and had made preparation for accomplishing her wicked design. She had first carefully fastened all the doors of the dwelling, and was passing down the backyard, intending to throw herself into the sea, when the knocking at the doors, one after another, arrested her steps, and prevented her carrying her intention into effect. The young woman's gratitude for her own deliverance had probably a good effect upon the old one's mind; and she ever after felt thankfulness to her

P

Almighty Saviour, who, by sending the affrighted girl there for refuge, had prevented the accomplishment of the meditated crime, and saved her soul from endless misery. This was the reason she had felt bound to show so much kindness and respect to her young friend. Through the Lord's merciful regard, and the quickening operations of his Holy Spirit, her despair of mind had long since subsided; although she still, at seasons, felt much distress in the remembrance of her wicked intention.

As she was now leaving the neighborhood, she felt it a duty to inform her young friend of the circumstance, requesting her not to mention it during her lifetime. The request was faithfully observed; and the aged woman, who lived several years after this conversation, was favored with a good degree of inward peace and quietness of spirit to the end, and her close was happy.

TRIALS.

FAITH IN TRIALS.

THE Lord sometimes takes away our comforts to teach us humility and dependence upon himself, and to fit and qualify us for usefulness in his church and family. An instructive account is recorded of an affectionate, religiously-minded woman, of an active, useful turn of mind, who had been engrossed by many outward blessings to the endangering the better part. Her heart was much upon her family and friends, and she delighted in some of the elegancies of life, which an ample fortune enabled her to indulge in. At last she was sensible that her affections were becoming too much set on worldly things, and she was enabled heartily to seek for aid in counteracting their evil tendency. She wished to retain all her blessings, and enjoy them to the full, and yet not to be injured thereby. The Lord saw meet to order it otherwise; an affectionate husband, her two children, and other near relatives were taken from her, and some pecuniary losses reduced her estate. These trials made the defects of her Christian character more apparent. She became melancholy at her bereavements, and her gloom increased as months rolled by. She did not flinch from performing the duties of life, but she entered into them without pleasure; and nursing her sorrow, her health appeared to be giving way. The Lord, however, whom she continued to love under all, gave her a visitation in mercy, which, through his help, aroused her from her gloom. She visited, during the winter season, a friend who resided in the country, whose house was surrounded with many rare and beautiful flowers and shrubs, of which she was very careful. The visitor, who much admired the grounds and the plants, one morning, on looking out of the window, was very much astonished to see many of the most ornamental branches cut from the fairest flowers and richest shrubbery, and scattered carelessly on the ground. Much had been done, and still the work of apparent desolation was going on. There was a gardener still ruthlessly cutting and hewing, and not knowing where he would stop, she asked her friend how she could bear to see her favorites so cruelly mangled, adding, "They will be totally ruined. Do stop him." Her friend replied in nearly these words: "I could not let *any one else* do it, but *he knows what he is doing*. They will be the more beautiful for all this." Whilst looking on this scene of devastation, the mournful visitor found her thoughts dwelling on the words of her friend, "*He knows what he is doing.*" Her mind reverted to her trials; to the stripping and pruning dispensation which her heavenly Father had meted out to her. She felt she had not exercised a similar faith in the discipline of her dear Saviour; she felt that *he* knew what he was doing. She appreciated the impressions made at that moment by the Holy Spirit, that everything had been apportioned to her in love. These simple words of her friend, through the blessing of her Saviour, were made instrumental in changing the whole current of her thoughts. She found she had many things left to be thankful for; and although never forgetting the loved ones she had lost, yet, with cheerful resignation, renewed health and spirits, she endeavored faithfully to pursue the path of duty. Ah! Christian, how much of thy trouble would be removed, how many of thy afflictions would be lightened, if thou couldst only refer all to thy Saviour, and say in meekness, "Thou knowest what thou art doing. Do with me as seemeth unto thee good."

THE OLD ROSE-BUSH REVIVED.

There is in the possession of the writer a rose-bush that had been robbed of its strength and beauty by shoots from its wild root, which bore no flowers. The pruning-knife had been freely applied, a year ago, to the barren growth; and indeed the whole top of the decaying shoot from the true graft, which had borne, in its vigor, beautiful flowers, was also cut away. This was done as the only method of saving it; yet we had little hope that any permanent good would be effected, as it appeared as though all that was of any value in the bush was fast dying. Two or three shoots started before winter, and grew with some rapidity; yet, as we believed they were from the natural wild root, little attention was given to them; and it was not until the time when other roses were blooming, that it was apparent that some were from the graft; for on one of them, rapidly opening its green mantle, was a promising rose-bud. On this discovery, the pruning-knife was freely applied to the fresh shoots of the wild root, which were absorbing the sap and weakening that growth which was doing its best to bloom. Strengthened by this pruning, the plant has perfected roses, beautiful in color as ever, although somewhat less in size and fewer in number than those it put forth before its strength had been given to the nourishment of the barren *suckers;* and it is evident that with careful attention, and a constant *pruning* down of all wrong growth, we may once more have the plant blooming in vigor, and bearing more abundantly than ever the sweet, beautiful roses of the true graft.

Whilst musing over this rose-bush, its threatened decay, and happy recovery, my mind seemed a little animated with spiritual good. I was led into a train of thought on the benefit often experienced by the Christian from right pruning, administered by the heavenly Husbandman; even from the frequent application of the sharp knife of affliction, not merely trimming off wrong branches, but cutting down, as it were, to the root all growth not from the grafting of grace. Memory recalled the records of many persons,—the good, the wise, the useful in their generation,—who, in early life, and some of them until far past the meridian of their day, had given the sap of their strength to the *natural* shoots, which bore no good fruit, and nothing to admire at best but *showy, useless leaves*. A graft had, by Divine visitation, been set in some of them, but in the profusion of the natural growth, it had been dwarfed, and seemed dying or dead, whilst only fruits of evil hung round in abundance. These men and women exerted an influence in the world for evil; their fruit was bitter; they brought forth nothing to the praise of him, who, by the visitation of his Spirit, called them to grace and to glory; until, through his merciful chastisements and regenerating baptisms acting as a sharp pruning-knife, the evil growth within was little by little cut off. Then, indeed, the heavenly graft of early or later visitation found room to grow, obtained strength and nourishment to bloom and bear fruit. As the keen strokes of affliction, wielded by the skilful hand of him who doeth all things well, cut off and destroyed shoot after shoot of the *old wild stock*, the new growth waxed stronger and stronger, until its blossoms and fruitage were truly to the honor of the great·Husbandman, and to the praise of his redeeming grace. I thought of Samuel Fothergill, rioting in all wickedness,— of Daniel Wheeler, degraded and sunk in sin,— of Peter Yarnall, making a sport of religion, and everything excellent; and as I saw how, through the severity of Divine dispensations, their evil growth was removed, and in how large a measure, in after-life, they were enabled to bring forth the fruits of holiness, for their own good and the good of the church, I felt how merciful was the great Husbandman, that every branch bearing no fruit unto holiness should be taken away from us, and that every plant bearing fruit should have all evil growth purged from it, that it might "bring forth more fruit."

Whilst musing, without seeking for illustrations, there was suddenly brought to my remembrance one whom I had known many years ago, and of whom I had seen but little since. When I first knew him, he was just entering manhood, of fair abilities, and an excellent character in civil society; and who, by his consistent walking, gave cheering evidence that the great Husbandman had indeed engrafted in him a heavenly bud, which through assisting grace was growing vigorously, —bearing already some fruit, and giving large promise of more.

Time in its ever ceaseless movement carried us forward. Years passed. He was married, and his wife, in addition to earthly graces, had the adornings of the Spirit. The graft of grace given her had grown and produced good fruit. He had children born to him; and these outward blessings, a religious wife and healthy children, whilst adding to his earthly cares and comforts, should have increased his thankfulness to God and dedication to his service.

After a long time, being in the neighborhood in which I knew he had formerly resided, I found him in bodily health, but his very appearance proclaimed a *changed* man. His religious duties, even near home, were neglected; and I could but remind him of the dew of his youth, and the love of his espousals, now, alas! apparently forgotten. I found that the cares of the world, and probably the unsubdued love of it, had caused shoots to spring up from the old nature, which had very much weakened the graft from Divine grace. Many afflictions had been mercifully granted him to cut down the wild growth; near and dear ones had been taken away; but, however, after such a discipline, wrong things might appear momentarily to wither, yet for want of yielding all up to the great Pruner, with earnest desire for thorough repentance, and the perfect reduction of self, the evil shoots but grew more luxuriantly. He had a fresh sense given him how it was and had been with him, acknowledged his error, and thought he would improve. Alas! a mere sense of our error produces no improvement. He had not yet experienced a longing desire to feel the *pruning-knife*, — an earnest, beseeching love to him who wieldeth it, and a daily, hourly, craving for the removal of every budding of evil!

Fresh visitations of trial for his good are still mercifully granted him. Immediately, and instrumentally, he has evidently been sought after.

Stroke upon stroke has been given him to cut off the evil growth, to bring him back, if not as a branch to bear much fruit to the Lord's glory, at least as one of which the fruit, though scant and feeble, might be unto holiness, and through the mercy of him who seeketh to save, might in the end be unto everlasting life.

In my present musing, these things came into my mind, and whilst sorrowing over the present condition of this *once* promising plant, I could but feel the petition raised that still sharper strokes of the pruning-knife might be given him, even until driven to the Lord Jesus for comfort in his distress, he might be rightly enabled to kiss the rod, and him who hath appointed it. Oh, there is no time to delay! When the discipline of affliction and merciful chastisement is continually rejected, may we not fear that the time will soon come when the growth of grace being smothered, the growth of evil fruit will be so openly apparent, as to bring shame and reproach?

CHEERFUL RESIGNATION A CHRISTIAN DUTY.

Whatever our trials may be, whatever bereavements we may have experienced, a Christian has no right to murmur at them, or to nourish a gloomy disposition—dwelling continually and repiningly over his losses or his crosses. He has no right, by anything he says or does, to give his neighbors cause to believe that he thinks he has been hardly dealt with by his heavenly Father.

It is narrated that a minister of the Society of Friends called one day to see a female acquaintance who had during the previous year lost her husband. He found the window-shutters of the house closed, as if for a recent death, whilst everything in it wore a sable hue; and the widow herself, attired in deep mourning, gave evidence, by her sad, disconsolate countenance, that she was unprofitably, nay, sinfully dwelling on her great loss, to the neglect of present duty, and in forgetfulness that submission to the will of Divine Providence is a universal Christian requirement. Observing that she was nourishing such a rebellious spirit against the holy will of her Saviour, he addressed her in these words of solemn rebuke: "I perceive thou hast not yet forgiven the Almighty." This short sentence probably gave her a clearer insight into her own motives and feelings than she had before attained; and led her to seek, through the aid of the Holy Spirit, genuine repentance for the past, and strength to bear her burden with cheerful submission for the future. She was enabled to shake off her complaining gloom, to remember the many mercies bestowed upon her, and to seek for peace in a daily surrender of her will to that of the all-wise, all-merciful Controller of the allotments and vicissitudes of his children.

A writer has said: "To be good and to be disagreeable, is high treason against virtue." If this be true, and he must be hardy who, after serious reflection, will dare to gainsay it, then also must it be treasonable for one professing himself a Christian, to show by his continual gloom that he is rebelling in heart against the allotment of trial and suffering apportioned him. The Christian feels his earthly trials, but there is One who can and will, if he is sought unto in living faith, grant him consolation. The believer must mourn; yea, cold and dead, and unworthy of the name of Christian were he, who, when the ties of affection are severed by the removal of beloved ones to their heavenly home, does not deeply feel the bereavement. But he, who when in an earthly body shed tears over a dead Lazarus, is near, if they will seek for him, to soothe their sorrows, to grant to the resigned soul some sweet streams of inward refreshment, and the ability to say in tearful yet reverent acquiescence, "Thy will be done!"

In the midst of his trials, of whatever kind they be, the true Christian has much comfort, and real, if it be a subdued, and humble happiness. How is it with the man of the world, even amidst all his gayeties, and, it may be, his almost unbroken prosperity. Let the idol of the German literati, Goethe, answer for himself. When seventy-five years of age, he writes: "I have often been praised as an especial favorite of fortune; and I will not myself complain. But at the bottom there has been nothing but trouble and labour; and I can well say, that in my whole five and seventy years I have not had four weeks of real pleasure. It was the eternal rolling of a stone, that had always to be lifted up again for a new start." How could such a man have real pleasure? He did not know in what it consisted! he sought it not of him who can alone bestow it. How often do we find the Christian, even amidst all the pain of a diseased body, enjoying true happiness of mind. A Friend well known to the writer, who when visited during the paroxysms of extreme agony, which were rapidly breaking down a strong constitution, said with a sweet smile, in allusion to his suffering, "It is all of the body, within all is peace." What an excellent thing to be able to feel in the hours of suffering as John Camm did, who, having to endure a long season of agony whilst the bodily powers were gradually giving way, was yet able with thankfulness of heart to exclaim, "How great a benefit do I enjoy beyond many; I have such a large time of preparation for death;—dying daily, that I may live forever with my God in that kingdom that is unspeakably full of glory. My outward man daily wastes and moulders down, and draws towards its place and centre; but my inward man revives and mounts upwards towards its place and habitation in the heavens." So, although full of pain, and often terribly shaken with a racking cough, he yet could rejoice in a full assurance of faith, feeling in and over all his afflictions, as George Fox expressed himself when he too was passing through the last pangs of parting mortality, "All is well! The Seed of God reigns over all!"

MISTAKEN COMFORT.

Christian, if God is smiting thee with the rod of suffering or bereavement, be assured it is for thy good. Attempt not, I beseech thee, to flee from, but, on the contrary, draw nearer and nearer to, him, seeking for a spirit of humble acquiescence in his dispensations to thee. It has been said by some one, that if we would lighten the stroke of our punishment, we should draw near to the hand inflicting it. This is sound philosophy outwardly and inwardly. By drawing near to the Lord, our chastiser, we shall see the mercy which directs the stroke, and it will fall with much less of that condemning force, the fear of which increases our suffering. The Christian, therefore, for the honor of Truth, for the sake of others, for the good of his own soul, should seek to his God for ability to walk before men with a cheerful countenance, with a cover of humble resignation over his spirit, even when a song of rejoicing has not been given to his tongue. But let him not seek for comfort and consolation in outward things, especially those which, dissipating serious impressions, and restoring apparent cheerfulness to the countenance, tend to alienate the mind from God, the alone efficient comforter of his children.

An aged, religiously-minded woman told the writer, a few years since, that, being much cast down, and nervously distressed at the awful condition of things in our beloved country, and the uncertainty where and what further calamities would yet come, she had been persuaded by her children to retire to a quiet retreat, far from the turmoil of cities, and advised, nay, almost enjoined, to indulge herself in *novel reading*, to lighten her trouble of mind and quiet her nerves. Certainly, those who thus persuaded, and at last induced, her, as an experiment, to read one such work of fiction, were not themselves acquainted with the true remedy for their much-loved and honored parent. A permanent and abiding sense of the omnipotence and all-directing wisdom of God in the dispensations he directs or permits to come upon individuals or nations, and of his superintending providence and fatherly care over all who trust in him, was what she needed. No doubt she acknowledged all this in words; but a bare acknowledgment is often made where a real, supporting faith is not felt. Novel reading might change the tone of her mind; it might, for a brief period, drive from her thoughts the fearful images that oppressed it, but it could prove at best a temporary remedy, which would alienate from God, and thereby produce a condition far worse than the original disease. Her troubles, if they only had had the effect of driving her to cleave more closely and abidingly to her Saviour for comfort, would have brought her peace in him. Novel reading, whilst soothing, debases, and of necessity has in it and draws after it a curse.

INFLUENCE OF THE OUTWARD UPON THE INWARD.

It is recorded that an officer in one of the English expeditions in search of Franklin, the Arctic explorer, was of a frank and open disposition, fond of gayety, and very thoughtless as respected his future state. During his journey as leader of one of the sledge parties, his mind was awakened to serious considerations. He saw the utter worthlessness of many things highly prized, and eagerly sought after, in the world of civilized life. He thought, what would all the wealth of Europe avail him, if he should lose the judgment and self-possession which would enable him to conduct his party back to the ship? Then came the thought how would it be with him, if they should be stricken down by disease amid the snowy wastes?

The difficulty of directing their course, from the variation of the compass, was great, and much care was required to keep the chronometer from stopping; and feeling the responsibility heavy upon him, he walked much alone. After a time one of the party was struck with the snow-blindness, and soon afterwards another. These events added much to the weight of his care and anxiety. The next day, after the malady attacked them, before starting in the morning, the twenty-third Psalm was read, beginning, "The Lord is my shepherd." As they journeyed on that day, amidst all the fears which beset his mind relative to the safety of his party, this passage from that Psalm kept sounding through his mind, "Yea, though I walk through the valley of the shadow of death, I will fear no evil." At night, as he lay, kept awake by his anxiety, through the merciful visitations of the grace of God, he was brought to look back with contrition on his past life of folly, and to covenant in secret, that if spared to return to his native country, he would never forget how the Psalmist had been enabled to rejoice in communion with God. Lessons of instruction he had received in childhood came back to his memory, and a comfort he had not felt for years stole into his mind.

Greater trials came upon them than they had yet experienced; at one time they encountered a violent snow-storm, and were buried in the drift so deeply, that it was thirty-six hours before they could proceed. Provisions were growing scarce, and the weather was so thick that it was doubtful if they could find the ship. During this time of distress, his mind was consoled as the text, "The Lord is my shepherd, I shall not want," was again and again presented to it.

The company reached their vessel in safety, and the officer, it is testified, became, through the power of Divine grace, a wiser and better man. The visitations of mercy to his soul, in the hours of his lonely, anxious, Arctic travel, and in the wakeful watches, whilst his worn-out men were sleeping soundly around him, had been blessed to him.

Many of those who have been faithful laborers in the Lord's vineyard, have received sensible visitations and precious awakenings apparently springing from outward things; some, during seasons of quiet retirement, and when walking in solitary places; some, whilst musing amid rural scenery; others in feeling the fury of a storm, threatening to destroy them. When the Lord has prepared the heart for his service, there lacketh not outward events through which the sensible operations of his Holy Spirit take hold of the awakened mind. Sickness and the fear of death have driven many, with strong cries and earnestness of spirit, to seek to the great Physician of value, who, in his own time, as they continued depending upon him, healed all their maladies. Some have been driven by terrible, some drawn by gentle means into the paths of peace. Daniel Wheeler could trace deep and abiding effects on his mind received during a hurricane at sea; whilst Mary Haggar could remember visitations of Divine love granted her amid the flowers of a garden.

PRAY IN FAIR WEATHER.

In a recent number of a religious paper, an anecdote to this import is told. A number of years ago, a ship bound to New York, whilst far out in the ocean, suddenly encountered a dreadful storm. All hands were called to take in sail and put the ship in the best trim to stand such a hurricane, and all seemed too few. At this moment, one of the men, the most hardened, wicked person in the ship, was missing; the captain, himself an irreligious man, looked round for him and found him below, on his knees, repeating the Lord's prayer over and over again. Seizing him by the collar, the captain jerked him on his feet, and shouted with a voice heard even amid the roaring of the storm, "Say your prayers in fair weather."

The ship, through the good management of the skilful mariners, and the blessing of a merciful God, was saved, and in a few days reached her port. The man who prayed in the storm was at once discharged, having been through his wickedness a pest in the ship for the preceding fifteen months. But Divine grace had touched him. The blunt speech of the captain, "Say your prayers in fair weather," seemed ever sounding in his ears, and deep distress for his past sins and present state came upon him. Through the mercy of God, and the cleansing baptisms of his Spirit, the work of regeneration went on, until the late hardened sinner became a child of the kingdom, an heir of God, and joint heir with Christ.

On a certain occasion, years after this event, this man was engaged in preaching, and was surprised at perceiving the captain who had been made the instrument of good to him, sitting among his hearers. At once the scene of the storm came vividly before him, and with a voice so loud as to startle all present, he exclaimed, "Say your prayers in fair weather." When he had recovered in measure his composure, he proceeded to narrate the circumstance we have given above. The captain, on finding who the preacher was, and how it had pleased the Lord, of mercy and loving-kindness, to make use of him and his scornful exclamation in turning a hardened sinner into a preacher of righteousness, was much affected. His mind was awakened, and Divine grace operating therein, led him also forward in the path of purity and peace, until, through the baptisms of repentance and the renewings of the Holy Ghost, he too was made a partaker of the blessed hope of the gospel of life and salvation.

These words, "Pray in fair weather," so eminently blessed in these two instances, may well claim the serious consideration of each one of us. The paper in which the narrative is given, puts the inquiry to each of its readers, if they say their prayers in fair weather, or whether they wait until some storm, fraught with sorrow and danger, comes upon them, to drive them in anguish and terror to seek comfort and security in God. We have need to be doubly watchful and prayerful in times of prosperity. When God gives us most outward blessings, we are most likely to forget him. Reader, whether it be fair weather or foul weather with thee, seek ever for the spirit of prayer; then, through a full surrender of thy own will to the Lord Jesus, his redeeming and sanctifying mercy will prepare thee to bear the afflictions of time without terror, and the blessings of prosperity without injury to thy immortal soul.

AGITATION THAT PURIFIES.

The trials, the tossings, the varied afflictions of the Christian tend to his purification. If a man or a woman gives more than usual evidence of heavenly-mindedness, it will frequently be found that the path in which he or she has been led, has been, either from inward or outward conflicts, a peculiarly trying one. It has been stated, that if water, in a perfectly calm condition, was foul with mud, it would, for a long period, hold the impurity in suspension; but that if it was much agitated, or set in lively onward motion, the sediment quickly deposited, leaving the fluid pure and transparent. The soul that is passing from a state of nature to a state of grace, cannot fail to be agitated. The immense importance of the object at stake awakens intense anxiety, and fears and doubtings assail it. The white-robed, rejoicing company in heaven are those who have come out of great tribulation; yet this tribulation has no doubt been often much confined to inward spiritual conflicts. Some of those who have attained considerable Christian growth, who have exhibited in beautiful perfection the Christian graces, may have had small share of outward trials. Nevertheless, their cup has had its bitterness in it. They have tasted the wormwood and the gall; they have been tossed with inward conflicts, and have known seasons when there seemed to be none to comfort them, none that cared for their souls.

If the soul has been really awakened to a sense of its inward corruption; if it feel the necessity of knowing the Lord Jesus Christ for itself, and of attaining to a state of obedience unto him in his inward requirings, it will, it must, be shaken with inward conflicts. The fear of running too fast, the dread of lagging behind the heavenly guide, will agitate the mind. The old corruptions of nature often retard, the impatience of an unsettled state sometimes hurry it forward in zeal without true knowledge. If, however, the heart is really touched by Divine grace; if it is really longing for a perfect salvation through the one offering of the Lord Jesus Christ, and the sanctifying power of his inward baptism, it will, amid all the vibrations of its weakness, turn back to him.

THE WAY HEDGED UP.

Reader, is thy way hedged up? Are the inward trials and afflictions dispensed to thee of so trying and peculiar a character that thou canst not see how thou art to hold on thy way in patience and resignation any longer? Or, is thy pecuniary condition such that it appears to thee that the way is completely hedged up? Whatever thy situation, whatever the peculiar trials which beset thee, and appear to hedge thy way, remember, if thou art a believer in and a true-hearted lover and follower of the Lord Jesus Christ, all thy trials, all thy difficulties, nay, all thy bereavements, are in mercy, according to the declaration, "All things work together for good to them that love God."

A Christian narrates that on a certain occasion,

when his trials and afflictions were so great that he thought it almost in vain to endeavor to bear up under them, he was returning towards his house in the evening, and found a mass of thorns laid in his way. As in the dark he could not see to penetrate them, he tried to walk round them, but found thorns had been placed all across the road. He concluded some enemy had placed them there; but as he found it impracticable to pass, he turned backward, and, trying another way, was soon safely in his own house. In the morning he went to the place, that he might understand why the path had been hedged against him. Great was his thankfulness, when he reached the spot, to those whose kindness had induced them to place so thick a fence of briars as to baffle his attempt to pass it. From a quarry by the road-side the top had recently fallen in, so that had he passed on, broken limbs, or even loss of life, might have ensued. With gratitude he could lift up an offering of praise to his heavenly Father, whilst he acknowledged it had been a friend, and not an enemy, who had hedged up his way.

This occurrence led him to a consideration of the manifold trials which beset his path through life, and he felt an inward assurance that in these, also, the hand of a Friend had been at work. He was led closely to inquire, Am I in my proper path? Does my heavenly Father, by hedging my way with thorns, seek to turn my feet from certain danger, from probable or positive destruction? This is a question which may profitably engage all of us when our way is hedged up. Is my being here in my heavenly Father's direction? Have my steppings, which have brought me here, been taken in his fear?

FAITH.

WALKING BY FAITH.

THE natural man cannot appreciate the feelings which, operating in the heart of the humble Christian, enable him to walk by faith in the openings and leadings of the spirit of Truth. He has no faculty by which to take hold of, or to understand, such an intercourse between the soul of man and God his creator. He is like those individuals who, having no appreciation of certain colors, wonder at the remarks of those around them. Dugald Stewart had a natural defect in his sight, so that, we are told, "to him the cherries and the leaves on a tree were the same color; and there was no distinction of hue between the red coats of the soldiers, marching through a wood, and the green trees themselves." The fact that those who have not submitted to the visitations of Divine grace, and been happily made acquainted with the still small voice which reproves and instructs in the soul, may not understand the actions of the man who, endeavoring to perform his religious duty, walks by faith and not by sight, furnishes no more reason to doubt the reality of that which directs him, than the inability of Professor Stewart to distinguish colours does to prove that no such difference exists. These reflections have arisen while recording the following anecdote strongly exemplifying the walking by faith.

A member of the Society of Friends, who resided many miles from Philadelphia, several years ago, felt a strong religious concern to attend a meeting of which he was a member in that city. He was a worthy, exemplary man, and it was right for him to endeavor to be in attendance there, even if he had not felt it to be at that time particularly his religious duty. But he was one who, although rich in faith, was poor as respects worldly substance, and had no means of raising the small sum of ready money necessary to meet his expenses by the way. The impression of duty continued, and doubtless with many heart-sinkings and fears he set off on the journey. On crossing a stream he saw something shining in the water, which proved to be a silver coin. Taking it, he passed on his way, thankful to his heavenly Father for this merciful provision, and paying therewith all unavoidable expenses, until he arrived at a neighborhood of Friends, where he was freely entertained, and from whence he was enabled to reach the city without further outlay.

THE MYSTERIES OF PROVIDENCE.

The attributes of the Almighty, his creating power in nature, and in the sanctifying and justifying operations of his grace, can never be understood and comprehended by the weak, circumscribed faculties of man. His dealings with the children of grace, the peculiar tribulations meted out to some, the comparatively sunny paths through which he leads others, are doubtless in true wisdom, and tend to the perfecting of his glorious purposes. We may not be able to perceive any fitness in the dispensations of his Providence, through which we or our friends are, through his assistance, slowly working our way to the kingdom of purity and peace, whither he calls us; yet through faith in him, and in his unbounded wisdom and mercy, *we know* that the path in which he leads all his spiritual children is the very path most conducive to individual holiness and the good of the church militant.

It is useless to perplex ourselves by an attempt to sound unfathomable depths with the short line of our limited understanding. An illustration in point is told relative to Augustine, who, says the story, had been perplexing himself respecting the nature of the deity, the mysteries of the Godhead. The more he mused, the more difficult did the subject appear to him. With his mind agitated by the failure of his intellect to grasp the subject, he walked out on the sea-shore, that at least his body might be invigorated by the cool, bracing wind. As he paced along, still straining his intellect to compass things beyond human comprehension, he perceived, as he thought, a child busily engaged bringing water from the sea in the hollow of his hands, and pouring it into a small hole he had scraped in the sand. Augustine felt interested in the little laborer, and ceasing from the vain and fruitless exertion of thought he had been engaged in, he paused to consider and question. "My child, what art thou doing?" he asked. "Mine is an easy task," said the boy; "it is only to sweep the wide ocean into this narrow hole." "Foolish boy! to expect those vast waters could be held in that small pit," said the learned man, astonished that even a child should have been so unreasonable as to deem it a possibility. As he so spake, the little child appeared to change into the form of an angel of light, and with answering reproof thus addressed him: "Child of dust, thy object is still more hopeless. Dost thou conceive that thou art able to comprehend the nature of the most High within the compass of thy own shallow understanding? Far sooner, Augustine, far sooner could I accomplish this work, than any finite mind understand his nature who is infinite."

Whether Augustine narrated this as a vision, or as a parable, we know not. In either case the moral is so plain that we may profit by it.

We cannot comprehend God, neither can we always see the design of the operations of his providence. Yet it is often the case that apparent mysteries are made plain to us, even on this earth. If he leads some of his children through bloody or fiery martyrdom into his kingdom of glory, it has often been his good pleasure thereby to awaken hardened spectators to turn to and embrace the truth, and to quicken lukewarm believers to seek for a greater portion of that grace which had enabled a brother or sister to thank God whilst exulting in the fires, or in the jaws of wild beasts, or whilst yielding their lives under the gallows. Some children of grace have had lifelong conflicts with pain, and afflictions of various kinds; and although the workings of Providence may at times appear very mysterious to them, yet we have evidence that, from the holy, heavenly example of meek, unrepining patience manifested by them, there have at seasons been merciful extendings of saving visitations to others. Yea, others, seeing their good works of cheerful submission, have through Divine grace been enabled to glorify God in this their day of visitation.

The removal of valuable laborers from the church militant in the maturity and vigor of their days, before the spiritual eye has become dim, or the strength and alacrity of spirit for doing the Lord's work has abated, is often a mystery, as well as an affliction to the flock and family. Yet, at times, a benefit to others may spring out of such afflictive dispensations.

It has been noticed that when large, full-grown trees which had cast a goodly shadow have been removed, it is often the case that plants which had been sheltered by them, but shaded also, and thereby stunted in growth, have become more thrifty and vigorous; and thus it is with some of the members of the church, who have depended too much on the leading and labors of such honorable members, who have been taken to their everlasting rewards. Those who have lived too much under this shadow of such, are now required to come forward and take a more active part in religious concerns, to their own growth and establishment in the truth.

HOW LITTLE WE UNDERSTAND.

We drop a hard peach-stone in the ground, and covering it with earth, leave it. We know that if we crack it open we shall find nothing within but a kernel, with a reddish skin; yet, we confidently expect to see the following spring a green shoot piercing the ground where we have deposited the stone, which, if left unmolested, will soon grow into a tree. We cannot understand the process, yet we have an undoubted faith that it will take place, and nature does not disappoint us. The stone and the kernel were red; the soil, whose juices furnish much of the nourishment to the young growth, is a dingy brown, or it may be dull yellow, yet the young stem comes forth of a bright, lively green. The most acute chemist cannot understand the operations of nature by which these changes are effected; like the ignorant and the simple, he sees and believes without comprehending. The plant grows on. A fresh crop of leaves is thrown forth from the stem every year, and in the third and fourth spring, beside the green leaves, there shoot out crimson blossoms, rich and sweet. The naturalist knows that this varied growth of leaves and flowers is fed by the same sap; and whilst watching their beauty and variety, he feels that the subtle chemistry at work is beyond his comprehension. Before him are the scentless green leaves and the fragrant rose-tinted blossoms, from whose cups the bees draw forth the clear honey to store their comb with sweetness. No one can tell the reason why, though experience daily proves the truth of it, that buds from many different peach-trees, inoculated into one, will always bear fruit of the kind borne by the tree from which the bud was taken. Many varieties — some sweet, some more lively, some even tart — have been seen all growing from one trunk, all fed from one fountain of sap. How much is there to admire in nature? How much which we must believe, but cannot comprehend.

A little child can tell that the peaches grew on the tree,— he can eat them and be satisfied,— and a philosopher can do no more. So, in a religious sense, we often find that very children can feel and feed on spiritual truths, when the wisest father and mother in the church cannot do more. Saving faith does not require great intellect in its possessor. A man of wisdom is often compelled to believe in spiritual operations which he cannot understand, and well may it be so with the babes in Christ.

When the blind beggar, as narrated in the New Testament, called upon the Saviour to have mercy on him, he was healed. His faith saved him; yet he knew not, even after the cure had been effected, how the all-healing word and will had reached his malady; yet he could say, "One thing I know, that whereas I was blind, now I see!" Would that we all, wise men and children, old and young, might come to the same blessed experience.

RICH IN FAITH.

It is often the case that the poor in this world's goods are rich in faith, and those without earthly inheritance are heirs of the kingdom of grace and of glory. The illiterate, as to human knowledge, are sometimes learned in the school of Christ; and those very poorly clad, as to outward attire, are found inwardly adorned with spiritual graces, with jewels far more precious than ever shone in earthly diadems.

Heber tells us that, on a certain occasion, he paid a visit, with a friend, to the inmates of a country almshouse. Among the tenants they found an aged man, very deaf, one of whose legs was so shaken with the palsy that the wooden shoe on its foot kept a constant pattering on the brick floor. Although rendered nearly helpless by various infirmities of the body, they found him sound in mind, cheerful in disposition, and, in the present feeling of the Saviour's love and heartfelt faith in its eternal endurance, very happy under all his privations. His name was Wisby. When the visitors inquired of him what he was doing, he sweetly answered, "Waiting." To the question, what he waited for. He replied, "For the appearing of my Lord;" adding, "I expect great things. He has promised a crown of righteousness to all that love his appearing." When asked the foundation of his hope, he pointed to the text, "Therefore, being justified by faith, we have peace with God through our Lord Jesus Christ, by whom also we have access by faith into this grace wherein we stand, and rejoice in the hope of the glory of God."

Heber, in moralizing on the condition of mind in which they found this poor invalid, says, "Although we may possess untold wealth, yet, if we are not the possessors of the faith which made Wisby happy, we are poor. With that faith, being rich towards God, we would count it all joy, even though we were as poor as Lazarus or Wisby in worldly possessions. Our heavenly inheritance is as sure as the promise of him who cannot lie, yea, as transcendently glorious as a throne, a crown, and eternal happiness can make it." He concludes, "Better have Wisby's hope than Victoria's sceptre, Lazarus' rags than Dives' purple. Better is poverty with piety, than riches with perdition."

Another religious writer relates that on one occasion, more than twenty years since, he received a lesson from a poor man, a suffering invalid, yet one rich in faith and patience, and abundantly supported by the love of God, which had been a lesson to him ever since. The man had been a common laborer, and now in his age was so afflicted with peculiar infirmities, that he was confined to his chair, being unable to lie down night or day. He had, through great mercy, in the days of his health, been favored to witness the washing of regeneration, and the renewing of the Holy Ghost, and being thereby an heir of the kingdom of God, he now felt him as a loving Father dealing with him as with a beloved child, and administering to him the consolations of his grace. On the occasion referred to, to the inquiry as to how he was, he replied, with a cheerful smile and a strong provincial pronunciation, giving greater emphasis to the Christian pleasantry with which he spoke, "I am promoted noo. I was lang the Lord's *workin* servant, and noo he has promoted me to be his *waitin* servant."

The writer who gives the anecdote says that at times, when he has felt weary on his heavenly journey, and been disposed to complain at his lot, he has recalled this old suffering Christian's words of cheer, and has thereby silenced his murmuring thoughts. He tells us he has found it far easier to do the Lord's will in active service, than to bear it in silent, submissive, quiet endurance. Greater grace is requisite cheerfully to *wait* the Lord's time in suffering long continued, with few to sympathize in our affliction, than to *work hard* in what appears to be active benevolence and public labor, when we feel that the hearts of our Christian brethren and sisters are with us in our work, and bidding us heartily God speed. " The silent, secret bearing of his will, in faith and hope, is as pleasing to God as the most faithful public witnessing." The true Christian who has been enabled, through the strengthening influence of Divine grace, to *work* according to the Lord's will, *should be;* if he has been made conformable to the example of his Divine Saviour, he *will* be, as ready to serve him by *waiting*. This condition is hard for flesh and blood to attain; yet it *may* be, it *must* be, known by the perfected Christian. He cannot reach it through his own exertions, but the message to Paul, " *My grace is sufficient for thee,*" is intended for the support of all the true-hearted children of our Lord Jesus Christ in every exigency and close trial.

An English woman, who spent some time in a small village in Germany, gives the following interesting account of an old peasant she met with there. His name was Gottlieb, which means, "God's love," or "the love of God." Although the name gave no heavenly help to the peasant, yet, through the Lord's assisting power, he had been created anew in Christ Jesus, and richly adorned with the grace of the Spirit. Love to God was the pre-eminent feeling of his soul, love to his fellow-creatures a mainspring of his actions.

During the winter season he was confined to a little room in his small tenement, being unable to bear the cold winds, but when the warm days of summer came, he spent much of his time in the fresh air, moving about with a kind word of comfort, or it may be of exhortation, to those he met with. Although poor, he had a small spot of ground just out of the village, on which grew two or three large apple- and pear-trees. There was a little shed near the trees, and in that he sometimes lay and rested after having been employing himself in gathering the fruit which had fallen. Once, whilst walking, the English visitor came up to him as he was stooping to pick up an apple, and asked him if he did not weary of the work of stooping so often after the fruit, and also of lying there so much alone. He smiled kindly, and offering her a handful of fine ripe pears, said, "No, no, I don't weary; I am just waiting — waiting. I think I am about ripe now, and I must soon fall; and then, just think, the Lord will pick me up! Oh! thou art young yet, and perhaps just in blossom; turn well round to the Sun of righteousness, that he may ripen thee for his service." On another occasion he addressed her, pointing along the public road, "That seems a straight road, but I can't see the end of it; but the road to heaven is a straighter road than that; and, blessed be God, I can see the end of it clearly. Perhaps God is letting thee see a little bit of the way at a time. Oh, then, walk straight in that little bit with his help, and as thou goest along, thou wilt see it better and better, till the bright end comes in view."

She says that not long after this last conversation, the end to him came. In holy confidence, and a most loving faith, he entered cheerfully into that blessed country on which he had for so long a period fixed the earnest and desiring gaze of his spiritual eye. His season of waiting was over, and now the fulness of perfect peace was his forever.

BENJAMIN TROTTER.

Benjamin Trotter, a beloved minister of the gospel in this city, having retired from business with but a small amount of property, his friends, as he grew aged, felt many fears whether he had a sufficiency to make him comfortable, and various proffers of pecuniary assistance were made him; all these he quietly yet gratefully refused, because his Master had promised to the effect that his little store, the meal in his barrel, and the oil in his cruse, should last him to the end of his life. He lived very frugally, from day to day waiting for the coming of his Lord, yet day by day performing the duties laid upon him by his Divine Master, with cheerful alacrity. At last the end came. As a shock of corn fully ripe, he was gathered to the heavenly garner; as a waiting pilgrim, thankful for the preservation vouchsafed through a long life, and for the holy comfort and heavenly enjoyment granted him whilst waiting for his admittance into the heavenly Jerusalem, he gladly laid down, with his feeble frame, the staff of faith, which had supported him, passing into the certainty of his eternal rest and peace. Just enough of his property was left to pay all funeral expenses, and thus he and his anxious friends realized the faithfulness of the promise of his Lord and Saviour. Poor in earthly treasure, yet rich in faith, he waited in love, in hope, in assurance, until death led him into his inheritance of glory, to spiritual riches far transcending in value aught which this world possesseth, or than man can conceive.

Rich in faith was our friend John Letchworth, who, though poor as to this world's goods, in the closing hours of his life looked sweetly forward to the mansion prepared for him in heaven, and to the treasures there laid up for him. "I am poor," he said; "but I serve a rich Master, who loves his own."

SUPPORT IN THE TIME OF TRIAL.

The true Christian depends upon his Saviour, and in that dependence finds strength to enable him to bear every trial, every calamity, which may be apportioned him in his earthly pilgrimage. Yet he sometimes finds it hard to realize the presence of his Divine Master, which is to support him in safety over the threatening billows. It is narrated of one of the Protestant martyrs that whilst being led to the stake, finding the sensible presence of his Saviour withdrawn from him, he exclaimed in anguish, "I cannot burn! I cannot burn!" Some of the priests standing by, deeming that through terror he was willing to recant, approached him to witness his confession. They mistook their man. His confidence in the truth of the principles he was to suffer for was unchanged, but he wished to feel the consoling presence of his dear Saviour with him to enable him to witness a good confession to his glory in the flames. In great earnestness of spirit he sought the Lord, and being favored to feel the manifestation of the love of God sweetly strengthening his soul, he clapped his hands, and with a loud voice he exclaimed, "*Now* I can burn! *now* I can burn!"

By faith his hold was firm on the support which would bear, and he little heeded the fiery waves of bodily suffering he had to pass through before entering the haven of eternal rest and glory.

OBEDIENCE NECESSARY.

Esther Tuke remarks, "All who are called to service in the church, have not every evil root wholly plucked up—but these, in obedient minds, wither and die; and their infirmities are healed in the way, like the lepers who went as they were bidden."

INFIDELITY.

HENRY HOWARD.

HENRY HOWARD, a resident of the State of Georgia, was an infidel; at least he professed to be one, and his evil course of life, and wicked principles, gave great sorrow of heart to his wife, who longed for his present happiness and eternal well-being. They had a slave named Peter, who was a Christian indeed, and who, loving and beloved, passed quietly on his way, showing charity and kind feeling to every one, and having the respect, yea, kind wishes and love of all, and perhaps of none more sincerely than his unbelieving master. One night, Peter retired as usual to his cabin for needful repose, but knew not that his earthly labor was over. His heavenly Master during that night quietly released his purified spirit from its worn-out tenement of clay, and gathered him into his heavenly rest. In the morning the body was found cold and stiff. There was great grief manifested in the household when the death became known, and his late master seemed especially affected by it. He pondered much during that day over the many marks of piety which had distinguished the deceased, and he could not but feel what an awful difference there was between his own spiritual condition and that of his late servant. Serious thoughtfulness accompanied him to bed the following night, and the conclusion he had come to was made manifest by the words he spoke to his wife after they had retired, "Old Peter's gone to heaven." His wife, deeply stirred at the thought of the unsanctified condition of her husband's heart, added, with sorrowful emotion, "and his master is going to hell." Startled by the idea which his wife's few words had brought forcibly before his mind, he became thoroughly aroused to a sense of his condition, and after a season of great inward conflict and distress was, through the Lord's saving grace, brought forth purified in heart, and with a living faith in the Lord Jesus as the Saviour and sanctifier of his people, and was enabled to prove the genuineness of his faith by the constancy of his obedience. He felt that his late slave was a rich inheritor in the kingdom of God, and that he, the rich owner of a large earthly estate, was now a poor forgiven servant of Jesus Christ, called to walk in humility and dedication of heart until the end of his earthly labors should come. The words of his wife had proved words spoken in season, and he felt grateful to her for uttering them, and thankful to the Lord who had given them such effective power. He was afterwards, according to his measure, a laborer in the gospel of life and salvation.

REMARKABLE VISIT OF SARAH TAYLOR.

About the middle of the last century, Sarah Taylor, of Manchester, Eng., a humble-minded minister of the Society of Friends, engaged in a family visit to the members of her own religious society in the city of Norwich. She was generally kindly received; but two brothers, Edmund and John Gurney, who had joined a club of infidels, refused to receive a visit from her. This honest-hearted lover of the souls of men was much distressed at their conduct, and one night retired to bed not a little depressed about this matter, no doubt endeavoring, before giving herself to sleep, in humility to cast her burden upon her Lord and Saviour. At last she slept, and when the sound sleep of the early part of the night was past, she dreamed. In her dream, she thought that she awoke, and finding that day had broken, arose, dressed herself, and went down stairs. She opened the front door, and walked out into the street. The public lights were not all extinguished, and this, with the daylight, which was increasing, enabled her to see the names of the residents of the different houses on their door-plates. She thought she passed through several streets, making several turns, until at last she came to a house on which she saw the name of Edmund Gurney. Stepping up and ringing the bell, a porter quickly opened the door. She asked if Edmund Gurney was in. The man replied that he was in the garden, but he had ordered him not to admit any of the Quakers into the house. Sarah dreamed that she passed right by the astonished man, and seeing a side door, she opened it, and finding it was the way to the garden, she followed one of the walks until she came to a summer-house. A man was sitting therein, who, as she stepped within the door, said, "I believe the devil could not keep the Quakers out." Sarah dreamed she sat down on a bench, and he, who had risen on her entrance, sat down beside her, when she thought she was favored so to speak to him that the witness for the Truth in him was reached, and he was much affected and tendered. When her service seemed over, she left him, and then she awoke, and behold it was a dream. Looking out of the window of her room, she saw that day was breaking, and solemnly affected by the vision she had been favored with, she arose, and dressed herself for going out, just as she had done in her dream. On opening the door looking into the street, everything seemed so entirely as she had seen it, that without hesitation, or speaking to any one in the house, she started onward, taking her dream for direction. As she passed along, the same houses, with the same names on the doorplates, appeared as in her dream, and she followed, tracing them from street to street, until the house with Edmund Gurney's name on it stood before her. She rang the bell; the porter opened the door, and to her inquiry if Edmund Gurney was in, he said, "Yes;" but added, "He has commanded me not to admit any of the Quakers." This would probably have discouraged Sarah, if it had not been for the dream; but as all things had as yet turned out as she had seen in her vision, she determined to trust it further, and so pushing by the man, she opened a side door, and let herself into the yard. The garden appeared exactly as seen in her dream, and she soon found the summer-house, where Edmund Gurney was sitting with a book in his hand. As she entered, he arose, and approaching her, said, "I believe the devil could not keep the Quakers out."

Sarah sat down, and he took a seat beside her. She soon found her heart tenderly concerned for him, and her mouth was opened to address him in the persuasive utterance of gospel love. She told him he had professedly adopted sentiments which his heart refused to own, and that he was reading infidel books to strengthen him in infidelity. Edmund was affected under her ministry, and he knew her message to him was the truth. When she arose to leave him, he pressed her to stay and breakfast with him, but this she declined, saying she had nothing further to do there. Bidding him farewell, she returned to her lodgings, her heart warmed in grateful admiration of the Lord's wonderful leadings and marvellous loving-kindness.

Edmund Gurney, through the Lord's renewed and strengthening grace, was thoroughly aroused from the slumber in which the evil one had sought to keep him to his utter ruin. He never again attended the infidel club, and as in deep abasement and sorrow of heart he repented for the past, submitted to the baptisms of the Holy Spirit, and bowed in reverent obedience to the Lord's teachings, he grew in religious experience, and in time came forth in the ministry. The effect of the blessed change wrought in Edmund was, through the Lord's mercy, made of heart-cleansing efficacy to his brother John. He also came to see that the root of infidelity is wickedness, and publicly renouncing all connection therewith, he witnessed, like his brother, true repentance towards God and soul-saving faith in our Lord Jesus Christ.

PROFESSED INFIDELS OFTEN INSINCERE.

Many *professed* infidels are not such in reality. They feel that the whole tenor of their lives is contrary to Christianity, to the pure, holy requirings of the gospel of our Lord and Saviour Jesus Christ; and they know without a change of heart and a love for him who died for them, which they have not, they cannot, if the doctrines of Christianity be true, be saved. The natural man is enmity against God, and in the condition in which they are, they wish that salvation by Christ, through his precious offering, and the sanctifying influences of his grace and good spirit, with the attendant consequences of damnation to the unbelieving and unholy, were *not* true, and in desperation they declare they do not believe in him. This is often *all* in self-defence, and however much they may desire their assertions were true, they, in the secret of their hearts, do not *believe them*.

"CALL UPON ME IN THE DAY OF TROUBLE."

About the beginning of the present century, a native of Sweden named A. E. Kothen, having occasion to go from Stockholm to Copenhagen, by sea, found, when he came to the place from which he expected to embark, that the regular vessel between the ports had sailed. On inquiry, he discovered a fishing-boat going that way, in which he took passage. The boatmen observing he had several trunks, concluded he must be rich, and consulted together in the Finnish language, which they supposed he did not understand, to throw him into the sea, and keep his property. This he overheard, and it gave him great uneasiness. To show them he was not laden with money, he took occasion to open one of his trunks containing books. On seeing this, they said one to another: "'Tis not worth while to throw him overboard, as we do not want books." They then asked him whether he was a priest? Fears for his life induced him to deceive them, and he told them he was one. At this they appeared pleased, saying they would have a sermon the next day, it being the Sabbath, as they called it. This, however, had a tendency to increase the anxiety and distress of his mind, believing himself to be as incapable of such an undertaking, as it was possible for any man to be; for he knew but little about the Scriptures, neither did he believe in them, nor in any Divine revelation whatever manifested to man.

They came to a small island of rocks in the sea, about a quarter of a mile in circumference, where were a number more such like men. By this time he found he had fallen into the hands of a company of pirates, who had chosen that little spot to deposit their treasure. He was taken to a cave, and introduced to an old woman; the men telling her they had got a priest, and should have a sermon the next day. She said she was glad, for she had not heard one for a long while. His case appeared desperate indeed. Preach he must, and he knew nothing about it. If he refused, he expected death would be his portion; and, if he undertook it, and did not succeed, it might be the same. In this deplorable situation he passed the night, not having power to settle his mind upon any thing to offer to the people; and to call upon God, whom he had believed to be inaccessible, appeared altogether vain, and he could not devise any way whereby he might be saved. When morning came, he arose and walked to and fro, still shut up in darkness and distress, striving with all his might to command his thoughts. The time for the meeting to begin came, and he returned to the cave, where he found them assembled, a table with a Bible on it, and a seat provided for him.

Upon sitting down they all continued, he believed

the space of half an hour in profound silence, when the exercise and anguish of his soul were as great as was possible for human nature to bear, without any way opening to address the people. At length these words came before him: "Verily there is a reward for the righteous; verily He is a God that judgeth in the earth." With these words he arose, and having delivered them, some other pertinent matter presented, and so on from less to more, until his understanding became opened, and his heart enlarged, in a manner wonderful to himself, to treat on subjects suiting their condition; such as the excellent rewards for the righteous; the just judgments of God awaiting the wicked; the necessity of repentance and amendment of life; the universality of the love of God to the children of men. This had such a powerful effect on the minds of these poor wicked wretches, that they were exceedingly broken into tenderness, weeping to such a degree that the floor was wet with their tears; and he no less astonished at the unbounded goodness, power, and love of an Almighty Creator, in thus interfering for the saving of both his natural and spiritual life: and well might he exclaim, "It was the Lord's doings, and marvellous in his eyes." Under an awful sense of the favor, his heart became filled with such thankful acknowledgments as were beyond the power of language to convey.

After the meeting ended, the poor creatures were very loving and affectionate, willing to show him all the kindness in their power. The next day they fitted out one of their vessels, and carried him whither he wished to go. From that time, he became an entirely changed man, and a sincere believer in the efficacy and power of the unchangeable Truth, as it is in Jesus Christ, the Saviour of the world.

The foregoing narrative was related by Stephen Grellet, an eminent minister of the Gospel, who in the course of a religious visit to the South of France, where this individual was then residing, became personally acquainted with him.

INDIVIDUAL EXPERIENCE.

Among certain scientific men, sentiments are from time to time advanced which have a subtle tendency to destroy a belief in the direct and merciful superintendence of Divine Providence in the affairs of men. Those who hold these views may not directly deny the existence of the Supreme Being, but by professing to discern in mere matter, and the forces inherent therein, as expressed by a late writer of this class, "The promise and potency of every form and quality of life," they practically ignore and disregard the need of, and the direct control of, the Ruler of the universe in the events and operations of our daily lives.

These " materialistic " doctrines are by no means new, having been held by some of the ancient heathen philosophers, and though repeated in the experience of the present day of greater enlightenment, they but illustrate anew the truth of the ancient scripture declaration, " The world by *wisdom* knew not God." Obedience to Christ, as he is revealed in our hearts, as the Light of life, is the one safe abiding place of the Christian. If we are founded on that Rock, all the floods of infidelity, and the storms of temptation of whatever kind, will beat upon us in vain. The Spirit of the Lord will lift up a standard against them. On the other hand, if we depart from that sure foundation, we know not how far and how fatally we may fall. " This is the condemnation, that light is come into the world, and men loved darkness rather than light, *because their deeds were evil.*" If we indulge in anything which we feel to be at variance with the pure leadings of the Holy Spirit in our hearts, we so far turn our backs to the light, and open the way for further degrees of darkness and death to come over us. Thousands who once knew better, have in this way become blinded, so as even to deny the Lord that bought them.

The case of a young man, blessed with pious parents, who had endeavored both by precept and example to train him up as a consistent member of religious society, furnishes a striking illustration of these truths. Becoming actively engaged in business, he too much neglected that inwardness of mind and habitual sense of the Divine presence which would have preserved him from the snares of the evil one; he gradually laid aside some of that simplicity in language, dress, and manners in which he had been educated. As he advanced in this downward course, he felt darkness and doubt increasing in his mind. He no longer experienced those seasons of heavenly tenderness and sweet consolation, with which he had been favored in his more innocent days; and was tempted to doubt the genuineness of those impressions made directly on the heart of man by the agency of the Holy Spirit, and the kind care of a superintending Providence, in the affairs of life. In this blinded and dangerous state a renewed visitation of Heavenly Love was remarkably extended to him, in the silent part of a religious meeting; and a convincing evidence was thus afforded that a compassionate Redeemer was in love and pity for his benighted condition, operating in his soul; his eyes were opened to see his dark state, and he was enabled to say with the patriarch of old, "Now mine eye seeth thee, wherefore I abhor myself, and repent in dust and ashes." Living faith was again raised in his heart, and gratitude for his escape from that evil spirit which ever seeketh to blind the minds of them which believe not.

He who has submitted his heart to the gracious visitations of his Saviour and has known the feeling of condemnation for sin; the godly sorrow and repentance which follow; the sweet, tendering influence which often, at an unexpected moment, is spread over the heart, causing it to rejoice in the feeling of Divine love; the solemn quiet which settles over the mind, hushing everything into stillness as in the presence of the Holy One; and the whole train of blessed experiences, which attend the sincere follower of Christ,— he has within him, in these things, an answer to every infidel suggestion. He knows that these feelings are not at his own control, that they come and go at the bidding of a higher power than his own; and he regards as simply absurd the doctrine that they have no other source or meaning than the mutual action of particles of matter among themselves.

INTEMPERANCE.

"NEVER TEMPT A MAN TO BREAK A GOOD RESOLUTION."

IN the autobiography of John Trumbull, the celebrated painter, a circumstance occurred, which is well worthy of preservation. In the wars of New England with the Aborigines, the Mohegan tribe of Indians early became friends of the English. Their favorite grounds were on the banks of the Thames, between New London and Norwich, and in the year 1776, about which time the incident occurred, a small remnant of them still existed on a part of their ancient domain. He says, "The government of this tribe became hereditary in the family of the celebrated chief, Uncas. During the time of my father's mercantile prosperity, he had employed several Indians of this tribe in hunting animals, whose skins were valuable for their fur." Among these hunters was one, named Zachary, of the ruling race — an excellent hunter, but "a drunken and worthless Indian." When he had somewhat passed the age of fifty, several members of the ruling family, who stood between him and the chieftainship, died, and he found himself with only one life between him and that office. At this he reflected seriously: "How can such a drunken wretch as I am aspire to be a chief of this honorable race? What will my people say? and how will the shades of my noble ancestors look down indignant upon such a base successor? Can *I* succeed to the great Uncas? *I will drink no more.*" He solemnly resolved never again to taste any drink but water, and he kept his resolution.

John Trumbull says, "I had heard of this story, and did not entirely believe it; for, young as I was, I already partook of the prevailing contempt for Indians. The annual election of the principal officers of the (then) colony was held at Hartford, the capital. My father attended officially, and it was customary for the chief of the Mohegans also to attend. Zachary had succeeded to the rule of his tribe. My father's house was situated about mid-way on the road between Mohegan and Hartford, and the old chief was in the habit of coming a few days before the election, and dining with his brother Governor. One day the mischievous thought struck me to try the old man's temperance. The family were seated at dinner, and there was excellent home-brewed beer on the table. I addressed the old chief:

"'Zachary, this beer is excellent — will you taste it?'

"The old man dropped his knife and fork, leaned forward with a stern intensity of expression—his black eye, sparkling with indignation, was fixed on me.

"John,' said he, 'you do not know what you are doing. You are serving the devil, boy! Do you not know that I am an Indian? I tell you that I am, and that if I should but taste your beer, I could not stop till I got to rum, and again become the contemptible drunken wretch your father remembers me to have been. *John, while you live, never again tempt a man to break a good resolution.*'

"Socrates never uttered a more valuable precept. Demosthenes could not have given it in more solemn tones of eloquence. I was thunderstruck. My parents were deeply affected; they looked at me, and at the venerable Indian, with deep feelings of awe and respect. They afterwards frequently reminded me of the scene, and charged me never to forget it. Zachary lived to pass the age of eighty, and sacredly kept his resolution.

"He lies buried in the royal burial-place of his tribe, near the beautiful falls of the Yantic, the western branch of the Thames, in Norwich. I visited the grave of the old chief lately, and repeated to myself his inestimable lesson."

A FATHER SAVED.

James Stirling, the temperance lecturer of Scotland, was a remarkable man, and his life was a remarkable life. With a very limited education, he had improved his mind by considerable reading, whilst tending his flocks as a shepherd lad. At that time he appeared to be a religious character, and very favorably impressed those acquainted with him as respected his piety. Having afterwards removed to Paisley to learn the shoemaker's trade, he fell amongst profligate companions, who shamed him out of his religion, and induced him to become a drunkard. This he was for forty years, except during a few intervals, the longest of which, perhaps, was about the period of his marriage. The condition to which he was reduced by his cravings for and indulgence in intoxicating liquors, was that of the very lowest, most degraded of drunkards. We need not give any extensive outlines of the sad, disgusting picture which he and his biographer have drawn, but we shall quote his description of his cure, first premising that his wife appears to have been a religious woman. "I had been all day in the public-house; and at night, when I came home, my wife, as usual, was reading a chapter to the children. When she was so engaged I went in, slipping like a condemned criminal. The portion of Scripture read was the twenty-fifth chapter of Matthew, in which these words occur: 'When the Son of Man shall come in his glory, and all the holy angels with him, then shall he sit upon the throne of his glory: and before him shall be gathered all nations; and he shall separate them one from another, as the shepherd divideth his sheep from the goats: and he shall set the sheep on his right hand, but the goats on the left.' Our youngest boy, then about four years old, was lying with his head on his mother's lap, and just when she had read these awful words, he looked up earnestly in her face and asked, 'Will father be a goat then, mother?' This was too strong to be resisted. The earnest, innocent look of the child, the bewilderment of the poor mother, and above all the question itself, smote me to the heart's core. I spent a sleepless, awfully miserable night, wishing rather to die than to live such a life.'"

From this time James Stirling became a changed man. Through the blessing of the Most High resting on the question of his child, a great and permanent effect was produced upon him. He ceased attendance at the public-houses, he avoided all intoxicating drinks, and he soon gave, in his consistent Christian conduct, evidence that he had witnessed the washing of regeneration, and the renewing of the Holy Ghost. One writing of him says: "He began to rise immensely in character, and usefulness, and honor, and, with the exception of the spirit dealers, was treated with wonderful deference by all classes—the rich and the poor. He felt he was no longer the poor, self-degraded and despised thing he had been; a new impulse had been given him, and henceforth he devoted all the energies of his naturally vigorous and powerful mind to the promotion of everything that was good." He says of himself: "All things put on a new appearance—my wife, my family, my trade, my countenance, my clothing. I saw all nature happy around me. My heart was happy within me—happy at having overcome my besetting sin—happy in the inward beaming sunshine of content. Those sights and sounds that delighted my youthful fancy became delightful again." He was renewing his youth,—his heart became as the heart of a little child.

We shall not further follow the life of this renewed man, except to say that as a temperance lecturer he was *remarkably* eloquent, attractive, and convincing. For the twenty years he lived after his recovery, he proved that the change had been thorough. His Christian life was evidently increasing in spirituality and grace. Yet he frequently passed along under much depression of spirit when, in the remembrance of what he had been, he was made, as it were, to possess the sins of his youth. At such seasons he was sometimes in the very *depths*, and felt as though he could not even cry for deliverance. No doubt but these fiery trials were for his further refinement, and all administered in mercy by his blessed Saviour, who, in his own good time, scattered the clouds and gave him to see his face with comfort. On the twenty-sixth day of the Eighth month, 1856, he was in loving mercy relieved from further earthly conflict, being then eighty-two years old.

EVIL OVERCOME OF GOOD.

A recent writer relates the following incident: A little boy in Connecticut of remarkably serious mind and habits, was ordinarily employed about a mechanic's shop, where nearly all the hands were addicted to the common use of intoxicating liquors. The lad had imbibed temperance principles, and though often invited could never be induced to partake with any one in this habit. On one occasion, three or four of the "harder" drinkers in the shop resolved to force a dram of rum down his throat. Seizing an opportunity when he was left alone in the shop by themselves, they invited him to drink. He refused. They then told him they should compel him. He remained calm and unmoved. They threatened him with violence. Still he neither seemed angry nor attempted to escape, nor evinced the least disposition to yield; but insisted that it was wicked, and he could not do it. They then laid hold of him,—a man at each arm, while the third held the bottle ready to force it into his mouth. Still their victim remained meek and firm, declaring that he had never injured *them*, and never should, but that God would be his friend and protector, however they might abuse him. The man who had held the bottle, resolute to that moment in his evil purpose, was so struck by the non-resisting dignity and innocence of the lad, that, as he afterwards confessed almost with tears, he actually felt unable to raise his hand. Twice he essayed to lift the bottle, as he placed the mouth of it in the child's mouth, but his arm refused to serve him. Not the least resistance was made at this stage of the proceeding otherwise than by a meek, protesting look; yet the ring-leader himself was overcome in his feelings, and gave over the attempt, declaring that he could not, would not, injure such an innocent, conscientious, good-hearted boy. Thus doth the Lord deliver those that trust in him. Thus may evil be overcome with good.

A REPROOF BLESSED.

An aged man related the following incident: "I was once travelling," said he, " in the State of New York, and night coming on, I put up at a rum-tavern. Soon after several of the neighboring men called in to tell stories and patronize the bar. They all seemed given to profaneness; but one of them excelled the others in profanity. Their oaths were so horrid it almost made my blood run cold. It seemed like blasphemy. I groaned in spirit, and, after one of these terrible oaths, I cried out: 'Oh, dear!' The chief swearer immediately came to me, and acknowledged the wickedness of his habit and said: 'Will you pardon me?' 'No,' said I, 'none but God can pardon you; but if you will swear no more, I will overlook the past.' He made a fair promise. After, this, there was no more swearing for some time. Towards bed-time these villagers must have another drink. They then commenced swearing again. Again I sighed 'Oh, dear!' Again my pardon was asked. I told them it was *rum* that made them swear. We parted, never expecting to see or hear from each other again.

"After two and a half years, I had occasion to pass that way again, and stopped to bait my horse at the same tavern. The landlord was not in, but his wife eyed me closely, and said: 'Did you not spend a night here two or three years ago?' Yes. 'Do you remember reproving a man for swearing?' Yes. 'Well, that man, and all his companions were led, by that reproof, to give up swearing and drinking; and what is better still, they have all become Christians. So have I and my husband, and we now find we can keep a tavern without selling rum."

REMARKABLE WARNING.

On board of the vessel in which Thomas Chalkley was returning to England, from a religious visit to this country, in the year 1698-9, was a doctor, an intemperate man, who, as they were approaching land, had a remarkable dream, which he related to Thomas Chalkley, as follows: "He dreamed that he went on shore at a great and spacious town, the buildings whereof were high, and the streets broad; and as he went up the street he saw a large sign, on which was written in great golden letters, SHAME. At the door of the house to which the sign belonged, stood a woman with a can in her hand, who said to him, Doctor, will you drink? He replied, with all my heart; for I have not drank anything but water a great while (our wine and cider being all spent, having had a long passage), and he drank a hearty draught, which he said made him merry. He went up the street reeling to and fro, when a grim fellow coming behind him, clapped him on the shoulder, and told him that he arrested him in the name of the governor of the place. He asked him for what, and said: What have I done? He answered, For stealing the woman's can. The can he had indeed; and so he was had before the governor, which was a mighty black dog, the biggest and grimmest that ever he saw in his life; a witness was brought in against him by an old companion of his, and he was found guilty, and his sentence was to go to prison, and there lay for ever."

Thomas Chalkley remarks in his Journal: "He told me this dream so punctually, and with such an emphasis, that it affected me with serious sadness, and caused my heart to move within me; for to me the dream seemed true, and the interpretation sure. I then told him he was an ingenious man, and might clearly see the interpretation of that dream, which exactly answered to his state and condition, which I thus interpreted to him: 'This great and spacious place, wherein the buildings were high, and the streets broad, is thy great and high profession. The sign, on which was written *shame*, which thou sawest, and the woman at the door, with the can in her hand, truly represent that great, crying, and shameful sin of drunkenness, which thou knowest to be thy great weakness, which the woman with the can did truly represent to thee. The grim fellow who arrested thee in the devil's territories, is death, who will assuredly arrest all mortals: the governor whom thou sawest, representing a great black dog, is certainly the devil, who, after his servants have served him to the full, will torment them eternally in hell.' So he got up, as it were in haste, and said, God forbid! it is nothing but a dream. But I told him it was a very significant one, and a warning to him from the Almighty, who sometimes speaks to men by dreams."

A few days after this occurrence they met in the English channel, with a Dutch vessel loaded with wine, brandy, fruit, and other such commodities from Lisbon; and sent a boat to her to buy a little wine to drink with their water. Thomas says, "Our doctor, and a merchant who was a passenger, and one sailor, went on board, where they stayed until some of them were overcome with wine, although they were desired to beware thereof. When they came back, a rope was handed to them, but they, being filled with wine to excess, were not capable of using it dexterously, insomuch that they overset the boat, and she turned bottom upwards, having the doctor under her. The merchant caught hold of a rope called the main-sheet, whereby his life was saved. The sailor not getting so much drink as the other two, got nimbly on the bottom of the boat, and floated on the water till our other boat was hoisted out, which was done with great speed, and we took him in; but the doctor was drowned before the boat came. The seaman who sat upon the boat saw him sink, but could not help him. This was the greatest exercise that we met with in all our voyage; and the more so, because the doctor was of an evil life and conversation, and much given to excess in drinking. When he got on board the aforesaid ship, the master sent for a can of wine, and said, Doctor, will you drink? He replied, yes, with all my heart, for I have drank no wine a great while. Upon which he drank a hearty draught, that made him merry, as he said in his dream; and notwithstanding the admonition which was so clearly manifested to him but three days before, and the many promises he had made to Almighty God, some of which I was a witness of, when strong convictions were upon him, yet now he was unhappily overcome, and in drink when he was drowned. This is, I think, a lively representation of the tender mercy and just judgment of the Almighty to poor mortals; and I thought it worthy to be recorded for posterity, as a warning to all great lovers of wine and strong liquors. This exercise was so great to me, that I could not for several days get over it; and one day while I was musing in my mind on those things relating to the doctor, it was opened to me that God and his servants were clear, and his blood was on his own head; for he had been faithfully warned of his evil ways."

DEATH.

SUSTAINING GRACE.

THE following incident related by Dr. Robinson, affords matter for serious reflection. He stated that at one time his father, awaking in the night, saw or appeared to see a sea-captain, a near neighbor of his walking backward and forward across his apartment. Surprised at his appearance there, he inquired why he visited him at such an unseasonable time. He replied, "The grace of God in the soul, at such an hour as this, is worth millions of worlds," and immediately vanished from sight. It then occurred to Robinson, that his neighbor was at sea, and feeling much impressed with the occurrence, he rose and noted down the time. He afterwards learned that, at the very hour this appearance took place, his friend was knocked overboard from his vessel and was drowned.

Ah! when death stares the Christian in the face, when he sees there is no escape,— that for him a few more swiftly passing moments only are allotted in this world, how sweetly comforting to feel the grace of God sustaining the soul. To him, it is worth indeed millions of worlds. The deathbed of that ancient laborer in the gospel of Christ, Richard Hubberthorn, is a fitting illustration. His natural disposition was meek and lowly, and he loved peace amongst men; but when, through the tender mercy of the Lord, he experienced the converting visitations of heavenly love, we are told, "He went through great afflictions, through the dispensation of the grace and spirit of Christ Jesus, until such time as the same power that killed did make alive, that wounded, also healed." Being raised up by the holy spirit of the Lord, he was made a minister of the everlasting gospel, and accordingly went forth in the name and power of the Lord Jesus Christ, and travelled to and fro in England for the space of nine years, and many were the seals to the power and verity of his ministry, and of his faithfulness among the Churches of Christ. "He was very wise, and knew the season when to speak and when to be silent. When he spoke, it was with such discretion and plainness of words, that reached perfectly the matter intended; and his speech being with grace, and his ministry savory, God made him and his service a blessing to many. He was not easily moved into grief by adversity, or into joy by prosperity; a faithful contender for the living faith once delivered to the saints, which stands in the power of God, and worketh by love."

So he lived faithful to God; and being imprisoned for attending a religious meeting, he sealed his testimony with his blood, dying in the thronged and foul prison-house of Newgate. He, whom he had served, was with him through the valley of the shadow of death; and that grace which he had preached unto others, gave great comfort and sweet support as the end of his earthly course drew near. He told his friends, "There is no need to dispute matters. I know the ground of my salvation, and am satisfied forever in peace with the Lord." His longing after immortality seemed to increase, and on the day of his departure he said to a Friend, " Do not seek to hold me. It is too straight for me! Out of this straightness I must go." And so trusting in and supported by Divine Grace, he went to his heavenly home rejoicing in a sense of acceptance.

How does the power of Divine Grace pour into the souls of some rich streams of consolation when the hour of death and the pains of a dissolving tabernacle are upon them. Thomas Loe, an able gospel minister in his day, very powerful in confounding opposers of the truth, and yet remarkably pleasant and sweetly agreeable in conversation, full of kind sympathy for those in affliction, to whom he was qualified to speak encouragingly from experience, closed a life of dedication to the Truth, and sufferings for its support, by a death of unusual comfort, yea, glory! In an outburst of heartfelt adoration and praise he exclaimed: "Glory to thee, O God, for thy power is known. God is the Lord." Then addressing William Penn, who had been convinced of the Truth through his ministry, he said, "Dear heart, bear thy cross! Stand faithful for God, and bear thy testimony in thy day and generation, and God will give thee an eternal crown of glory, that shall not be taken from thee. There is not another way than that the holy men of old walked in, and it shall prosper. God has brought immortality to light, and immortal life is felt: glory, glory, for he is worthy. My heart is full, what shall I say? His love overcomes my heart; my cup runs over, my cup runs over! Glory, glory to his name forever! He is come. He has appeared, and will appear. Friends, keep you testimony for God! Live with him, and he will live with you."

So expressing his gladness to see his friends, and his sense of the Lord's mercy, and declaring the glory of the Holy One, of which he had been permitted to see the day, he closed with ascriptions of praise to the Lord, saying: "Glory, glory to thee, forever." Thus, warmed with love and devotion to the very close, participating even here in the blessed employ of redeemed souls in glory, he was permitted in great joy to pass the gates of death, to praise the Lord God and the Lamb, in that city where there is no more death, neither sorrow nor sighing.

"READY TO BE OFFERED."—PAUL.

What a blessed condition the apostle had attained to. He felt that his sins had gone beforehand to judgment, and that through the mercy of God in Christ Jesus, they had all been blotted out and a free pardon granted him. In this assurance, he knew that there was laid up for him a crown of righteousness. Yea, he already felt in the inward comfort of the Holy Ghost, a foretaste of the joy which should afterwards be revealed in its fulness. To him, to depart and to be with Christ, was far better than to remain toiling upon earth, yet for the love which he bore his Divine Master, he was willing to continue in his prison-house of flesh just so long as that All-wise, and All-loving One should see it was best. Yet he was ready to be offered. He had nothing further to do, but in holy trust and confidence, whilst performing present duty, to wait the moment of his dismissal from time. How different his condition from that of the fearful, doubting ones, who know not whether they are accepted of God, yea or nay! How still more widely different from those who feel they have not the love of God in them, that it is not, and has not been as their meat and drink, to do His will? Such oftentimes have a vague hope, that they shall, somehow or other, find a rest with the righteous, although they have not whilst on earth followed the dear Saviour as cross-bearing disciples.

An anecdote is related by an attorney, to this import. He had a case, in which the whole estate of a client was at stake; on the result of which his future affluence or poverty depended. On the morning of the day in which the lord-chancellor was to deliver the judgment, he called on his attorney in a state of great excitement. His case was to come up — was everything ready! The deep feeling evident in the client, struck the attorney with fear for the result. Learned counsel had given a favorable opinion of his cause, but the attorney it appears had doubts, and the chancellor decided adversely. Of the poor client, the attorney writes, "never shall I forget the agony of despair depicted in his countenance at that moment, as, rushing from the court, he hissed into my ear the fearful words, 'Oh! I am undone.'"

The attorney himself moralizes on the case, comparing it to that of those who are about closing their earthly accounts, and know that their case is to be called up that day, or at least in a very short period. As death leaves us, judgment will find us. There is no place for pardon, or repentance, to those whose day of life has closed. Their case is then forever fixed. If they have gone down to the grave in their sins, their doom is fixed forever, where the worm dieth not, and the fire is not quenched. In vain may friends — like the learned counsel in the poor man's case referred to — give favorable opinions. God, who seeth the heart, giveth a final decree, according to the blessed counsel of his immutable justice, in accordance with the precepts and declarations He has given unto men, through the Gospel revelations of his dear Son. Sympathizing and loving ones may bid them confide in the mercy of God in Christ Jesus, priests may undertake to make good any defect in their heavenly title, but the fond wishes of the one sort, and the pretended absolution of the other, are equally unavailing. To the unregenerated soul, the issue of the case will be: "Depart from me ye that work iniquity."

How soon death may call our case up for final decision, we none of us know; but it must be in a little while, to the longest liver; it may be very soon to some of us. We cannot tell but our *case may* come on this day; nay, we know not but that before the hour we have now entered on shall be finished, our eternal condition shall have been forever fixed. It behooves us, dear reader, to be in earnest in our inward aspirations after a clean heart and a right spirit. Our God, though he be rich in mercy, and ready to forgive the contrite in spirit, will surely punish the rebellious and backsliding, and every son or daughter of Adam who does not come unto him, through Jesus Christ, out of whom there is no salvation, must expect no mercy.

"But if we walk in the light, as he is in the light, we have fellowship one with another, and the blood of Jesus Christ his Son cleanseth us from *all* sin." As we daily strive to be found walking in this holy light, all our life long, it will be of secondary consequence when or how our dismissal out of this "earthly house" shall take place, for we know that the immortal part will then have "an house not made with hands, eternal in the heavens."

BE NOT DECEIVED.

There is no doubt that many trembling, fainting Christians, who, under an awful sense of the purity of the immaculate One, and the holiness that becometh his worshippers, look backwards, as they approach the grave, with fearfulness on their earthly pilgrimage, and their want of thorough dedication of heart, shall yet, through the mercy of God in Christ Jesus, receive the glorious welcome: "Come ye blessed of my Father." The inward work of sanctification has been going on in them in the midst of their fears and faintings; and whilst it may be acknowledged their salvation is all of free mercy, yet it is "by the washing of regeneration, and the renewing of the Holy Ghost." Happy will it be for those whose terrors are all witnessed on this side of the grave; to whom death is swallowed up in victory,—for whom the pains and sorrows of the parting moment of the earthly struggle, give place to the peace of God, and those good things which eye hath not seen nor ear heard, which are in store for those who love him.

But how awful will it be for those who go down to the grave in a condition of unconcernedness, a kind of dreamy hoping for heaven, if they waken up to a sense of condemnation, and hear the language uttered: "Verily, I say unto you, I know you not."

A captain of Holland, who was wrecked at sea, and with his crew tossed about in an open boat for eight days, gives an interesting account of their feelings and condition. Hunger occasioned them intense suffering, they felt little sleepiness towards the last part of their voyage, but when it did overtake them, they all had similar dreams. "Each time it was a well-laden table, a substantial dinner, that stood before us, and to which we set ourselves with lively shouts of joy. Every one of us dreamed this at least ten times. The waking up to the truth of our situation was horrible."

Far more horrible will it be, to waken up from our dream of carnal security, and find that our portion is forever fixed in the unutterable agony of that condition where the worm dieth not, and the fire is not quenched.

SET UP BEACON MARKS.

It is related of an Indian that when passing through a swamp, if he found any spot particularly difficult to cross, he invariably set up a stake in it as a Beacon Mark, to warn others of the danger, as well as to enable himself to recognize and avoid the place. It was a wise as well as kind act in this man, and it would be well if, in our every day walk, we were concerned to set up Beacon Marks to enable others to see where we had met with difficulties and dangers, spiritual as well as temporal. If we are really and truly actuated by the spirit of the petition " Lead us not into temptation," it is certain that we shall feel bound, as far as we can, not only to avoid placing incitement to evil in the way of others, but that we shall desire that they may be preserved from the sins into which we have been led.

After General Lee, of the rebel army, had fortified Richmond by forts and batteries of various kinds, he buried, all around its approaches, torpedoes which would explode if a heavy man or a horse trod over them, and scatter death and terror around. To prevent their own army, and those who came with provision for his needs, from falling victims to the murderous power of these hidden instruments of destruction, marks were placed over them to designate the places: which marks were to have been removed should General Grant's army approach. On the morning of that day, when General Lee fled from Richmond, too many other things claimed attention, and the little Beacon Marks were left unmoved, and thus many hundred lives were probably saved.

Sometimes individuals moving along in the

paths of vanity and frivolity, are suddenly arrested by severe illness, and in mercy brought to a sense of their sad fallen state, and the need they have of the washing of regeneration, and the saving, soul-cleansing baptisms of the Holy Spirit, and are then introduced into much mental agony, and taught to cry mightily to the Lord Jesus for help. His mercies are over all his works, and it pleases him, graciously to regard the supplications of such, and through the powerful operations of his grace to prepare the spirit at times through a few days of agony and remorse, to receive that inward cleansing in which it finds forgiveness for past transgressions, and a preparation for an admission into the kingdom of glory. Such persons thus introduced into the Christian family,—and made partakers of the salvation which comes by Jesus Christ, often attain, before the close comes, to great peace. All this is in full accordance with Divine mercy. It is through deep tribulation we must enter the kingdom,—it is through obedience that we grow in knowledge and experience; yet he who is perfect in wisdom sees meet, in some cases, to cut short the work in righteousness. He sees that deep agony of spirit has been felt, that the saving change has been wrought in suffering and remorse, through the fiery baptisms of the Holy Spirit, and as the will of the creature is subdued, he receives it into rest.

These redeemed ones, before they put off the shackles of mortality, in their true remorse, not unfrequently wish to set up Beacon Marks, to prevent others from making shipwreck on the shoals of sin where they themselves were long aground. Oh! the earnestness of their desires, that their dear friends and relatives should not resist the convictions of grace, should not follow the fashions, the manners and the customs of this vain world. But oh, how seldom are such Beacon Marks known to their fashionable friends. Death removes them before they have time or opportunity of spreading the warning themselves. Their friends in preparing obituary notices, often confine themselves to the expression of a hope that through mercy, they have been admitted into rest. Thus the Beacon Marks which their sudden removal from time might have erected in the view of thoughtless friends are not set up. Their friends lately may have known them as thoughtless and gay as themselves,— they may have seen them but a little while ago, flaunting with ribbons, or mingling with them in vanity and folly. Now, in a few days, they are noticed as having entered the heavenly city of purity and peace. Oh, did we only bear in mind the duty that devolves upon us of setting up "Beacon Marks," we should more frequently dwell upon the agony of mind, the deep contrition of those who having despised or *shrunk* from bearing the cross of the Saviour whilst in health, have found upon a sick-bed that the subjection of their own wills, as to dress and address, as to manners and walk amongst men, is an absolute *necessity* to every one seeking to enter the kingdom.

When there is any Beacon Mark to set up in the account of the closing hours of our deceased friends, let not a false delicacy prevent its erection. Surely if through the Lord's merciful providence one soul should be rightly warned by such a memoir, or should be encouraged to take up the cross whilst health and vigor are granted them, it would amply repay whatever cost such a testimony might be to our feelings.

DEATH SOMETIMES NOT TERRIBLE.

An account has been given of a little girl, not quite ten years old, who was drawing near to the close of her life. Her friends, who were gathered around her dying bed, found from her broken words, that she felt a dread, a natural dread, at passing alone through the awful river of death.

She may have felt that the dear Saviour had died for her, and that he would receive her; but oh, this dark river, this mighty mysterious river, must be passed. Before the close came, however, she ceased to speak of its loneliness and darkness, and just as she entered it, her face brightened suddenly, a sweet confiding smile lightened her features, and with accents of trustful courage she exclaimed, "Oh, it's only a brook!" Happily she entered and passed over to the heavenly Canaan, for her Saviour, the true Ark of the Covenant, gave her gentle spirit a passage as upon dry ground.

James Simpson, an able minister of the Gospel, was a nervously eccentric man. To him death was in prospect a very fearful thing—a river turbid and tumultuous, the thought of which produced terror whenever he dwelt upon it. Yet, when his last sickness came, and the solemn moment of departure drew near, through the merciful condescension of his dear Saviour, he, too, found the dreaded *river* a mere *brook*. His pulse having sunk, he was enabled to pray that, if his day's work was done, his bands might be loosed, and he received into rest. In the feeling of his Lord's sustaining presence he then exclaimed, "It is done! It is done!" and almost instantly, in holy, humble triumph, had passed over the brook.

It sometimes pleases the Lord, in his infinite wisdom, to cause that death should appear more and more terrible to his faithful servants, as they approach it. He would drive them to trust in himself for comfort, he would show them that they are not to rely upon past services in this solemn hour for hope. Yet when these have endured all their fearful forebodings of the dark, bitter, overwhelming flood—they find, to their eternal rejoicing, that the Lord upholding them, death was only a shallow brook, quickly to be passed over into the land of rest and peace.

Another humble Christian, looking towards the close of his earthly pilgrimage in sweet trusting faith in his long-loved Redeemer, was heard to say: "Though I enter the valley of the shadow of death with awe, I can truly say it is not with dread;" and, perfectly resigned in the belief that his sins had been blotted out, he calmly and patiently awaited his dissolution.

THE SAVIOUR TAKES CARE OF HIS LAMBS.

The love and tender mercy of our Lord and Saviour Jesus Christ are often marvellously displayed toward the workmanship of his holy hands, and more particularly so toward those young in life, who have learned to love and serve him.

Some years ago a little girl, who had been well instructed in the school of Christ, felt willing to part with her earthly friends, and to go to the Saviour, which was far better. When the time of her departure seemed drawing near, she expressed a willingness to die, but added, "I fear to go down into the dark valley *all alone.*" To some words of consolation offered her, she replied, "I am a poor, weak, timid creature, and I dread the last struggle with the king of terrors." One, present, told her to trust in the Saviour. This seemed to reach her state, and with a renewed feeling of loving confidence she exclaimed, with a sweet smile, "I will trust Him." The dear Saviour was very merciful to her; for, in a few minutes after saying those words, she appeared to sink into a sweet sleep, and without a bodily struggle which could be perceived, was quietly gathered to glory.

Of one little boy of eight years of age, the following interesting incident is narrated. He was taken suddenly very ill, and after a few days the physician told his parents that he could not survive the attack. His affectionate father thought it right that his little boy should be aware of his situation, and therefore told him what the doctor thought. After doing so, he asked the little sufferer if he was afraid to die. The child received the intelligence with much calmness, but, instead of replying to the query, he requested his father to read to him out of the Bible what the Saviour had said about little children. The father read to him the passage, "Suffer little children to come unto me, and forbid them not." When the father had finished, the grace-supported child looked up at him, and said, "No! I am not afraid to die. When I die, Jesus will take care of me. No! I am not afraid to die!"

INFLUENCE OF THE HOLY SPIRIT.

BARBARA HOYLAND.

VARIOUS are the methods which Divine goodness uses to arrest the careless and unconcerned, and awaken them to a sense of the importance of religion, and of the necessity of their earnestly seeking for the pearl of great price. Yet, in every case, it is the convicting and persuasive energy and power of the Holy Spirit which is the real agent of conversion. Sometimes he is pleased to operate on the heart, without instrumental means, sometimes through those who have been anointed and qualified to preach the gospel, and sometimes by what may seem as merely accidental occurrences.

Barbara Hoyland, who became a valuable minister of the gospel, received an awakening visitation in early life, a visitation which, through the Lord's grace, saved her from utter ruin, as she believed, through the Divine blessing upon what might seem like a trivial incident. She was brought up in the observance of the rites and ceremonies of the Church of England, by her parents, and early in life was favored with the visitations of Divine grace, and manifested some seriousness and religious tenderness of spirit. When twelve years of age, she was sent by her parents to a dancing-school, through the influence of which, and the young persons she was introduced to there, a great change for the worse took place in her character. Her father, too late, discovered it, and earnestly sought to break up all her intercourse with those who had there been her associates. But he died; and when about sixteen, she was exposed to a temptation, which, if yielded to, would have been her ruin. Whilst hesitating and unsettled, she was one evening sitting with her mother, when they observed a moth fluttering and playing round the candle, until at last the flame caught it, and burned its wings, so that it soon expired in apparent agony. Musing on this, her mother said, "How like incautious youth! playing round the flame till drawn within its power, caught and consumed." The incident, and the remark of her mother, were effectual, through the accompanying visitations of the Lord's Holy Spirit, for her spiritual awakening. She turned from the seductive attractions, sought comfort and strength in the Lord Jesus, became his faithful follower, and in life and conversation, as well as by the ministry of the gospel, preached powerfully through her day.

REFINEMENT NECESSARY.

The operations of one of our large iron-works, where the metal is reduced from the ore, have furnished food for profitable reflection. The rough pile of brown, clayey-looking earth and stone, which lay by the side of the furnace, would seem to one ignorant of iron manufacture very unlikely to yield such a valuable product as the pure metal. In it, indeed, the iron is largely mixed with impurities, which must be removed. A portion of these is washed away by a stream of water, which separates much of the clay that is mechanically mixed with it. But the heap which remains is still ore, and in it the iron is so intimately united with other substances, that nothing will effect their separation but being plunged, with an abundant supply of fuel, into the capacious furnace, where it is subjected to the action of the most intense heat. The air which supplies the combustion is forced into the seething mass by powerful machinery, and is itself first heated so as to augment the temperature within. The most refractory ores, when long enough exposed to this fiery ordeal, are softened and melted, the iron separates from its associates which had so closely held it and sinks to the bottom of the furnace, from whence in due season the workman allows it to escape—and casts it, while yet fluid, into such shape as best suits his purpose.

What a lively illustration does this process furnish us of the manner in which our heavenly Father accomplishes the great work of transforming apostate man from earthly to divine. The restraints of civil society, the humanizing influence of polished companions, and the influence of education, may be compared to the stream of water which washed away the loose particles of earthy matter that were mingled with the ore; but the corrupt tendencies of the human heart, and its unwillingness to bear the yoke of Christ, and resign its own selfish will, are so closely entwined about it, forming as it were part of its very nature, that they are to be removed only in the furnace of affliction, under the direction of Him, whose baptism is with fire, and of whom it was predicted that He should be like a refiner's fire. Let none then seek to escape from this needful and profitable experience, but patiently abide the fiery trial, so that in the right time they may be brought forth prepared to be made into whatever vessel it pleases the Master Workman.

Though the iron, as it first comes from the furnace, is valuable and useful for many things, yet there are some purposes for which it is not adapted without passing through still further processes. For its further purification, it is broken into fragments, and placed in a puddling furnace, where it is melted by the flames continually directed upon it. Exposed to their action, the impurities are gradually consumed, and when this has been fully accomplished it is withdrawn from the furnace, and, while still soft and pliable, it is so beaten and moulded as best to fit it for the uses and purposes for which it is intended.

It is the concurrent testimony of experienced Christians that those who are designed for especial service in the church, must submit to repeated baptisms of various kinds, to fit them for the work to which they are called. The prophet Jeremiah compares the word of the Lord to the fire and the hammer; and those only can hope to become useful vessels in his house who submit patiently to the severe and ofttimes painful operations of the Refiner and Purifier.

He who is infinite both in wisdom and goodness knows how to dispense to each one what is needful to His humbling and purification—and it is in great mercy that He administers trials and afflictions. It was under a fresh sense of this truth that a deeply experienced Minister of the Gospel, Isaac Penington, gave the following exhortations:

"Prize inward exercises, griefs, and troubles; and let faith and patience have their perfect work in them." And again, "The more thou art weakened and distressed, the more thou art fitted for, and the more abundantly shalt thou partake of, His mercy and strength; waiting upon Him in the meek, quiet, patient, and resigned spirit which He will not fail to work thy mind into; that, in the issue of all, thou mayest reap the quiet fruits of righteousness and heavenly peace from His hand."

THE SWEET INFLUENCE OF GOSPEL LOVE.

Oh! that every awakened soul would daily seek after the sweet influences of gospel love! It sweetens society; it begets its likeness in others; it excites gratitude; and even if bestowed on the ungrateful (as saith our dear Redeemer,— love's holy and exhaustless fountain—the rain falls on the just and the unjust), it brings its own sweet reward with it; for it attracts the approbation of God. Where, then, will be contempt; where the indulgence of evil surmisings and hard thoughts; where either studied or careless detraction; where even the needless disclosure of real failings; where the least place for any enmity? These hurtful practices and pride, the promoter of many such things, will fall before the prevalence of pure, Christian love; and surely when these are exterminated from the heart, is it not so far prepared for its best and most sacred purpose,— to be a temple of the Holy Spirit!

PROVIDENCE OF GOD ASSERTED.

In the time of the Revolution, an encampment of about five hundred men was stationed near the dwelling of David Sands, in New York State. During their stay, D. Sands and wife became very uneasy, particularly his wife, who felt a presentiment that some trial was approaching. In a short time afterwards, she was alarmed one night by a noise she heard in the house, after they were gone to bed, which her husband apprehended might be only the wind rustling among the trees. In a few minutes they were more certain, finding some persons near their room, and distinctly hearing them say, "Some of the family are awake, we will shoot them." In this alarming situation, personal safety seemed the first object, and they soon determined to attempt an escape, which was the more easily effected as their chamber was on the first floor. In getting out through the window, one of the company, stationed to keep guard on the outside, discharged a piece at them, the ball of which grazed the forehead of D. Sands; however, they escaped, but with very thin clothing; and as it was a very cold night, and they remained in the open air till break of day, these circumstances, together with their painful anxiety, rendered it a most suffering time. When they returned to their dwelling, they found it plundered of all the cash, about fifty pounds, most of their bedding, and much of their furniture. A servant and two children, who were sleeping in another part of the house, were not disturbed.

After considering what was best to be done, David found his mind most easy in determining to go to the encampment. On his arrival, he saw several officers conversing together, who said to him: "Mr. Sands, we have heard of the depredation committed at your house, and desire to know what you think can be done to discover the offenders." After some solid consideration, he informed them he had on the road felt a belief that, if the men were drawn up rank and file, about fifty in a company, he might be able (if he followed the best direction), in passing through them, to detect those concerned in the robbery. The officers wondered at his proposal, thinking it very improbable he should discover them in such a manner without any outward knowledge of the persons. But they complied, and gave the necessary orders.

On passing down the first rank he made a stop near the bottom, but went on to the next, where he soon made a stand at one of the men, and looking him full in the face, said to him, " Where wast thou last night?" He answered: "Keeping guard, sir, and a very cold night it was." " Didst thou find it so when at my house?" replied David; at which the man trembled much, and showed evident signs of guilt, on which he was ordered out of the ranks; and in like manner four others were discovered. Then he went to a young officer, whom he asked how he came to aid and accompany his men in pillaging his house. He positively denied the charge, but D. Sands further interrogated him, by saying: "Let me feel thy heart, and see if that do not accuse thee." On putting his hand to it, it throbbed up to his neck, and so loud, that D. Sands called to the other officers to come and see, and hear how it accused the officer. He was therefore considered to be guilty. Two others, which made eight concerned, deserted before the search commenced, and which accounted for the stop he made in the first rank.

The officers now desired to know what could be done for him. He said he should like to have his furniture, bedding, etc., returned; he wanted his bedding in particular; on which they brought the greatest part, with half the money, assuring him the rest was lost. They were brought to trial before the civil power, but as David declined appearing at the stated time, they were, of course, acquitted; but this not exempting them from the trial by martial law, and their guilt appearing beyond a doubt, the officers had them bound together and taken to David Sands' house, informing him their lives were at his mercy, and he was to determine their sentence; upon which he gave them suitable advice, and then forgave them; and as they were weary with long travelling, he ordered them comfortable refreshment.

At this time, his wife observing one of the men, said, "Thou art he that shot at us." Her husband made answer, "He has been told of it before." David Sands was informed the officer could not be pardoned, as the punishment of such a crime was death to him, who should have been an example to his men. But David, being very solicitous to preserve his life, asked if nothing could be done to release him from that punishment. They informed him there was but one way, which was for him to desert the regiment, which was permitted. . They likewise said some punishment must be inflicted upon some of the men, to deter others from the like practices. Therefore some of them underwent a slight flogging.

Several years after this occurrence, David Sands was travelling on a religious visit, and after appointing a public meeting, a person came up to him and begged his pardon. He was, indeed, about to kneel down, but David Sands prevented him, saying, he thought he was not the person he meant, as he had no knowledge of him. But the man confessed he was one of those concerned in pillaging David's house, and was one of the two who deserted to avoid discovery, and that he had not been easy in his mind since, but hoped he should meet with his forgiveness. David Sands told him it was out of his power to forgive sins, but he hoped the Almighty would forgive him, as he himself had long done. The man informed him the other person was at a short distance off, who came to David, asking his excuse and confessing his crime, desiring him, at the same time, as a confirmation of his entire forgiveness, to go with him to his house, telling him he had married a young woman of the Society of Friends, but that he had not had true peace of mind since they had done him that injury. David consented to go, and found it as the man had said.

SILENT WORSHIP.

The value of silent worship is far from being properly estimated. Many people think the time passed in silence, in meetings for Divine worship, is almost wholly lost. But when we consider that all true worship consists in an intercourse between the soul and its Almighty Creator, we cannot doubt that a state of inward silent prostration of soul before the Majesty of heaven is a fit condition for the acceptable performance of Divine worship. There are many living witnesses to the truth of the Psalmist's testimony, when he says, "I waited patiently for the Lord, and he inclined unto me and heard my cry." It is a practice among many of the Methodists to await the opening of the New Year in solemn silence, and one of their preachers, speaking of an occasion of this kind, says, "During the time we sat in silent meditation and prayer, the whole assembly felt the overwhelming power of Divine grace."

A number of persons, whose minds had been powerfully awakened during what is called a revival among the Methodists, found themselves much drawn, after a time, into a state of stillness and inward waiting on God. Finding the comfort and benefit of this exercise, they met together for the purpose; their preacher heard of this, advised against it, and reasoned the point without being able to convince them—their own experience being more than a full answer to all his arguments. They still continued their silent meetings, and were evidently growing in the root of religion, that inward life which is hid with Christ in God. Pained at his want of success in producing a change in their views, and hoping to accomplish by an experiment what he could not by words, after setting forth the ridiculous appearance which he thought one of their assemblies would present —sitting in perfect stillness, he said in substance: "Well, come now, we will hold a silent meeting in the chapel; and you'll see what will come of it—what a dry, dull time it will be." Accordingly, at the next meeting they all sat in silence; there was neither hymn, nor sermon, nor prayer, nor benediction, vocally uttered. But we may well believe, that those spiritual worshippers, whose souls had oft been strengthened and refreshed in silence, did not sit in listless indifference, but wrestled in spirit for the Divine blessing on the opportunity. Nor was it withheld. After they had remained some time together, the Lord's power broke in upon them in a marvellous manner, contriting their spirits, and bedewing many cheeks with tears. The solemn and precious feeling spread from one to another, until it seemed to cover the whole assembly like a heavenly canopy; and, under its humbling influence, the minister no longer able to restrain the fulness of his emotions, broke forth with tears in these memorable words: "Surely the Lord is in this thing, and I knew it not." With this exception, the meeting continued to its close in silent waiting, and separated under a deep solemnity.

"BRIDGE UP."

An invitation came from a kind friend to accompany him in a ride into the thinly settled and wooded district of the middle portion of lower New Jersey, locally known as "The Pines;" and the early morning of a bright, pleasant day, in the early part of summer, saw us on our way, with a ride of forty miles before us, over roads, the sandy portions of which were rendered heavy by the long-continued dryness of the weather.

We had travelled but a short distance, enjoying the fresh air of the morning, listening to the songs of the Robin, Golden-crowned Thrush, and Song-Sparrow; and admiring the richness of the foliage, and the brightness of the verdure, as yet unbrowned by the summer's sun; when my companion unexpectedly halted at a road which crossed our path, and turned aside, regretting the necessity of making a détour, which would lengthen our journey. Noticing my surprise, he pointed to a small board, which had escaped my notice, stuck up near the side of the road, on which were written the words: "Bridge up," indicating that the repairs then in progress of a bridge a mile before us would prevent our passage. If he had not observed the caution, and had gone on, he would have been compelled to return, and thus added needlessly to the exertion and fatigue of the day.

This little incident furnished food for profitable reflection. Who is there, in his journey through life, that does not often find his onward career checked by a caution, a warning, an impression on his mind, that there are dangers in advance, that a "Bridge is up," on the road he is travelling, and that it is needful he should alter his course, if he would pursue his journey in safety? He may be a man in active business, enlarging the sphere of his operations, and, stimulated by a growing ambition, adding one thing after another to his concerns. The warning signal may be very unwelcome to him, and he may refuse to listen to it; or persuade himself that his own skill and energy will enable him to overcome all the difficulties he may encounter; and thus he may go on, as many a one has, until financial troubles overtake him.

He then finds his business beyond his control, his receipts insufficient to meet the obligations he has incurred, his credit weakened, and after struggling in vain to extricate himself from the quicksand in which he is sinking, ruin and distress overtake him.

If he avoids a catastrophe of this kind, and pecuniary success attends his labors, it may be that his mind becomes gradually more and more centered in the pursuit of wealth; his spiritual greenness withers, and though the desire of his heart is answered, yet leanness enters into his soul. This is a result even more to be deplored than the former. For the man whose business hopes have been blighted, may be so humbled by the dispensation, as to turn his thoughts to the Source of all good, and in repentance and contrition, may be led to acknowledge his transgressions, and seek for reconciliation and forgiveness; and thus, through the aboundings of Heavenly goodness, he may know his afflictions to be blessed, and to be a means to lead him back to the safe enclosure of submission to the will of God.

A late valued minister, William Evans, in the early part of his business life, becoming discouraged as to success in the avocation he followed, made some preparation to enter into another employment, involving greater risks, and giving promise of larger returns. From time to time doubts and uneasiness respecting the change attended his mind, but he reasoned them away. Yet they continued and increased, until, he says: "One day sitting in our religious meeting, it plainly appeared to me, that though the mind may be able to compass much, yet beyond its capacity it cannot go. If all its energies are enlisted in the concerns of the world, and their pressure is as great as it is capable of bearing, the all-important work of religion must be neglected. This appeared to me must inevitably be my case. My time and talents would be wholly engrossed, and I must abandon all prospect of usefulness in religious society for the servitude of a man of the world. It seemed, if I pursued the prospect of adopting the proposed change of business, that I would be lost to religious society, and to the work of religion in my own heart."

This merciful and clear notice of "Bridge up," was heeded, and circumstances that soon after occurred, showed that, by so doing, he saved himself from the spiritual decay with which he was threatened, and also from pecuniary difficulty, which would probably have resulted disastrously.

It is not in business matters alone that a warning voice is thus extended. The Spirit of our Redeemer, given to guide and direct us in our journey to heaven, raises in the heart a protest, intelligible to him that reverently listens and obeys, against all that would lead to evil. This is the every-day experience of the Christian. At one time we are called upon to abstain from fleshly lusts which war against the soul; or perhaps to lay aside a book which may tend to sow tares in the mind, or to dissipate, by its light and hurtful character, the serious impressions which have rested on our spirits; or we may be made sensible that some irreligious friend is leading our mind away from its true centre; or that our affections are becoming too strongly placed upon some favorite pursuit, which is thus coming between us and that which should be the supreme object of our attention. He who has long been pursuing the path of the pilgrim to the better land, has learned, by bitter experience, how dangerous it is to disregard any of these notices of "Bridge up," kindly placed by the master of the highway to keep his followers in the right path. Like my friend, they have learned by experience to be on the watch for them, and are prepared to point them out to their more unwary companions, and exhort them to be on their guard.

COBWEBS.

While gathering flowers in the early morning when they were yet sparkling with dew, a writer relates, that she noticed in one place that a spider had spun his web above a sprig, upon which were several blossoms; carefully reaching underneath the web, she plucked the flowers, and found that they were as dry as though no refreshing moisture had been deposited around them, *so slight a thing as a cobweb had intercepted the dews of heaven.*

How much of instruction does this little incident suggest to the thoughtful mind. A continuance in anything that is wrong, even if it seem to us but a trifling matter — a mere cobweb — may effectually prevent us from experiencing those sweet refreshing seasons with which the Lord favors at times His honest-hearted, faithful servants; and may keep us in a dry, barren condition, where there is no growth experienced in the life of religion: "Where there is neither dew, nor rain, nor fields of offering." Nor does this seem strange when we reflect that the great object of the Lord's dealings with us, is to humble us and make us thoroughly submissive to His will; and that without this there can be no admission into His heavenly kingdom. So long as we refuse to submit fully to His government, we are living to some extent in a state of rebellion.

When under Divine visitation we may at times have felt our hearts solemnized by the influence of heavenly good, and have clearly seen that we ought to give up ourselves, body, soul and spirit, without reservation, into the hands of our Creator, who was waiting to redeem us from all evil, and to purify us unto himself; but oh! the unwillingness we felt to part with some cherished project; some gratification of the appetite; some mental indulgence. Perhaps, in after years, we may look back on such periods, and be surprised to see what mere cobwebs we allowed to intercept the flow of heavenly love to us. Many years ago, the late Samuel Bettle attended the meeting at Westtown Boarding School, Chester Co., Pa., and was powerfully engaged in testimony therein. Among his listeners, was a boy who had in his possession several flying squirrels, which abound in the neighborhood. The regulations of the school prohibited keeping such pets, and the child felt condemned for his violation of the rules, and under the softening influence that prevailed in the meeting, resolved to give up this indulgence, which he clearly saw to be wrong for him. After the meeting, as he walked with a companion, he unbosomed his feelings and expressed his intention of releasing the squirrels. His companion was a more hardened character, and simply remarked that he had had such feelings, but that it would all die away in a few days, and so in measure it proved. It is not the magnitude or smallness of the offering required, but the willingness to surrender what is called for that opens the way to receive the rich blessings of the Lord.

During a season of Divine visitation, a respectable farmer in a certain neighborhood was strongly impressed with the importance of religion, and under much exercise of mind; but he seemed unable to arrive at any settlement in the Truth. An interested friend, who was anxiously concerned about him, knew not how it was that with so much apparent earnestness and sincerity, so little progress appeared to be made. He knew not of the cobweb that was spread over his soul; but it was all explained when one day his friend met him and told him that there had long existed some unpleasantness between him and a near relative, who, he thought, had improperly treated him. He had become convinced that this hardness of feeling must be removed from his own heart, or it would shut out the sweet enjoyment of Divine love; and he had become humbled enough to go to his relative and ask for forgiveness for all that he himself had unkindly said and thought about him.

He met with a kind welcome and a hearty response, and now all hardness between them was done, and great was the tide of peace that flowed into his soul.

How great is the goodness of our heavenly Father, and how does he visit, and re-visit his children; even the rebellious, seeking to draw them into his safe enclosure, that He may be good unto them and bless them. Oh, that all might turn to Him with full purpose of heart, and love and serve Him faithfully!

MINISTRY.

A GOSPEL MINISTRY.

WILLIAM PENN'S observations on this important subject are worthy our attentive consideration. He says: "There is such a thing as a very small gift in a great many words; and there is such a thing as a large gift in a very few words. We do not want an eloquent ministry; we do not want a flowery ministry; we want a *living* ministry; we want a baptizing ministry—a ministry that will break a hard heart, and heal a wounded one; a ministry that will lead us to the fountain, and leave us there."

PROVIDENTIALLY DIRECTED SERMONS.

It is recorded that a clergyman, who had prepared with more than usual care a written discourse to deliver to a large congregation, whilst on the way to the place of worship saw a half leaf of a printed book lying on the ground, which he took up. What the book was, of which it had been a part, he never knew; but there was a text of Scripture on the fragment, and a remark there which he read, that took such hold of his mind, that he believed it to be his duty to preach on it. So with his carefully prepared manuscript in his pocket, he spoke to the audience as his mind seemed led. He treated on sceptical sophistries, and closed with a solemn appeal to such as give way to such shallow reasonings, to examine Truth in its own spirit, and earnestly seek, through the Lord's assistance, to become Sons of God. He was much favored in this his unpremeditated ministry; so much so as to call forth this remark from the most spiritually minded members of the church: "Most assuredly of God to the congregation." He told them he hoped it was so, and said he had no thought of taking that text, or delivering such a sermon when he left his own house. They, as well as he, could feel there was something about this discourse which was not to be found connected with his usual written essays. In a few weeks after the delivery of this sermon, a young lawyer called upon him to say that, through the blessing of God on that discourse, he had been delivered from deep inward conflicts with sceptical temptations. An entire change of heart and life followed; he found it necessary to give up practice at the bar, and to seek after a profession which did not present so many difficulties in the way of being a truly consistent Christian—whose meat and drink it is to do the will of God, and to promote peace and harmony amongst all men.

Another preacher has left it on record, that, on a certain occasion as he was just ready to commence the delivery of a discourse, deliberately prepared at home, he observed four men enter the place of worship. Immediately, as they entered, his mind was turned in such a remarkable manner to the Scripture account of the general deluge, and trains of thought so presented on this subject, that he felt impelled to speak on it. There was no time for delay, and believing it to be his duty, he spoke as matters were opened to his mind. He treated on the reasons for the deluge, the useful results springing from it, and Noah's wisdom, in obedience to the Lord's command, in preparing for it. The congregation seemed unusually attentive, and, to the speaker himself, the new train of thought into which he had been led, and the solemn feeling which accompanied the delivery, were intensely interesting. Several months had passed away, when one day three men called to see him. They were three of the four men whose entrance into his meeting-house had been so particularly observed. They told him that all four of them had been avowed deists; that, upon the day alluded to, they had been seeking amusement together, and as they were returning, the Scriptural account of the deluge had been the subject of their conversation and ridicule; that they had heard in his discourse, to their amazement, not a few of their own sophistries repeated in the very language in which they had uttered them, and with clearness and power solidly refuted.

These four men were all, in the long suffering mercy of God, through the instrumentality of that discourse, brought under deep religious concern for the well-being of their immortal souls; and there is good reason to believe, in time, witnessed the new birth unto holiness, and walked thereafter in the lowly path of self-denial, as true-hearted followers and disciples of the Lord Jesus Christ. Of one of them, who had deceased when the account was taken down, it is stated, that he left behind him a blessed testimony—in the minds of those who witnessed his departure—that he had exchanged mortality for immortality, the trials and tribulations of this life for joy unspeakable and full of glory.

POOR PREACHING AND POOR HEARING.

An author, probably a preacher himself, after stating that he had heard much about poor preaching, gives it as his opinion, that there is also a great deal of poor *hearing*. He enumerates first *drowsy hearing*, the hearers being evidently dull and sleepy, if not soundly asleep. The second is *inattentive hearing*, when the mind is wandering, and taking little or no heed to what the preacher is saying. The third is *captious hearing*, when the listener keeps his attention alive only that he may find fault. He is a fisherman always on the alert to catch bad fish, and in this business being very expert, he is seldom without success. The fourth specimen of poor hearing of which he speaks is *hearing for other people*. The hearer is apt to say to himself, whilst dissecting the sermon he is listening to: Ah, this fits John; that is well adapted to Stephen's case; and thus, whilst looking around the assembly, is distributing all the advice and the reproof to others,—being unwilling to keep aught so unpalatable for himself. This the author referred to deems a certain way of "offering the sacrifice of fools."

Poor preaching there will ever be, so long as the professed ministers of the gospel trust to their own wisdom, and the knowledge obtained from study as the fountain from which to draw their sermons. Poor hearing will always be found, unless those assembled are really craving spiritual food, and desiring to be fed by the Lord Jesus Christ himself. If they are seeking instruction from Him, without placing their trust and confidence in man, their hearts will be open to receive the instruction the Lord may give to his anointed servants to distribute, and they will prove good. hearers — thankfully taking whatever of reproof or consolation the Holy Spirit may show them is fitted to their state.

If the ministers of the gospel do indeed dwell in their services under the influence of the Spirit of the Lord Jesus, and draw their supplies of doctrine and of power from Him alone, they will at times experience through his assisting grace, ability given them to arouse the drowsy, to draw the attention of those of wandering minds, to cause the captious to forget his criticisms, and even so to turn the attention of the hearer for others to himself, as to forget that there are others present to whom the words of the preacher may be applied.

Reader, be not thou one of the hearers who are drowsy in spirit, or inattentive, or captious, or one who listens merely for others. If the ministry under which thou art sitting at any time has evident tokens of Divine authority, do thou, with a lively spirit and an attentive mind, give it kindly entrance, and be sure in the first place let it have a self-application.

MUSIC AND DECORATION IN PLACES OF PUBLIC WORSHIP.

R. H. Herschell, a converted Jew, remarks upon this subject: "I firmly believe that, if we seek to affect the mind by the aid of architecture, painting, or music, the impression produced by these adjuncts is just so much subtracted from the worship of the unseen Jehovah. If the outward eye is taken up with material splendor, or forms of external beauty, the mind's eye sees but little of 'Him who is invisible;' the ear that is entranced with the melody of sweet sounds listens not to the 'still small voice' by which the Lord makes his presence known."

"A WORD SPOKEN IN DUE SEASON HOW GOOD IS IT."—Prov. xv. 23.

In the fifth month, 1782, as Rachel Kirk (afterwards Price) was passing by the gate of Friends' meeting-house, at Second and Market sts., Philadelphia, she was stopped by Samuel Emlen, an eminent minister who at times was led to speak in a prophetic manner. He took her hand, and asked: "Whence comest thou?" Having told the place and her name, she informed him of the settlement in life of her sister Rebecca, whom he had met before, and whom he remembered and loved; he paused and said: " Rachel, it will be thy turn next, and be careful that thou place thy affections upon virtue. Let not anything short of virtue sway thy mind. If anything inferior should gain pre-eminence in thy view, difficulties may ensue; but if virtue and piety govern thy mind in making a choice of a companion, you may walk, hand in hand, happily together through life, and be true helpmates to each other." Still holding her by the hand, he continued,—"Farewell: now mind what I say." Two young men were at that time seeking the acquaintance of Rachel Kirk, with a view to marriage, one of whom was a person of polished manners and specious address and appearance, whom inclination might have prompted her to accept, the other a plain, unassuming man of solid character. That casual meeting — casual so far as man can discern — produced a lasting impression. Narrating it to her children, after she had lived in wedlock for more than half a century, and known the experience of a long life, she said, "I thought it a remarkable interview with an entire stranger. But it was of great use to me in settling my mind to make a prudent choice, which was soon after brought to a trial, having but a few days previously become acquainted with Philip Price, with whom his prediction has been verified, and as far realized as can be expected in this probationary state of trial." Assisted by the opportune advice, she preferred the serious, virtuous, and solid character, and enjoyed the felicity of a congenial companionship through life, but witnessed the moral declension of the more gay and showy suitor, who had had a momentary power to hold her choice in suspense.

PREACHING BY EXAMPLE.

Many conscientious Christians who are not called to the work of vocally upholding and advocating the gospel of Christ Jesus, are yet efficient preachers thereof in life and conversation. Some by their humble, self-denying example, when surrounded by the votaries of pride, of fashion, and of self-indulgence;— some by their honest, upright dealings in the walks of trade and business, when most around them seem grasping after all they can gather of this world's goods, without respect to the law of doing to others as they would others should do to them; — some by cheerful content in poverty; some by holy resignation in sickness and sorrow. These are all teaching the great lessons of Christian principle, — these are all preachers of righteousness, in a greater or lesser degree to those around them.

A striking remark was once made by a religious man, to one who complained of the distance which he lived from the place of worship. The latter was deemed a pious man, and was diligent in his attendance at religious meetings, although he lived six miles from the house in which they were held. On this occasion, however, he spoke of the distance *he* had to travel, whilst some of the members had but a few steps to walk. His religious friend told him to remember that he had weekly the privilege of *preaching a sermon six miles long.* To all the residents by the road side,—to all those he met or passed on his way,—he upheld by example the duty of assembling for the worship of Almighty God. These silent sermons may have been blessed to many.

We have it on record that a meeting of the Society of Friends in one of the Southern States, which, by the moving away to the west of many members, and the remissness in spiritual zeal of some who remained, had been entirely dropped, was resuscitated through the faithfulness of one young woman, who regularly, on meeting days, went and sat alone in the old house. Her diligence preached with prevailing power. Some who beheld her going, and others who heard of it, were led to consider their own responsibility, as dependent creatures, and the duty they owed to their Almighty Care-taker, to offer him worship and praise for the unnumbered blessings received at his hands, and were drawn, by a heartfelt sense of duty, to meet with her.

A somewhat similar instance occurred in the experience of John Carter of North Carolina, during last century. He had felt it his duty when a young man to repair to the old house on meeting days and to sit there, though alone. He had continued this practice for some time when, on one of these occasions, a great exercise came upon him to stand up and audibly proclaim what he then felt of the love of God, through Jesus Christ, towards sinful man. It was a great trial of his faith, but he yielded to the apprehended duty. Shortly after he had again taken his seat, several young men came into the house, in a serious manner, and sat down in silence by him, some of whom evinced brokenness of heart. After the meeting closed he found that these young men, his former associates, wondering what could induce him thus to go alone to that house, had approached softly to look through the cracks of the door at what he was doing: and in this situation were so affected, by what he had declared, that they were induced to come in. Some of these young men continued to meet with him; zeal for religion revived; others joined them; and, in time, a large meeting of Friends was held there. John Carter himself became a valuable minister amongst them.

TIMES OF REFRESHMENT.

Many portions of our country, during the summer season, have at times experienced the effects of a prolonged withholding of those refreshing showers which are so essential to the maintenance of vegetable life, and the health and comfort of us all. In some neighborhoods, the broad leaves of the Indian corn have rolled up, and presented that parched aspect so distressing to the farmer; the pasture fields have become brown and dry, and furnished but little food for the animals that fed in them; and the cucumber, melon, and similar vines, have wilted under the hot sun. One who listened to the conversation of those who met in such districts, would hear sage comments on the weather, doubts as to the future of the crops, and discussions upon the amount of drought that corn would bear, and the necessity of moisture when the grain was about developing. Even those not directly interested in farming could not but enter into sympathy with their friends and neighbors. It often required some effort, during these periods, to refrain from indulging in *impatient* longings for rain, and to maintain that state of quiet submission to the Divine will which, when associated with due diligence in the performance of our allotted labors, is the safest resting-place for short-sighted, dependent mortals.

When at length these seasons of drought have been ended, and the hoped-for rains have come, a great change appears in the landscape. A fresher greenness clothes the fields of grass, and the curled corn-blades open out their broad surfaces as they feel the influence of this "sweet reviver of the famished land." The spirits of the people are as much enlivened as their fields, and they now look forward with confident hope of receiving a reward for their labor and care.

Can we not see in all these things an emblem of the condition into which the church is sometimes brought? There are times when little apparent fruit is seen from the most earnest labors of the spiritual husbandmen. The seed which is sown remains in the heart apparently without germinating — the soil appears to be without moisture, and no growth is visible. The hoe of church discipline may, indeed, loosen and mellow the soil, as well as prevent the growth of noxious weeds, but it cannot supply that penetrating and all-powerful Grace, which alone gives spiritual greenness and life to the plants. Disheartening as it may seem to the workman in such a field, it is still his duty faithfully to stir the ground, prune the straggling branches, and to watch over and care for the poor shrivelled plants, as the Master of the vineyard may direct. In the vicissitudes of the heavenly seasons, the rains will descend and water the ground — there will come a time when it will please the Lord of the harvest, not only to send forth laborers, but to visit His Church with a renewed outpouring of His Grace and good Spirit. Then, indeed, the toiling husbandmen will see of the travail of their souls and be satisfied. Sons and daughters, who had wandered far from the safe inclosure of the sheep-fold, will be brought back; new growth will be developed in some who had seemed like stunted plants, and heavenly life and beauty will again adorn the garden of the Lord.

THOMAS BROWN.

Human wisdom is not an essential attribute of Christian character. Some who have been valuable ministers of the gospel of Christ, and through his aid have been enabled to turn many to righteousness, have been in point of intellect considerably below the average of the human race. For the service to which they were called by their Divine Master, they were furnished at the time with the necessary qualifications to enable them rightly to perform it. Sometimes they were eminent in the ministry, even as to the beauty and force of the language they employed, although in the common affairs of life, they took rank with the simple, and in some instances were unacquainted with the meaning of the words which, in their public ministrations, they used with perfect propriety.

Thomas Brown, who died in Philadelphia in 1757, was an illustration of these remarks. He was an illiterate and, as regards the ordinary business of life, a simple-minded man; yet he was entrusted with a remarkable gift in the ministry, in the exercise of which he was at times led (to use his own language), "to extol the divinity of that religion that is breathed from heaven, and which arrays the soul of its possessor with degrees of the divinity of Christ, and entitles him to an eternal inheritance." His friends say of him: "Though not a man of literature, he was often led into sublime matter, which was convincing and persuasive in setting forth the dignity and excellence of the Christian religion." He was frequently drawn to speak in a remarkable manner upon the glories of the celestial kingdom; and on one occasion the celebrated George Whitefield, who had attended a meeting of Friends in the hope of hearing him, was so impressed by his communication and the Divine authority accompanying it, that he said he felt himself like a child in comparison with him.

George Dillwyn says: "Divine Wisdom sometimes sees meet to endue the instruments he makes use of with qualifications far above their natural powers, and this to enable them to distinguish between the heavenly treasure and the earthly vessel that contains it; that so none may deck themselves with jewels not their own, or give the praise to the creature, which is due to the Creator, and to him alone!"

JOHN JUSTICE.

The Apostle Paul, in speaking of his call to the work of the ministry, declared: "For I neither received it of man, neither was I taught it, but by the revelation of Jesus Christ." Immediate revelation still continues to be the only source of true gospel ministry, and it is by attention and obedience to the Lord's will, thus inwardly manifested, that a minister can be qualified to communicate exhortation, reproof, warning or consolation to his hearers. As this is the ministry of Christ's appointment, so it often pleases him to make use of it as an instrument in the accomplishment of his blessed purposes, and at times to open the minds of individuals in a remarkable manner to receive it. Of these remarks the following circumstances, narrated by the individual to whom they occurred, are an illustration.

John Justice, late of Bucks Co., Penna., was in early life a zealous member of the Methodist Society, and, at the time the following incident occured, was living in Philadelphia. Several times while going to his place of worship he had been impressed with a belief that it would be right for him to go to a meeting of Friends; but he set aside the impression, as he afterwards related, on the ground that he did not believe in the doctrine of a Divine Revelation to the souls of men, and that until convinced thereof, he could not be a member of that religious Society. On a certain First-day morning, however, as he was on his way to his place of worship, the impression was again so forcibly renewed, that he almost involuntarily turned, and retraced his steps towards the building in Key's alley, in which the meeting was then held.

As he went towards the house, musing upon the singularity of the intimations he had received, he resolved that, if he must attend that meeting, he would avoid observation, and then, if anything particularly applicable to him was said, it could only be by Divine revelation. With these thoughts he quietly entered and, taking a seat near the door, leaned down so as to be partly concealed by the benches in front. Whilst in this position, considering the circumstances which had led him there, a piece of writing appeared to be presented to his view. It remained visible long enough to be deliberately read; after he had perused it, it was removed, and another manuscript appeared to be presented to him, which also remained in sight long enough to be read, and was then removed. The contents of these writings made a strong impression upon his mind. Shortly after the last had disappeared, Samuel Smith, a minister of that meeting, arose and commenced his discourse with the words written on the first paper which had been presented to John Justice's mental vision, the contents of which he repeated verbatim, and also a *part* of the contents of the second paper, which comprised his whole sermon. His astonishment at this remarkable occurence was great; but it was increased when, soon after Samuel Smith had sat down, Thomas Scattergood another minister of the same meeting, arose, and commenced his discourse at the part of the second paper where Samuel Smith had ended, and repeated the remaining portion of it: after which he addressed an individual who was present in a very affectionate manner, describing John's state, as though he had been familiar with his most secret thoughts and exercises from his youth to that day.

The power which accompanied his ministry, and

the accuracy with which he described his condition, left on John's mind no doubt that nothing short of *immediate Divine revelation* could have informed and enabled him thus to minister to his spiritual wants. The events of that day wrought a full conviction in John Justice, that a Divine qualification was necessary effectually to preach the gospel, and from that time he attended the meetings of the Society of Friends. He afterwards became a member, and for many years before his death was an approved minister among them.

GRAFTED INTO CHRIST.

A certain rose-bush, which, though of small growth, had borne beautiful roses, one summer appeared unusually weak, and bloomed feebly. But there were strong and vigorous shoots, lifting up green leaves and spreading branches far above those which had heretofore furnished beauty and fragrance. The summer passed; and it was a matter of wonder that such a luxuriant growth, such a fine appearance of green leaves, should be unattended with a single bud. At last, the cause was apparent — the rose-bush, which had borne the beautiful flowers, was but a graft upon a wild stock, and the much-promising, nothing-yielding shoots, were from the old root. On closer investigation, it was found that the leaves, although flourishing in appearance, were very different from those which grew on the graft.

Christian, if thou art bearing fruit to the praise of the blessed Saviour, it will be found only on the branches springing from the graft he himself has placed in thee. Take heed, lest in running into things ostensibly good, thou shouldst be found encouraging a growth, vigorous in appearance, and drawing human attention from afar, which will not produce the true fruits of the Spirit, and which may cause a withering and blight to come over that growth in thee which was of Divine nourishing, and whose fruit and flower were acceptable to thy heavenly Father, and comforting to his saints on earth. The works of charity and labors of love into which any are led by their heavenly Father, are to be accounted amongst the fruits of the Spirit, and being brought forth through grace, have no tendency to dwarf any growth from the root of Divine life.

The experience of an excellent man,—a religiously minded exhorter amongst the Methodists, who was willing to spend and be spent in works for the good of others—is instructive. He was frequent in his exhortations in meeting-houses and beside sick-beds. He labored abundantly in First-day schools, and wherever he thought he might do good. His time, not devoted to making a preparation for the wants of the body, seemed fully occupied in these—as he deemed them—religious engagements. In the midst of his hurry and zeal to work, however, the thought sometimes pressed on his mind, that he was not growing in grace; nay, more,—he feared that in the inward life and power of religion he was withering. This conviction increased, until he found that his peace and safety consisted in ceasing from all these engagements, that in quietness he might seek after a more intimate acquaintance with his heavenly Father, and witness a fresh visitation of love, and a renewal of inward life and greenness. The suckers, which had been draining his spiritual life, were cut off, as it were, in one day. In his silent watching and waiting, he witnessed a new growth inwardly; and although his path afterwards was attended by much sickness and suffering, yet knowing his way and work to be ordered of the Lord, he was kept in patience until the period came when his earthly service being accomplished, his Divine Master gathered him home in love.

WORK OF THE MINISTRY.

This is the great fundamental,—that "God is light, and in Him is no darkness at all." The great work of the ministry, is, to turn mankind from the darkness, wherein is the power of Satan, unto this light, wherein is the power of God. As Isaac Penington remarks, "The ministry of the Apostles was to turn men from Satan's kingdom to this kingdom; from his large compass of dominion in the heart to this narrow seed; from his great territories of darkness to this little principle of light; from his great power of death to this little weak thing of God; wherein the eternal power and godhead is made manifest, as this comes to be opened and increased by the Spirit."

The great work of the ministry, then, is to turn people from everything outward to the kingdom of God which is within, and to His law written upon the heart. And the Psalmist, in speaking of the happiness of the godly, says: "His delight is in the law of the Lord; and in his law doth he meditate day and night." This is the Christian's privilege.

"There is," says a well-known author, "in silent worship something so beautiful, so sublime, so consistent with the relation in which we stand to God, that it appears strange there should exist a single doubt of its propriety."

INDEX.

AFFLICTION, Observations on the uses and benefits of, 229.
Agitation that purifies, 247.
Anguish of soul at times experienced by the Christian on reviewing the actions of his unregenerate days, 29.
Augustine, Narration by, illustrating the impossibility of finite nature comprehending the infinite, 254.
Augustine, Humility of, in the prospect of death, 127.
Ann Young's text, 196.
Awakening inquiry, An, 61.

Barclay Robert, and the highwaymen, 91.
Baxter Richard, Dying expression of, 50.
Be faithful to impressions of duty, 135.
Be not ashamed of the cross, 115.
Be not deceived, 305.
Berridge John, Anecdote of, 115.
Be ye not conformed to this world, Anecdote entitled, 34.
Bettle Samuel, Remarkable preservation of the life of, 207.
    Incident connected with the ministry of, 334.
Bird tamed by kindness, and comments, 14.
"Bridge Up," Incident entitled, and comments, 328.
Brown Thomas, Observations on the ministry of, 350.

"Call upon me in the day of trouble," 275.
Camm John, Thankfulness of, upon the bed of death, 238.
Capital punishment, Remorse of Judge Wilson for passing the sentence of, upon a criminal, 65.
Captain Yonnt's dream, 204.
Carson Hannah, a poor colored woman, and Nathan Rothschild, Contrast between, 60.

Carter John, A religious meeting revived by the faithfulness of, 347.
Chalkley Thomas, Remarkable warning recorded and interpreted by, 292.
Child, Gratitude of a, 21.
    Influence exerted by a, upon a drunken father, 28, 286.
    The lost, 141.
    Remarkable expressions of a, 154.
    Evils intended to a, overcome by good, 289.
    Notice of the happy death of a, 310, 312.
Children, Series entitled, 149.
    Anecdotes of kindness to, and comments, 18.
    Prompt obedience of, to the commands of Christian parents, a duty, 1 9.
    Narrative of sufferings of, for religion, 152.
    Are a heritage of the Lord, 154.
Chinese convert, Remark of a, on the fashionable life of professed Christians, 34.
Cheerful resignation, a Christian duty, 235.
Church, Times of refreshment in the, 348.
Cobwebs, 333.
Cope Samuel, Anecdote of, 131.

Daily mercies, 188.
Death, Series entitled, 297.
    Of a fellow-being, To be accessory to, abhorrent to the Christian, 65.
    Sustaining grace in the prospect of, 297.
    On the importance of a timely preparation for, 301.
    The danger of being deceived in the prospect of, 305.
    Sometimes not terrible, 310.
    Beacon marks sometimes to be set up in preparing notices of, 306.
Deliverance from shipwreck, 184.
Dillwyn George, Anecdote of, 190.
    Observations of, on the ministry, 352.
Divine intimations, Observations of Thomas Story on, 169.
    The necessity of strictly heeding, 328.

Du Plessis, Humility of, in death, 126.
Due attendance of religious meetings, 108.

Emlen Samuel, Anecdote of, 312.
Erskine Henry, relieved from want, 209.
Evans William, Providentially restrained from business embarrassments, 331.
Evil overcome of good, 289.
Evil prevented, Anecdote of, 42.
Example, Influence of, 28, 35.
 Setting good grafts by a Christian, 38.
 Preaching by, 345.

Faith, Series entitled, 252.
 In Trials, On exercising, 227.
Faithfulness to convictions, 116.
Family, Advice on spreading a feeling of love in the, 10.
 Care of a religious man in reference to speaking of money transactions in his, 63.
Father saved, A, 286.
Fault-finding, Remarks on, 120.
Fell Leonard, attacked by a highwayman, 208.
Florence, Establishment of a beneficial institution in, by a religious-minded laborer, 40.
 Trivial origin of a sanguinary war by, 70.
Forgiveness of injuries, 110, 335.
Fothergill Samuel, Anguish of, in reviewing his evil course in early life, 31.
 Touching incident in the life of, 158.
From whence come wars and fightings? Incidents entitled, 70.

Gentleness and gratitude, On the happy influence of, in our every-day life, 9.
Gerhardt Paul, Incident in the life of, 105.
Go to Launceston, Anecdote entitled, 177.
Goethe, Remark of, on the disappointed happiness of his life, 238.
Good out of evil, 223.

Grafted into Christ, 355.
Guidance in giving, 201.

Healy Christopher, Anecdote of, 116.
Heart of man deceitful above all things, The, 82.
He is dead! Solemn incident entitled, 54.
Heaven — Home, 49.
Herschell R. H., Remarks of, on music in places of worship, 342.
Honor thy father and mother, 156.
How little we understand, 257.
Howard Henry, a professed infidel, Instrumentality of a slave in the conversion of, 269.
Hoyland Barbara, Merciful visitation of Divine Grace to, 315.
Hubberthorn Richard, Rejoicing of, on the bed of death, 298.
Human life soon over, 44.
Humility, 123.

Indian, Remark of an, on refusing to drink intoxicating liquors, 283.
Indians, Notice of the Protest and Memorial of the Cherokee, and succeeding events, 92.
Individual experience of the gracious visitations of the Saviour, an answer to infidel suggestions, 279.
Individual Influence, Series entitled, 28.
Infidel, Remarkable conversion of an, 275.
Infidels, Professed, often insincere, 275.
Infidelity, Series entitled, 269.
Influence, No one without, 28.
    Of example, 35.
    Of the outward upon the inward, 241.
Influence of the Holy Spirit, Series entitled, 315.
Intemperance, Series entitled, 283.
    James Stirling, reclaimed from, through the instrumentality of his child, 286.
    Reproved, 291.
Intemperate doctor, Remarkable warning to and death of an, 292.
It costs too much, 57.

INDEX. 363

Jordan Richard, Remarkably preserved from shipwreck, 184.
Justice John, Incident in the life of, 352.

Kindness, Series entitled, 9.
    Rewarded, Anecdote of, 12.
    Anecdote and comments on the power of, 14.
    To children, On showing, 18.
    Want of proper thought often the cause of unkindness, 23.
Knox, Expression of, on his death-bed, 127.

Larks sent to the starving, 183.
Lawrence Amos, Anecdote of, 132.
Leaky roof, The, 128.
Lee Thomas, Instructive incident in the life of, 163.
Letchworth John, Incident in the ministry of, 175.
    Faith of, in the decline of life, 267.
Lights in the world, Christians called to be, 32.
Little wonts, 120.
Loe Thomas, Happiness of, on the bed of death, 299.
Long life undesirable, 45.
Lost child, The, 141.
Love of money the root of evil, The, 59.
Love your enemies, 86.

Marks of the Lord Jesus, The, 72.
Marsh James, Anecdote of the kindness of, to children, 19.
Martyr, Dying experience of a, 267.
Materialistic doctrines, Remarks on, 279.
Maximilian, an early Christian, Account of the martyrdom of, for his testimony against war, 78.
Ministry, Series entitled, 337.
    Necessity of watchfulness in those engaged in The, 144.
    Observations of Wm. Penn on the, 337.
    Human wisdom not essential to gospel, 350.
    Immediate revelation the only source of the gospel, 352.
    Work of the, 358.
Mistake providentially directed, A, 214.

Mistaken comfort, 239.
Music and decorations in places of public worship, On, 342.
Mysteries of Providence, The, 254.

Napier, Sir William, Anecdote of the kindness of, to children, 20.
Neri Fillippo, Anecdote of, 61.
Never tempt a man to break a good resolution, 283.
No one without influence, 28.
Novel reading tends to alienate from God, 240.

Obedience necessary, 268.
Old age, Religion the effectual comforter of, 45.
Old rose-bush revived, The, 229.
Our little treasures, 21.
Our past lives, 51.
"Out of the mouth of babes and sucklings, etc," 152.
"Out of sorts," 118.

Particular Providence, A, 190.
Penington Isaac, Remark of, on the benefit of spiritual exercises, 319.
Penn William, Dying injunction of Thomas Loe to, 300.
  Observations of, on gospel ministry, 337.
Politeness, Anecdote and definition of, 25.
  Remarks on Christian, 27.
Poor preaching and poor hearing, 340.
Power of kindness, The, 14.
Pray in fair weather, Incident entitled, 245.
Prayer, Remarks on the efficacy of, 166.
Preaching by example, 345.
Prevention of war, 98.
Price Rachel, Incident in the life of, 342.
Professed infidels often insincere, 275.
Profanity checked, Anecdote of, 40.
  Reproved, 291.
Providence directing, 163.

Providence of God asserted, 321.
Providential deliverances, Series entitled, 163.
Providentially directed sermons, 337.

"Ready to be offered,"— Paul, 301.
Refinement necessary, 317.
Regeneration, On the necessity of, 51.
Relief from starving by providential means, 171.
Relief in extremity, 173.
Religious Duties, Series entitled, 101.
Remarkable preservation of life, 206.
Remarkable warning, 292.
Reproof blessed, A, 291.
Retirement essential to the Christian, 101.
Retribution, 92.
Riches, Series entitled, 57.
    Caution of Cecil to a friend concerning, 48.
    Remarks on the undue pursuit of, 63.
Rich in faith, Anecdote of persons poor in earthly treasure, yet, 260.
Rothschild Baron, Remarks of, on the accumulation of wealth, 59.
    Nathan and Hannah Carson, Contrast in the circumstances and happiness of, 59.
Rutherford, Dying expressions of, 128.

Sands David, Remarkably guided in detecting robbers, 321.
Saviour, The, takes care of His lambs, 312.
Scattergood Thomas, Incident in the ministry of, 352.
Scotton Robert, Anecdote of, 108.
Set up beacon marks, 306.
Setting good grafts by a Christian example, 38.
Shortness and uncertainty of life, Series entitled, 44.
Silent worship, 326.
Simpson James, Incident connected with the ministry of, 108.
    Fear of, in the prospect of death, dispelled, 311.
Smith Samuel, Incident in the ministry of, 357.

Spirituous liquors, Remarks on the temptations to the use of, 129.
    Remark of an Indian on abstaining from, 283.
    James Stirling reclaimed from the use of, through the instrumentality of a child, 286.
Steinhofer, C. G., Protected from injury, 192.
Story Thomas, Remarkable experience by, of the operation of Divine power, 166.
    Observations by, on Divine intimations, 169.
Strawberry bed, A, 144.
Superintending Providence, A, account of the visit of a Friend to Bucks county, Pa., 212.
Support in the time of trial, 267.
Sustaining grace in the hour of death, 297.
Sweet influence of gospel love, The, 320.

Tamerlane, Remarks on the early and later character of, 82.
Taylor Sarah, Remarkable visit of, to a professed infidel, 271.
Tearing down a wall, 138.
Temptation, On resisting the first approaches of, 128.
    The approaches of, frequently insidious, 138.
Tertullian, Observations of, on the marks of a Christian, 74.
Thornton James, Remarks of, on the attendance of religious meetings, 109.
" Thou shalt not kill," 65.
Times of refreshment, 348.
Tobacco, Observations of Richard Williams on giving up the use of, 135.
Trials, Series entitled, 227.
Trotter Benjamin, Faith of, in the decline of life, 265.
Trust in the Lord, 105.

Walking by faith, 252.
Want of proper thought often the cause of distress to others, 23.
War, Series entitled, 65.
    Trivial origin of a, 70.
    Testimony of Tertullian against, 74.
    The unresisting testimony of a Friend against, blessed to a persecutor, 75.

War, Example of the early Christians in reference to, 78.
  Remarks on the career of Tamerlane, 82.
  Zulu, the Greek chief, brought to see the inconsistency of, with the Christian religion, 86.
  Conduct of Robert Barclay when attacked by highwaymen, 91.
  Retribution by, in the former country of the Cherokees, 92.
  On the prevention of, 98.
Warning by a dream, 216, 292.
Watchfulness over self, Series entitled, 118.
Way hedged up, The, 249.
Whiting George, A kind act of, rewarded, 12.
Wilberforce William, Remarks of, on long life, 45.
Wilson Judge, Remorse of, for sentencing a criminal to death, 65.
Widow protected, A, 219.
Woolman John, Expression of, on Christian graces, 73.
Woman the messenger of mercy, 210.
"Word spoken in due season, how good is it, A," 342.

Zulu, Basil Patras, a Greek chief, brought to see the inconsistency of war with the Christian religion, 86.

THE END.

The following are some of the publications of the Tract Association of Friends, and are to be had at their Depository, No. 304 Arch street.

BIOGRAPHICAL SKETCHES,

AND

ANECDOTES OF FRIENDS.

This work comprises brief biographies of Friends who lived in this country in the last and early part of the present century, who became conspicuous for their devotion to the cause of Truth. It is interspersed with numerous anecdotes and records of religious experience exemplifying the doctrines and testimonies of the Society of Friends.

∴ Price, in cloth, $1.25 per single copy, or $12 per dozen. Pp. 427.

DIVINE PROTECTION THROUGH EX-
TRAORDINARY DANGERS DURING THE IRISH REBELLION IN 1798.

A narrative of the preservation of the family of Jacob and Elizabeth Goff, members of the Religious Society of Friends of the county of Wexford, Ireland.

∴ Price, in cloth, 15 cents each, or $1.50 per dozen. Pp. 41.

MARY DUDLEY AND DAUGHTERS.

An abridged Memoir of the life, convincement, and religious labors of Mary Dudley, an approved minister of the Religious Society of Friends, and of the lives and happy death of her daughters, Hannah and Charlotte Dudley.

∴ Price, in cloth, 50 cents each, or $5.00 per dozen. Pp. 288.

A SHORT ACCOUNT OF ANN REEVE,
OF GREENWICH, NEW JERSEY,

Who died at the age of fourteen years.

∴ Price, in paper covers, 10 cents each, or $1.00 per dozen. Pp. 12.

MEMOIR OF RACHEL C. BARTRAM,
OF PHILADELPHIA.

A member of the Religious Society of Friends.

∴ Price, in paper covers, 12 cents each, or $1.25 per dozen. Pp. 28.

SELECT READERS.

In compiling these Readers care has been taken to select such pieces as would be interesting to the pupils, and at the same time be adapted to improve them in reading, and to avoid matter containing erroneous or improper sentiments.

The Series consist of

SELECT READER, No. 1; pp. 144. Price, $1.00 per dozen, or 10 cents each.

SELECT READER, No. 2; pp. 240. Price, $2.00 per dozen, or 20 cents each.

SELECT READER, No. 3; pp. 408. Price, $5.75 per dozen, or 55 cents each.

THE MORAL ALMANAC,
PUBLISHED ANNUALLY.

Containing, besides the calanders sixteen pages of instructive miscellaneous reading matter.

∴ Price, per gross, $2.88, or 4 cents each.

JUVENILE BOOKS.

MEMOIR OF SAMUEL W. CLARK AND CHARLES COLEBY.
—— ELIZABETH C. SECOR AND MARY POST.
—— AMY ELIZABETH LLOYD.
—— WILLIAM TYLER BARLING.
—— MARY SAMM.

∴ Price, 80 cents per hundred, or 1 cent each.

TRACTS.

The Tract Association of Friends now publishes a series of 117 Tracts. Price of the whole series, bound in two volumes, $1.20 per set. They are sold separately at the rate of sixteen pages for a cent. Among them are the following:

NO.		PAGES.
1.	Memoir of John Woolman	24
2.	On the Universality of Divine Grace	12
4.	Evidences of the Truth of the Christian Religion	36
7.	On the Effects of Ardent Spirits	8
9.	Detraction	8
10.	The Poet Cowper and his Brother	12
13.	William Penn's Exhortation	4
15.	Remarks on the Doctrine of the Influence of the Holy Spirit	8
18.	On Profane Swearing	4
20.	Popular Amusements	4
22.	Christianity and Infidelity Contrasted	12
24.	On Worship, Ministry, and Prayer	16
26.	"What shall we do to be Saved?"	12
27.	On the Holy Scriptures	4
36.	A Familiar Exposition of the Leading Prophecies regarding the Messiah	16
37.	A Memoir of Sir Matthew Hale	8
38.	A Sketch of the Life and Character of Dr. John D. Godman	16
39.	A Memoir of William Churchman, a poor cripple	8
46.	The Principles of Peace Exemplified	12
47.	Account of Charles Dunsdon, of Semington, Wiltshire, England	16
48.	Oaths, their moral character and effect; extracted from Essays on the Principles of Morality; by Jonathan Dymond	12
49.	The Rights of Self-Defence; by Jonathan Dymond	8
56.	Clarinda, a Pious Colored Woman of South Carolina	4
57.	On Military Glory	8
60.	On Baptism	8
61.	An Address, by the late John Barclay	4
63.	The Origin and Objects of Civil Government	12
65.	Salvation by Jesus Christ	16
66.	On Theatrical Amusements	8
73.	Sketch of the Life and Character of William Penn	32
74.	John Davis, "a brand plucked from the burning."	12
76.	Humphrey Bache, or Restitution the Fruit of Conversion	8
77.	Reasons why Women should be permitted to exercise the Gifts of the Holy Spirit in reference to the Ministry of the Gospel	8
80.	Some Account of the Life and Convincement of Thomas Story	16
81.	The Sufferings of Richard Seller on board the flag-ship Royal Prince, for his testimony to the unlawfulness of war	8
82.	A concise Account of the Religious Society of Friends, commonly called Quakers	20
83.	The Example and Testimony of the early Christians on the subject of War	4
84.	Memoirs of the Life of Daniel Wheeler, a Minister of the Gospel in the Society of Friends	32
89.	A Memoir of Thomas Chalkley, chiefly extracted from a Journal of his Life, Travels, and Christian Experiences	24
90.	Thomas Lurting; or, the Fighting Sailor transformed into a Peaceable Christian	8
92.	Two Instances of Divine Preservation at Sea	4
93.	A Brief Memoir of George Fox	60
94.	Why is a Man obliged to Pay his Debts?	4
98.	Robert Barclay	20
101.	A Proper Use of Riches, exemplified in the Life of Richard Reynolds	8
104.	Remarks on Gay and Costly Apparel	12
109.	The Kingdom of God Within	8
110.	On Lying	8
113.	The Power of Divine Grace	12
115.	Samuel Fothergill	20
116.	"Because of Swearing the Land Mourneth."	1
117.	What is it?	4

William Penn's Exhortation (in German) 4

www.ingramcontent.com/pod-product-compliance
Lightning Source LLC
Chambersburg PA
CBHW020310240426
43673CB00039B/760